Crisis, Representation and Resilience

Methuen Drama Engage offers original reflections about key practitioners, movements and genres in the fields of modern theatre and performance. Each volume in the series seeks to challenge mainstream critical thought through original and interdisciplinary perspectives on the body of work under examination. By questioning existing critical paradigms, it is hoped that each volume will open up fresh approaches and suggest avenues for further exploration.

Series Editors
Mark Taylor-Batty
University of Leeds, UK
Enoch Brater
University of Michigan, USA

Titles
Brecht and Post-1990s British Drama
Anja Hartl
ISBN 978-1-3501-7278-4

Drag Histories, Herstories and Hairstories: Drag in a Changing Scene Volume 2
Edited by Mark Edward and Stephen Farrier
ISBN 978-1-3501-0436-5

Contemporary Drag Practices and Performers: Drag in a Changing Scene Volume 1
Edited by Mark Edward and Stephen Farrier
ISBN 978-1-3500-8294-6

Performing the Unstageable: Success, Imagination, Failure
Karen Quigley
ISBN 978-1-3500-5545-2

Drama and Digital Arts Cultures
David Cameron, Michael Anderson and Rebecca Wotzko
ISBN 978-1-472-59219-4

Social and Political Theatre in 21st-Century Britain: Staging Crisis
Vicky Angelaki
ISBN 978-1-474-21316-5
Watching War on the Twenty-First-Century Stage: Spectacles of Conflict
Clare Finburgh
ISBN 978-1-472-59866-0
Fiery Temporalities in Theatre and Performance: The Initiation of History
Maurya Wickstrom
ISBN 978-1-4742-8169-0

For a complete listing, please visit
https://www.bloomsbury.com/series/methuen-drama-engage/

Crisis, Representation and Resilience

Perspectives on Contemporary British Theatre

Edited by
Clare Wallace, Clara Escoda, Enric Monforte
and José Ramón Prado-Pérez

Series Editors
Mark Taylor-Batty and Enoch Brater

methuen | drama
LONDON · NEW YORK · OXFORD · NEW DELHI · SYDNEY

METHUEN DRAMA
Bloomsbury Publishing Plc
50 Bedford Square, London, WC1B 3DP, UK
1385 Broadway, New York, NY 10018, USA
29 Earlsfort Terrace, Dublin 2, Ireland

BLOOMSBURY, METHUEN DRAMA and the Methuen Drama logo are trademarks of Bloomsbury Publishing Plc

First published in Great Britain 2022
This paperback edition published 2023

Copyright © Clare Wallace, Clara Escoda, Enric Monforte and José Ramón Prado-Pérez, and contributors, 2022

The authors have asserted their right under the Copyright, Designs and Patents Act, 1988, to be identified as authors of this work.

For legal purposes the Acknowledgements on p. ix constitute an extension of this copyright page.

Series design by Louise Dugdale
Cover image: *Lung E15* © Joe Twigg

All rights reserved. No part of this publication may be reproduced or transmitted in any form or by any means, electronic or mechanical, including photocopying, recording, or any information storage or retrieval system, without prior permission in writing from the publishers.

Bloomsbury Publishing Plc does not have any control over, or responsibility for, any third-party websites referred to or in this book. All internet addresses given in this book were correct at the time of going to press. The author and publisher regret any inconvenience caused if addresses have changed or sites have ceased to exist, but can accept no responsibility for any such changes.

A catalogue record for this book is available from the British Library.

A catalog record for this book is available from the Library of Congress.

ISBN: HB: 978-1-3501-8085-7
PB: 978-1-3501-8683-5
ePDF: 978-1-3501-8087-1
eBook: 978-1-3501-8086-4

Series: Methuen Drama Engage

Typeset by Integra Software Services Pvt. Ltd.

To find out more about our authors and books visit www.bloomsbury.com and sign up for our newsletters.

Contents

Acknowledgements   ix
Notes on Contributors   x

1   States of emergency: Performing crisis *Clare Wallace and Clara Escoda*   1

Part 1   Corporealites

2   Ageing as crisis on the twenty-first-century British stage *Siân Adiseshiah*   21

3   Creative contexts and crises of care: Ella Hickson's *The Writer* *Vicky Angelaki*   39

4   'I'm not afraid of being labelled a dirty boring feminist': Reproductive work, feminism and/in crisis at the Royal Court *Elisabeth Massana*   55

Part 2   Collective action

5   'We need to make the world we live in': Crisis and utopia in Jack Thorne's *Hope* and Lung's *E15* *Enric Monforte*   73

6   Peopling the theatre in a time of crisis *Sarah Bartley*   89

Part 3   Nationscapes

7   Fields in England: Contemporary English drama and the countryside *David Pattie*   109

8   'Sinking giggling into the sea': Postdemocracy and the state of British politics in James Graham's *This House* and *Labour of Love* *José Ramón Prado-Pérez*   125

Part 4 Contact zones

9 Theatre of migration: Uncontainment as migratory aesthetic
   Verónica Rodríguez ... 143

10 The crisis of multiculturalism in Charlene James's *Cuttin' It*
    and Gloria Williams's *Bullet Hole* *María Isabel Seguro and
    Marta Tirado* ... 159

Part 5 New directions

11 'Imaging' crisis: Photodramas in focus *Elisabeth Angel-Perez* ... 177

12 Playing in the dark: Tim Crouch's *Total Immediate Collective
   Imminent Terrestrial Salvation* *Stephen Scott-Bottoms* ... 193

13 Re-membering assembly *Louise Owen and Marilena Zaroulia* ... 209

14 Perspectives from the cascade *José Ramón Prado-Pérez,
   Clare Wallace, Enric Monforte and Clara Escoda* ... 227

Index ... 232

Acknowledgements

Much of the research that is gathered in this volume was facilitated by the research project "British Theatre in the Twenty-First Century: Crisis, Affect, Community" (FFI2016-75443). We are grateful to Spain's Ministry of Economy and Competitiveness (MINECO) and the European Regional Development Fund (ERDF), which funded the project between 2017 and 2020, enabling meetings, two symposia and rich intellectual exchange at the University of Barcelona during that period. Thanks to this support, Siân Adiseshiah, Vicky Angelaki, David Pattie, Verónica Rodríguez, Clare Wallace and Marilena Zaroulia travelled to participate in events with Mireia Aragay, Clara Escoda, Elisabeth Massana, Enric Monforte, José Ramón Prado-Pérez, María Isabel Seguro and Marta Tirado; the outcomes of which are presented in this volume. "British Theatre in the Twenty-First Century: Crisis, Affect, Community" is the fifth research project undertaken by the Contemporary British Theatre Barcelona research group, recognized by the Catalan Research Agency AGAUR (2017 SGR 40), based at the University of Barcelona and led by Mireia Aragay. For more information on the group, please see www.ub.edu/cbtbarcelona/.

Contributors

Siân Adiseshiah is Reader in English and Drama at Loughborough University. Her primary research interests are in contemporary theatre, utopianism, and more recently, age studies and cultural gerontology. She is author of forthcoming monograph *Utopian Drama: In Search of a Genre* (2022) and *Churchill's Socialism: Political Resistance in the Plays of Caryl Churchill* (2009), and co-editor (with Jacqueline Bolton) of *debbie tucker green: Critical Perspectives* (2020), (with Louise LePage) of *Twenty-First Century Drama: What Happens Now* (2016) and (with Rupert Hildyard) of *Twenty-First Century Fiction: What Happens Now* (2013).

Vicky Angelaki is Professor in English Literature at Mid Sweden University. Major publications include the monographs *Theatre & Environment* (2019); *Social and Political Theatre in 21st-Century Britain: Staging Crisis* (2017); *The Plays of Martin Crimp: Making Theatre Strange* (2012) and the edited collection *Contemporary British Theatre: Breaking New Ground* (2013; 2016). She is co-editing *The Cambridge Companion to British Playwriting since 1945* with Dan Rebellato and the Palgrave Macmillan series Adaptation in Theatre and Performance with Kara Reilly. Her next monograph will be *Martin Crimp's Power Plays: Intertextuality, Sexuality, Desire*.

Elisabeth Angel-Perez is Professor of Contemporary British Literature and Drama at Sorbonne University in Paris. She has published extensively on modern and contemporary theatre and more particularly on theatre and trauma from Beckett, Pinter and Bond to debbie tucker green, Tim Crouch or Ella Hickson. She is also a translator (Barker, Crimp, Caryl Churchill, David Harrower, Lucy Kirkwood, Nick Payne, etc.). Her latest publications include *La Haine de Shakespeare* (2017), *Tim Crouch ou la scene émancipée* (2016) as well as editions of Harold Pinter's *Old Times* (2018) or Nick Gill's *Mirror Teeth* and *Sand* (2020). Her next monograph is entitled *Le Théâtre de l'oblitération: essai sur la voix photogénique dans le théâtre britannique contemporain* (2022).

Sarah Bartley is a community arts practitioner and Lecturer in Theatre at the University of Reading. She is interested in exploring the intersections of work, participation and policy at play within socially engaged performance. Sarah's previous publications explore artistic representations of the welfare state, the resurgence of people's theatres, and documenting the histories of prison arts practice in the UK. She is a researcher on the AHRC-funded project 'Clean Break: Women, Theatre, Organisation and the Criminal Justice System' (2019–2021). She published her monograph *Performing Welfare: Applied Theatre, Unemployment, and Economies of Participation* in 2020.

Clara Escoda is Lecturer in English Literature and Theatre Studies at University of Barcelona. She is author of *Martin Crimp's Theatre: Collapse as Resistance to Late Capitalist Society* (2013), and has written on Alice Birch, Martin Crimp and Kae Tempest's plays in journals such as *Performing Ethos*, *Contemporary Theatre Review*, *New Theatre Quarterly* or *Platform*. Her current research focuses on the intersections between feminism, affect theory and ethics.

Elisabeth Massana is Lecturer and PhD candidate in the English Literature Section of the Department of Modern Languages and Literatures and English Studies at the University of Barcelona. Her main research interests are in the fields of contemporary British theatre and performance with a focus on feminisms and queer studies. She has published on the work of debbie tucker green, nomadic spectatorship in post-9/11 theatre and contemporary British queer poetry.

Enric Monforte is Senior Lecturer in English Literature and Theatre Studies at the University of Barcelona. He specializes in contemporary British theatre, film studies and gender and sexuality. He has written on Mike Bartlett, Martin Crimp, Kevin Elyot, Mark Ravenhill, Simon Stephens, debbie tucker green and Roy Williams, amongst others. He has published *Gender, Politics, Subjectivity: Reading Caryl Churchill* (2001) and co-edited *British Theatre of the 1990s: Interviews with Directors, Playwrights, Critics and Academics* (2007), *Ethical Speculations in Contemporary British Theatre* (2014) and 'Theatre and Spectatorship', a special issue of the *Journal of Contemporary Drama in English* (2016).

Louise Owen is Lecturer in Theatre and Performance at Birkbeck, University of London. Her research examines contemporary theatre and performance in terms of economic change and modes of governance. Her writing has been published in various edited collections and in the journals *Performance Research*, *Frakcija*, *Contemporary Theatre Review* and *TDR*. She co-convenes the London Theatre Seminar and is director of Birkbeck's Peltz Gallery and co-director of the Birkbeck Centre for Contemporary Theatre. Her monograph *Agents of the Future: Theatre, Performance and Neoliberalization in Britain* is forthcoming from Northwestern University Press.

David Pattie is Senior Lecturer in Drama and Theatre Arts at the University of Birmingham. He has published widely in a number of areas; contemporary British theatre, Scottish theatre, Samuel Beckett, popular performance and popular theatre. He is currently working on a monograph on theatricality in popular music performance for Routledge and is finishing work on a co-edited volume on the Velvet Underground for Continuum.

José Ramón Prado-Pérez is Senior Lecturer in English Literature at Universitat Jaume I de Castelló, Spain. He has published on Caryl Churchill, Pam Gems, Punchdrunk and Theatre Uncut. He has co-edited *World Political Theatre and Performance* (2020). He has collaborated with Theatre Uncut as translator since 2013. Other research activities include founding and chairing the scholarly journal *Culture, Language and Representation* from 2004 to 2016.

Verónica Rodríguez is Associate Lecturer at Buckinghamshire New University, UK. Two of her main research areas are contemporary British theatre and the intersection of illness and theatre and performance practices, with a particular interest in women's health. She published *David Greig's Holed Theatre: Globalization, Ethics and the Spectator* (2019), with a foreword by Dan Rebellato. She has a forthcoming chapter on spectatorship and endometriosis in the *Routledge Companion to Audience and the Performing Arts* (2022). See https://veronicarodriguezmorales.com/.

Stephen Scott-Bottoms is Professor of Contemporary Theatre and Performance at the University of Manchester, UK. His previous work on Tim Crouch includes collating a special edition of *Contemporary Theatre Review* (21.4, 2011) on 'Tim Crouch, *The Author* and the Audience'. Books include: *Playing Underground: A Critical History of the 1960s Off-Off-Broadway Movement* (2004), *Small Acts of Repair: Performance, Ecology and Goat Island* (with Matthew Goulish, 2007) and *Sex, Drag and Male Roles: Investigating Gender as Performance* (with Diane Torr, 2010). His latest book, forthcoming from University of Michigan Press, is *Incarceration Games: Performing Social Psychology from Sing Sing to Guantanamo*.

María Isabel Seguro is Lecturer and PhD candidate in the English Literature Section of the Department of Modern Languages and Literatures and English Studies at the University of Barcelona. As a member of the research group 'Contemporary British Theatre Barcelona' she has also taken part in the research project 'Ethical issues in contemporary British theatre since 1989: globalization, theatricality, spectatorship'. Her interests include Asian American literature – on which she has published particularly on theatre – and Anglo-Irish theatre and drama.

Marta Tirado is Lecturer in the Humanities department at University Pompeu Fabra and in the Dramaturgy department at the Escola Superior d'Art Dramàtic Eòlia, Barcelona. She is currently researching her PhD thesis on Sarah Kane's work from an ethical perspective. She was dramaturg and assistant director in the first Catalan production of Kane's *Blasted*, *Blasted (Rebentats)*, at Teatre Nacional de Catalunya. Her research interests focus on the intertwining of ethics, aesthetics and spectatorship in contemporary British and Catalan theatre; she has published on these subjects.

Clare Wallace is Associate Professor at the Department of Anglophone Literatures and Cultures, Charles University in Prague. She is author of *The Theatre of David Greig* (2013) and *Suspect Cultures: Narrative, Identity and Citation in 1990s New Drama* (2006). She is a Key Researcher in the European Regional Development Fund Project 'Creativity and Adaptability as Conditions of the Success of Europe in an Interrelated World' (No. CZ.02 .1.01/0.0/0.0/16_019/0000734).

Marilena Zaroulia is Lecturer in Performance Arts at The Royal Central School of Speech and Drama, University of London, UK. Her research focuses on performance and the cultural politics of post-1989 Europe. She is the co-editor of *Performances of Capitalism, Crises and Resistance: Inside/Outside Europe* (2015). Her work has appeared in various edited collections and international journals, including *Contemporary Theatre Review*, *Performance Research*, *The Journal of Greek Media and Culture* and *RIDE*. Her monograph *Encountering Europe on British Stages: Performances and Politics since 1990* is forthcoming.

1

States of emergency: Performing crisis

Clare Wallace and Clara Escoda

'The crisis of theatre might well be its constant condition, determined by its own fatigue and opportunism, the economic constraints of show biz, the fragility of the inspiring artistic talent tending to slide into routine, and orchestrated by the overwhelming indifference to theatre of most potential viewers. But the theatre of crisis, the theatricalization of a crisis is no fancy and no myth but a viable option, given some distance, necessary for the collective and individual memory of the traumatizing experience to settle only to be unsettled again by the strikes of the stage acts. And the theatre of crisis, be it war, hunger, epidemics or civil unrest, can make sense if the artists focus not on the unfolding tragedy itself but on the ways it is being presented, reported, perceived and metaphorized by other dominant discourses.'

(Klaić 2002: 160)

'Don't weep. Create the new drama.'

(Bond 2020: x)

Politically, ecologically, economically, socially and culturally, the twenty-first century is awash with crises, so much so that it is a challenge to find our bearings. From global terrorism and the subsequent so-called War on Terror to forced migration, the financial collapse of 2007/8 followed by austerity measures, associated tensions in the European Union including the Eurozone debt crisis and Brexit, the rise of far-right populism, an epidemic of misinformation in the media, entrenched racism, surging

---

Clare Wallace and Clara Escoda's work was supported by the Spanish Ministry of Economy and Competitiveness (MINECO) and the European Regional Development Fund (ERDF) project 'British Theatre in the Twenty-First Century: Crisis, Affect, Community' (FFI2016-75443). Clare Wallace's work was also supported by the European Regional Development Fund (ERDF) project 'Creativity and Adaptability as Conditions of the Success of Europe in an Interrelated World' (No. CZ.02.1.01/0.0/0.0/16_01 9/0000734).

violence against women and sexual minorities, environmental disasters and climate change to a global pandemic, the list is long, rather obvious, and overwhelming. Feminist sociologist Sylvia Walby uses the word 'cascade' to describe the current proliferation of crises through society (2015: 14). They are overlapping, intersecting, enmeshed, sometimes nested, sometimes discontinuous, some swift, others gradual, some strike us as new, while many appear to replay historically earlier crises amid the conditions of the present producing an uneasy sense of déjà vu.

This collection of essays is the product of a collaboration that began in 2017 focused on crisis, affect and community in contemporary British theatre.[1] As we began the process of editing the various contributions at the start of 2020, we were overtaken by the then unanticipated, but now ubiquitous Covid-19 pandemic. So, while this book seizes upon crisis as a dynamic and integral feature/aspect of the post-millennial British theatre environment and its concerns, it does so, necessarily, from within, acknowledging our own immersion in evolving, unfinished, cascading emergencies, pressures and ruptures that shape our experiences of the world and, more specifically, our thoughts on theatre and performance. In this we echo the sentiments of Will Daddario and Theron Schmidt in their introductory article to the 2018 themed issue of *Performance Philosophy*, 'Crisis/Krisis'. Drawing on Naomi Klein's analysis in *The Shock Doctrine: The Rise of Disaster Capitalism* (2007), Daddario and Schmidt warn that 'crisis *works*... that is, the label... is not just descriptive but performative, producing helplessness, legitimating a particular response, and pre-emptively negating the possibility of critical thought' (2018: 1; original emphasis). Yet even while many current analyses of crisis like Klein's, converge in their diagnoses of the ills of the neoliberal system (and we turn to this discourse shortly), we also aim to explore crisis as transformative in ways that open possibilities of transvaluation, and of interrupting the cynicism of commodification. Understanding crisis as materially experienced and discursively produced, and navigating between the perpetual and the exceptional, events and systems, we want to preserve its complexity and plurality while seeking ways of evading futility, and modes of imaginative recognition, action, resilience and repair. Our overarching concerns here are the multifaceted relationships between twenty-first-century British theatre and crisis, the potential of critical creativity and the forms it takes. How does theatrical performance intervene in this discourse in ways that enable critical thought and communal solidarity in times of social atomization, disenfranchisement? What aesthetic strategies are British theatre makers crafting to communicate the structure of feeling,

---

[1] See Aragay, Delgado-García and Middeke 2021.

'characteristic elements of impulse, restraint, and tone; specifically affective elements of consciousness and relationships' (Williams 1977: 132) of the opening decades of the century?

Proportion, position, time

Before going further with our reflections on these relationships and issues, let us first take up the matter of definition. Crisis is a troublingly floating signifier, a term that accrues a multitude of meanings in adjectival combination. And there is clearly an incongruity between its diffuse and increasingly ubiquitous circulation, and its Greek etymology, κρίσις, that still bears the residual connotation of judgement and decision. Yet in current usage, crisis most frequently refers to pathology – the decisive point in the progress of a disease resulting in either death or recovery – or is used figuratively to signify, 'A vitally important or decisive stage in the progress of anything; a turning-point; also, a state of affairs in which a decisive change for better or worse is imminent; now applied *esp.* to times of difficulty, insecurity, and suspense in politics or commerce' (OED Online 2021). As is obvious even from such a standard dictionary denotation, thinking about crisis intrinsically means thinking about proportion, position. Approaching the topic from a social theory perspective Walby identifies, 'A crisis ... as an event that has the potential to cause a large detrimental change to the social system and in which there is lack of proportionality between cause and consequence' (2015: 14). Crisis, then, is not merely a synonym for change, though change is invariably brought by crisis. Rather it signifies change wrought by excess and disproportion, that develops in a non-linear manner and ruptures structures of control or efficiency within a system social or otherwise. Such definitions become meaningful when positioned in relation to causes, effects and contexts; a task that entails various perspectives and rationales. Throughout this book our focus on crisis corrals the aesthetic and performative with the social and political. Yet even looking back only as far as the twentieth century, it is clear that sociopolitical upheaval is hardly novel, neither are aesthetic ruptures of representational practice, so the crucial question is what is new or specific to the crises of the present?

The interleaving of modernity with an experience of crisis so central to the philosophical work of Walter Benjamin and the Frankfurt School is an intellectual heritage deeply imprinted on many subsequent considerations of contemporary conditions. More precisely, thinking crisis through and alongside the development of modern capitalism and, latterly, neoliberal globalization has become a major trajectory in current theorizations, and one that directly and indirectly informs the critical vocabularies of the contributors to this volume. By the turn of the century diverse economic, sociological and political scholarship converged on the ways in which crisis generation was intrinsic to the operations of an increasingly globalized neoliberal model. For instance, Ulrich Beck's influential 1980s research, published in English as *Risk Society: Towards a New Modernity* (1992), contends that this new modernity is characterized by risk production: 'Averting and managing these can include a *reorganization of power and authority*. Risk society is a *catastrophic* society. In it the exceptional condition threatens to become the norm' (24; original emphasis). Critiquing its normative economic rationale, Pierre Bourdieu's *Acts of Resistance* (1998) dissects neoliberalism as a utopian project, but one that presents itself as a 'scientific description of reality' (94). For Bourdieu, it is more accurately understood as a fantasy of boundless exploitation, facilitated by 'a *programme of methodical destruction of collectives*' (95–6; original emphasis). David Harvey similarly has illuminated the confluence of transformations wrought by capital in the later twentieth and twenty-first centuries throughout his contributions to anthropology, economic and political geography in *The Condition of Postmodernity: An Enquiry into the Origins of Cultural Change* (1989), *A Brief History of Neoliberalism* (2005) and *The Enigma of Capital and the Crises of Capitalism* (2010) among others. In particular, Harvey highlighted the disruptive force of postmodernity's accelerated 'time-space compression' (1989) alongside the erosion of values bound to the metastasis of contemporary consumer society. He has gone on to expose the ways neoliberalism equates individualism and entrepreneurialism with freedom and prosperity (2005: 2) despite the accumulation of evidence to the contrary (see 2010).

Unsurprisingly, the global financial crisis in 2007/8 concentrated unprecedented attention on the nature and costs of these developments. Sylvia Walby's socioeconomic analysis of crisis identifies the modalities of risk, catastrophe and disaster. She begins with the financial collapse of 2008 (in the UK) through its economic, fiscal, democratic and social impacts (2015). Walby sources the current crisis in unregulated finance and reminds us of the gendered realities of those who create and profit from such systems, as well as those who bear the brunt of the austerity policies introduced when failure occurs. In a more dynamically popular vein, activist Naomi Klein's *The Shock Doctrine* (2007) lays the blame with deregulated capitalism, a system that she argues 'has consistently been midwifed by the most brutal forms of coercion, inflicted on the collective body politic as well as on countless individual bodies. The history of the contemporary free market – better understood as the rise of corporatism – was written in shocks' (18–19).

Klein continues to map the destructive toll of the Western economic system on the environment in *This Changes Everything: Capitalism vs the Climate* (2014). Indeed, as this century progresses the realities of human-produced ecological change are increasingly devastating, and yet continue to elicit grossly insubstantial governmental and industrial responses.

Representation, agency, imagination

Crisis, then, concerns representation in several interleaved senses from political subjectivity, social identity to cultural practices. Zygmunt Bauman and Carlo Bordoni suggest that what marks contemporary crisis lies at the intersection of the state, modernity and democracy. For Bauman, 'the present crisis differs from its historical precedents in as far as it is lived through the situation of a *divorce between power and politics*. That divorce results in the *absence of agency* capable of doing what every "crisis", by definition, requires: choosing a way to proceed, and applying the therapy called for by that choice' (2014: 12; original emphasis). This leads to a state, described compellingly by Lauren Berlant as 'crisis ordinariness' that is 'not exceptional to history or consciousness but a process embedded in the ordinary that unfolds in stories about navigating what's overwhelming' (2011: 10). Berlant is attentive to representation beyond the strictly political senses debated by Bauman, Bordoni or Walby, to modes of aesthetically presenting and performing (in the midst of) 'crisis ordinariness' that are emblematic of a structure of feeling in the present. The wider resonances of Berlant's reading of diminished capacity and temporalities of dispossession are further refined by Winnie Balestrini, Leopold Lippert and Maria Löschnigg in a 2020 crisis themed issue of the *Journal of Contemporary Drama in English*. They trace the affects of crisis formations through Alain Ehrenberg's work on 'fatigue, exhaustion, and depression as physical and psychological states that have been deeply normalized in contemporary neoliberal societies' to Isabell Lorey's theorizing of 'precarization [that] ... entails assessing the cultural techniques individuals and communities develop and refine in order to live and cope with the contingencies created by a state of permanent crisis' (2020: 4–5). Their differing respective approaches notwithstanding, each of these sources underscore how the tensions between the utopian promises of ever more freedom, wealth, comfort, quality of life, and the realities of finite resources, extreme inequality, suffering, global conflict and environmental destruction are increasingly unignorable.

Such political and existential impasses are mirrored in cultural imaginaries, and have been amassing for some time. It is useful to recall

Arjun Appadurai's 'theory of rupture that takes media and migration as its two major, interconnected, diacritics' in *Modernity at Large: The Cultural Dimensions of Globalization* (1996), where he surveys 'their joint effect on the *work of the imagination* as a constitutive feature of modern subjectivity' (3; original emphasis). Appadurai's focus on 'the imagination as social practice' (1996: 31) does not disregard the roles of global capital flows and commodification, but addresses an expanded network of forces and activities at play across ethnoscapes, mediascapes, technoscapes, financescapes and ideoscapes (1996: 33) in ways that continue to resonate more than two decades later even when globalization has lost so much of its allure.

Indeed, Appadurai's mapping of the representational and affective economies of globalized modernity provides a route towards a cluster of publications that engage with imagination and identity within a complex and irregularly experienced neoliberal present. Mark Fisher (2009), Eric Cazdyn with Imre Szeman (2011), Neal Curtis (2013), Max Haiven (2014) and Jim McGuigan (2009, 2016) each have picked out the current contours of this ideational space, and, most importantly for our focus here, the challenges of imagining otherwise. As Fisher so lucidly puts it '[w]hat we are dealing with now is not the incorporation of materials that previously seemed to possess subversive potentials, but instead, their *precorporation*: the pre-emptive formatting and shaping of desires, aspirations and hopes by capitalist culture' (2009: 9; original emphasis). Curtis tracks the ways privatization infuses culture to produce personal individualism that is paradoxically perpetually performed in public but undermines the communal. Like Fisher, Cazdyn and Szeman provocatively focus on the temporal and conceptual foreclosure of neoliberal globalization, and the challenge of conceptualizing what might come next. Analogously, Haiven also concludes that '[t]he failure to acknowledge that the many global crises we now face are, inherently, crises of capitalism, represents a massive failure of the imagination' manifest in the 'parochialism' of the global north, dogmatic adherence to 'necroliberalism' and the normalization of an idea of 'ourselves as essentially isolated, lonely, competitive economic agents' (2014: ch. 1).

Despite Gerard Delanty's warning that 'we must not forget that neoliberalism... is not simply one thing that has remained constant but forms a constantly chang[ing] ensemble of ideas, discourses and practices' (2014: 212), these diverse works substantiate a sense of the magnitude and modalities of crisis in the twenty-first century. Acknowledging the plurality of origins and formations, Stuart Hall and Doreen Massey consequently describe crises as 'over-determined', occurring when '"relatively autonomous" sites – which have different origins, are driven by different contradictions, and develop according to their own temporalities – are nevertheless "convened" or condensed in the same moment' (2010: 59–60). The confluence of heterogeneous economic, ecological phenomena, with social and political crises of value, amplify their respective affects and effects, to the extent that in the opening decades of the twenty-first century, whether labelled as late, post, reflexive or liquid modernity, we might speak of a new ecology of crisis.

British conjunctures

Developments in a British context are usefully discussed by Hall with Massey who, drawing on the work of Antonio Gramsci, view the present through conjuncture, as 'a period during which the different social, political, economic and ideological contradictions that are at work in society come together to give it a specific and distinctive shape ... [usually driven forward by] a crisis, when the contradictions that are always at play in any historical moment are condensed' (2010: 57). The political ascendancy of a neoliberal monetarist programme is rooted in the transformation of Britain that begins in 1979 with the General Election victory of the Conservative Party led by Margaret Thatcher. For Hall and Massey, '[t]he post-war period, dominated by the welfare state, public ownership and wealth redistribution through taxation was one conjuncture; the neoliberal, market-forces era unleashed by Thatcher and Reagan was another. These are two distinct conjunctures, separated by the crisis of the 1970s' (2010: 57). The emergence of New Labour led by Tony Blair and the election of a Labour government in the 1990s altered the Thatcherist narrative, but in retrospect signalled less of a turning point in these developments than might have been anticipated. Despite the eruption of global terrorism and the conflicts in Afghanistan and Iraq in the early 2000s, it is the global financial crisis that marks a shift towards a new conjuncture, unfolding in the reckoning with austerity and the political backlash that rocks the foundations of the European Union. Thinking conjuncturally, however, is not to reinstate a simple linear historical trajectory, but to recognize 'point[s] where different temporalities – and more specifically, *the tensions, antagonisms and contradictions which they carry* – begin to come together' (Clarke 2010: 342; original emphasis). The resurgent nationalist impulses that gave rise to Brexit and 'Global Britain', in this respect, are illustrative of a 'ruptural fusion' (Hall and Massey 2010: 60) and, crucially, a distorted 'projective temporality' (Palladini 2015: 18) that anticipates a future by means of a return to an imagined past.

Theatre and performance

So, in what ways does theatre reflect on and participate in these crisis formations in the twenty-first century? Introducing a collection of essays by artists and scholars on theatre's situation at the turn of the century titled *Theatre in Crisis? Performance Manifestos for a New Century* Maria Delgado and Caridad Svich note,

> It is, after all, an art created under duress, under economic circumstances both trying and not, and within the often combustible environment of a rehearsal hall. It is also an art that has seemed to reach yet another break point in its identity, mode of presentation, and structural efficacy, given the rise of more popular forms of entertainment and instruction like film, television, and the internet.... art which uses conditions of crisis as its essential trope. Not merely rebellious, this is art that contains its struggle within the making and its articulation. It is art that reflects the crises of the past and tries to make active sense of the present.
> (2002: 6–7)

Plaiting together reflections on the pragmatics of funding and of institutions, the intrinsic role of peripeteia and crisis to dramatic structure with the aesthetics of performance, and theatre-world-spectator relations, contributors to Delgado and Svich's book offer some fine insights into the challenges of theatre practice within a predominantly Anglo-American frame that have been explored in scholarly work in the decades since. However, it is also worth remembering that 'British theatre enjoyed something of a qualified "golden age" in the 2000s, both artistically and economically' (Haydon 2013: 40). Andrew Haydon outlines some dynamic developments between 2000 and 2009, ranging from the rise of verbatim techniques, uses of digital technology and headphones, a panoply of site specific, site sympathetic and immersive work, the erosion of some of the traditional distinctions between drama and performance, as well as institutional changes at the National Theatre and the Royal Court Theatre among others.

Haydon's descriptive and carefully optimistic survey of the 2000s is critically counterpointed by Jen Harvie's nuanced assessment of conditions in British theatre and performance that dovetails with the social and political discourse synthesized above. In *Fair Play: Art, Performance and Neoliberalism* (2013), she sceptically weighs the current practices of socially engaged art (much of which adopts the new techniques described by Haydon) against the pervasive forces of neoliberal capitalism in a UK context. Attending to labour, entrepreneurialism, space and funding, she probes the ways in which art and performance function in this environment, in order to register the compromises and resistances in institutional, collective and individual practice.

More explicit crisis vocabularies featuring an emphasis on extremity, rupture, conflict and precarity/precariousness can be registered with an increasing tempo across subsequent theatre scholarship. For instance, the collapse of global financial markets in 2008 and the subsequent pressure on the 'metaphysics of Europe' provide the point of departure for Marilena Zaroulia and Philip Hager's edited volume, *Performances of Capitalism, Crises and Resistance: Inside/Outside Europe* (2015: 3). *Performing (for) Survival: Theatre, Crisis, Extremity* edited by Patrick Duggan and Lisa Peschel sets out to 'explore why people organize themselves into performance communities in sites of crisis and how performance – social and aesthetic, sanctioned and underground – is employed as a mechanism for survival' (2016: 1). Vicky Angelaki's *Social and Political Theatre in 21st-Century Britain* (2017) opens with a chapter titled 'theatres of crisis' to argue that a new theatrical discourse has developed, one that interrogates acts of spectatorship within an ethical frame. *Performance, Feminism and Affect in Neoliberal Times* (2017) edited by Elin Diamond, Denise Varney and Candice Amich collects provocative feminist perspectives on performance tuned by an awareness of affect as enabling thinking 'of new forms of relationality conducive to exploring the many vectors of feeling aroused by performance', and its activist, oppositional force (2017: 4). Tony Fisher and Eve Katsouraki's collection of essays *Performing Antagonism: Theatre, Performance and Radical Democracy* (2017) and Liz Tomlin's *Political Dramaturgies and Theatre Spectatorship: Provocations for Change* (2019) in contrasting ways assess the potential of political performance. Concurrently, Marissia Fragkou's *Ecologies of Precarity in Twenty-First Century Theatre* (2019) explores the affective currency of precarity as it percolates through the 'representational practices and identity politics in contemporary theatre' (15). Fragkou prefers the word precarity to crisis, a term she sees as aligned with 'a myopic and linear view ... as something which can be measured, controlled and resolved' (2019: 5). However, clear-cut distinctions between crisis and precarity are, as her insightful analysis soon reveals, difficult to sustain. We do not pretend that such publications represent an exhaustive survey, however they are indicative of a dynamic discourse around the ways theatre and performance mediates, reproduces or challenges the conditions of the present both within a British context and beyond.

A number of aesthetic tendencies might be observed across the work discussed in these publications; however, it would be hazardous to suggest a dominant mode. The uptick in work with dystopian qualities on British stages is elucidated by Dan Rebellato (and subsequently numerous others) as symptomatic not of nihilism, but of 'a constructive response ... to a key feature of contemporary neoliberal capitalism: its totalizing absorption of realism' (2017: par. 38). Meanwhile, Elaine Aston has made a contrasting case for a reappraisal of 'the heterogeneous mix of socially progressive realisms now circulating on the English stage' (2016: 33). Since early 2020, the Covid-19 pandemic has brought an unthinkable crisis to theatre with the closure of shared public spaces. Certainly, lockdown theatre in the shape of numerous Zoom-based online performances and streamed events has swiftly given rise to new forms of presentation – particularly a resurgence of monologues and the circulation of recorded performances. Accessible (in theory) to audiences across the globe, though arguably of predominantly an aesthetically flat and truncated nature, digitally mediated theatre and performance raises crucial questions about what we seek in theatre and what it means to be an audience.

More compelling are the still evolving outcomes for live performance culture, that despite the surge in publications and conferences assessing what has happened/is happening remain difficult to estimate. Some of the preliminary ones are relatively, if sadly, predictable: the closure of theatre buildings quickly led to the collapse of vulnerable projects, but also cut core institutions like the National Theatre, the Royal Court and West End Theatres to the marrow. Theatre's extensive reliance on precarious labour was brutally exposed, and the likely result of government support for the arts will be seen in the strengthening of institutions over small groups or individuals.

In symmetry with the opening of this section, we turn to another anthology that speaks directly to our topic. *Theatre in Times of Crisis*, edited by Dom O'Hanlon in 2020 which collects scenes and interviews with playwrights, is an early and stimulating example of creative efforts to respond to the current situation, and to reflect more generally on 'the idea of "crisis" and how that manifests on stage amongst different circumstances and through a range of characters, experiences and situations' (2020: xiv). O'Hanlon observes how through his interviews with writers (the anthology gathers an impressive cast of talents ranging from Lucy Prebble, James Graham, Simon Stephens, Tim Crouch to Mojisola Adebayo, Gurpreet Kaur Bhatti, Inua Williams and Tanika Gupta), the notion of states of emergency producing a 'moment of clarity' (2020: xviii) recurs forcefully. How such crisis-produced moments of clarity find expression in unique and impactful ways in theatre are likewise elaborated by the contributions to this volume.

Critical constellations

This book is structured around five interlocking clusters, intended to provide access points for exploring the discursive and performative contours of crisis. The first engages with the feminized body, pointing to ageist discourses that affect, primarily, women; at the lack of female presence in institutional spaces; or by highlighting the links between reproductive work and systemic violence against women in capitalism. Focusing on the post-apocalyptic dramas *Escaped Alone* by Caryl Churchill, and *The Children* (both 2016) by Lucy Kirkwood, Siân Adiseshiah analyses the intersection of crisis and ageing and the implications of this encounter. She argues that the resource demands of living longer have served to strengthen current articulations of ageing as consonant with narratives of crisis. In this context, Churchill and Kirkwood configure the intersection of crisis and ageing differently, and this difference has significant political effects. Indeed, Adiseshiah concludes that whilst *Escaped Alone* questions normative perceptions of old age, *The Children* leaves (neoliberal) ageist structures intact.

Turning to the assertion of female presence in institutional spaces traditionally associated with male authority, Vicky Angelaki reads Ella Hickson's *The Writer* (2018) as a performative intervention exposing contemporary crises of care and institutionalized absence of safety. Framing her analysis in relation to Walby's notion of 'male monoculture' (2015: 4), which describes the lack of egalitarian distribution in positions of power, Angelaki asserts that the play confronts the values of this monoculture at the heart of cultural production. Hickson's destabilization of perspective through a complex sequence of metatheatrical manoeuvres radically challenges both normative notions of creativity and normative dramatic assumptions of what makes good drama. Written and produced in the wake of the UK's recession, in the midst of Brexit, and uncannily anticipating the #MeToo movement, Angelaki ultimately concludes that the play is engaged both in the furthering of access and equality agendas, and in promoting the safeguarding and protection of the female artist against exploitative structures and norms.

The context of the #MeToo movement is also pivotal to Elisabeth Massana's chapter which focuses on two plays which opened at the Royal Court under the artistic direction of Vicky Featherstone: Cordelia Lynn's *Lela & Co.* (2015) and Vivienne Franzmann's *Bodies* (2017). Drawing on Silvia Federici's *Caliban and the Witch* (2004), Massana foregrounds the way experiences of capitalism and crisis are refracted through gender. Carrying out an analysis of their specific dramaturgical strategies, she contends that both plays expose how the control of and violence exerted upon the feminized body are intrinsic to expropriative logics of global capitalism. In doing so they challenge the notion of crisis as turning point and question any singular chronology of crisis when it comes to the feminized body.

The second cluster of chapters considers collective action and activism in performance. Synthesizing Hall and Massey's conjunctural approach to crises as 'moments of potential change' (2010: 57) and opportunities for counter-intervention, with Bourdieu's term 'forces of *resistance*' (1998: 103; original emphasis), and Walby's theorization of gendered crisis (2015: 10–11), Enric Monforte discusses Jack Thorne's *Hope* (2014) and Lung's *E15* (2015) as plays that dramatize the erosion of community following the 2008 financial crisis. For Monforte, *Hope* and *E15* present the foundational value of community as the only way to resist and survive the atomizing pressures of neoliberalism and austerity. Ultimately, Monforte suggests that both plays offer instances of 'utopian performatives' (Dolan 2005), fostering the creation of a local and global consciousness in the audience and promoting inclusive notions of community. Interpellating spectators to actively 'make the world we inhabit', the plays present themselves as examples, Monforte argues, of a theatre that actively contests the status quo.

Collective creative action is also the focus of Sarah Bartley's chapter, which explores the distinctive practices of Camden People's Theatre and Brighton People's Theatre and considers the utility of people's theatres in moments of social, political and artistic crisis in the UK. Taking up Lauren Berlant's concept of 'crisis ordinariness', wherein she recognizes 'the ordinary as an impasse shaped by crisis in which people find themselves developing skills for adjusting to newly proliferating pressures to scramble for modes of living on' (2011: 8), Bartley acknowledges the present as 'structured by a propagation of systemic crises' and postulates the potential of the people's theatre to offer ways 'of living on' under such conditions. Tracing the experimental and playful forms of both Brighton People's Theatre and Camden People's Theatre, Bartley proposes that People's Theatres 'respond to the affective conditions of anxiety, divisiveness, anger and isolation', which have proliferated in the fallout of the two macro-economic crises of 1992 and 2008 by giving voice to communities, engaging with the most socially and economically marginalized and bolstering a sense of resistant collectivity.

The third cluster of work here attends to the ways the disjunctions in the UK nationscape are reflected and reckoned with by contemporary British theatre. David Pattie's contribution centres on the ambivalent manifestations of Englishness that suffuse Jez Butterworth's *The Night Heron* (2002), *The Winterling* (2006) and *Jerusalem* (2009), Mike Bartlett's *Albion* (2017), and Simon Longman's *Gundog* (2018). For Pattie, a general sense of crisis becomes palpable in a turn to English countryside dramatic settings that, in the national imaginary, conventionally gesture towards an immutable identity. By representing the rural and the countryside as 'eerie', to use Mark Fisher's expression (2016), these plays undermine the idea of a fixed, unchanging Deep England. The 'eerie', as Pattie puts it, is associated with 'moments of dislocating emptiness, or moments where the apparently solid world reveals itself as unknowable'. Indeed, Pattie suggests that the idea of English national identity – not unlike the discourses that triggered Brexit – is not animated by a sense of shared, stable common values, but rather, as the plays distinctly show, is characterized by the 'troubling absence' of any sense of collective purpose.

By contrast, drawing on Jacques Rancière's notion of 'postdemocracy' (1999), José Ramón Prado-Pérez examines how James Graham's *This House* (2012) and *Labour of Love* (2017) respond to the progressive dehumanization of the practice of politics which characterizes current neoliberal, postdemocratic times. By staging British politics at crucial moments of conjuncture and through a form of comedy that engages spectators in critical laughter, Prado-Pérez contends that Graham's plays can be understood as resistant, because they reinstate 'regenerative politics as part of the social debate'. Leaning on Chantal Mouffe's notion of democratic 'agonism' (2000), which defends the crucial role conferred by disagreement and difference in the configuration of the democratic process, Prado-Pérez concludes that Graham's plays promote positive, affective bonds through comic, popular genres and dramatic agonism.

The fourth cluster turns to the tensions that revolve around exclusion, belonging and difference. Verónica Rodríguez analyses Clare Bayley's *The Container* (2007), a site sympathetic play about a group of migrants who are smuggled inside a shipping container lorry in order to reach the UK, and Phosphoros Theatre's *Dear Home Office* (2016), a performance devised by the company's refugee and asylum-seeking actors about their experiences. Rodríguez presents these works as examples of theatre of migration that 'uncontains' both a confined understanding of (the refugee) crisis, and the representation of the migrant and migration. Their experimental and experiential dimensions invite a recognition of connectedness. Via Mieke Bal's notion of migratory aesthetics, Rodríguez concludes that the aesthetic forms of *The Container* and *Dear Home Office* crucially allow for 'a weaving of the spectator into crisis/es and of her body into the body politic' enabling them to enter the sets of relations that are rendered obscure by the dominant crisis discourse.

María Isabel Seguro and Marta Tirado examine the conflicts of the prevailing liberal view of multiculturalism as it intersects with feminism with reference to Charlene James's *Cuttin' It* (2016) and Gloria Williams's *Bullet Hole* (2017), two plays that present the dilemmas of responding to female genital mutilation (FGM) in immigrant communities in the UK. Contesting Susan Möller Okin's controversial article 'Is Multiculturalism Bad for Women' (1999), Seguro and Tirado claim that the feminist view of multiculturalism risks reproducing the dichotomy already pointed out by Sara Ahmed of the 'happy/melancholic migrant' (2017: 549), whereby the 'happy' female migrant integrates successfully within the majority culture at the expense of sacrificing certain aspects of her family's cultural tradition, while the 'melancholic immigrant' would resist such assimilation. Seguro and Tirado conclude that, through performative strategies that expose 'the pain of the culturally, and physically, scarred female bodies', these plays illuminate the need for a global feminist perspective that prioritizes women's rights as a tool against FGM.

The final cluster in the volume considers modes of theatrical mediation of contemporary crisis formations. Elisabeth Angel-Perez, like Rodríguez or Massana, also claims that crisis can no longer be thought of as a state of exception with a clear chronology but must be recognized as structural. Angel-Perez reminds us that crisis has always been both the subject of drama and acted as a dramaturgic impulse, urging playwrights to experiment with new forms, and focuses on a new and especially innovative theatrical aesthetics, photo-based dramas, which both formally and in terms of content, capture the structures of feeling of our times of unrest. Focusing on Simon Stephens's *Rage* (2018), Lucy Kirkwood's *Chimerica* (2013) and Chris Thorpe's *There Has Possibly Been an Incident* (2013), Angel-Perez explores how these works render palpable 'the sense of ontological suspension attached to the notion of crisis'. As a result, such photodramas 'reconstruct this suspensive conversational space where the individual exists as part of a community in transition', thus crucially restoring 'a humanist vision to crisis'.

Analysing Tim Crouch's *Total Immediate Collective Imminent Terrestrial Salvation* (2019) Stephen Scott-Bottoms considers the ways this work implicates its audiences in a proliferating, yet elliptical, sense of crisis. With reference to Bruno Latour's recent writing on the politics of climate, Scott-Bottoms explores how Crouch augments a sense of cognitive dissonance by involving audiences in the co-production of a dramatic fiction that reverberates with an anxious paranoia about existence, control and the end of the world. Crouch creates a performative, affective space as a means, according to Scott-Bottoms, of 'inhabit[ing] the dissonance, the uncertainty, and the sheer, unholy mess of the crisis situation in which we now find ourselves. It approaches the abyss, and looks tentatively for ways to cross it'.

The closing chapter of the book takes a slightly different, collaborative form. Louise Owen and Marilena Zaroulia respond to one of the many online pieces of lockdown performance – Lost Dog's *In a Nutshell* (2020), a work that 'offer[s] a speculative fictional version of the future which speaks to that widespread closure'. Looking to Judith Butler's *Notes toward a Performative Theory of Assembly* and Rustom Bharucha's reflections on the pandemic and the theatre, they explore what happens to a sense of proximity, shared agential space and assembly, at a time when in-person meeting is impossible. *In a Nutshell*, they suggest 'condenses the different facets of the theatre, its utopian potential and its social and economic limitations, all of them hinging on the practices and constitution of theatrical assembly' – a gently performative contemplation of the civic value of theatre in times of crisis.

Resilience, resistance and repair

In closing we look back to Walby's synopsis of the four main routes crisis might take: 'system breakdown', 'a return to pre-crisis conditions', 'the renewal of the system along its existing path of development' or the birth of 'a new type of system' (2015: 34). As we scan the world, still in the grip of a global pandemic and bracing for its economic aftershocks, awakening to the hazards of environmental change while still addicted to everyday consumerism, it is obvious all four possibilities roil together, vying for precedence. It is difficult to be immune to the cruelly optimistic desire for everything to go back to 'normal'. Despite their varied approaches, each of the contributors to this book are united in a conviction that theatrical performance offers something of value in times of crisis in modes of disturbing our sense of the status quo, in challenging inequity and in advocating the communal. As Eve Katsouraki notes,

> [i]n this respect, theatre and performance become particularly good places for undoing an image or situation of the dominant discourse in society simply by... *presenting* it, whether on the stage of the public space or the stage of the theatre, in order to 'replace' it, which in itself is an antagonistic act – the act of 'negating' something in the present reality in order to expose it, subvert it and, ultimately, transform it.
>
> (2017: 290; original emphasis)

Resilience is a word widely co-opted for corporate and institutional ends, mobilized to disguise the need for systemic change, delegating responsibility to individuals for crises not of their making and beyond their control. We understand resilience as a response to risk, crisis or adversity, that implies transformation, not merely capacity to bounce back or the resumption of equilibrium/status quo (see also Katsouraki 2017; Steinbock, Ieven and de Valck 2021).

And what of repair? Throughout this volume we seek counter a prevailing notion of rupture with that of repair as a future oriented inclination of imagining otherwise, even in the midst of crisis. With this in mind, it seems apposite to turn once more to the ideas of Lauren Berlant, whose recent death adds a keen poignancy to thinking about crisis, loss and repair. Berlant's concept of 'cruel optimism' does not suggest that our attachments can simply be severed, rather that they need to be reformed, repaired, through the generation of alternative affective infrastructures and a reappraisal of the commons (Berlant 2016: 414). Throughout the chapters that follow, it is clear that such resistant resilience is intrinsic to the performative responses to crisis contemporary British theatre offers and to its sustaining critical potential.

References

Ahmed, S. (2017), 'Multiculturalism and the Promise of Happiness', in C. R. McCann and S-K. Kim (eds), *Feminist Theory Reader: Local and Global Perspectives*, 539–54, New York and London: Routledge.

Angelaki, V. (2017), *Social and Political Theatre in 21st-Century Britain: Staging Crisis*, London: Bloomsbury Methuen.

Appadurai, A. (1996), *Modernity at Large: The Cultural Dimensions of Globalization*, Minneapolis: University of Minnesota Press.

Aragay, M., C. Delgado-García, and M. Middeke (eds) (2021), *Affects in 21st-Century British Theatre*, London: Palgrave Macmillan.

Aston, E. (2016), 'Room for Realism?', in S. Adiseshiah and L. LePage (eds), *Twenty-First Century Drama: What Happens Now*, 17–35, London: Palgrave Macmillan.

Balestrini, N. W., L. Lippert and M. Löschnigg (2020), 'Theater of Crisis: Contemporary Aesthetic Responses to a Cross-Sectional Condition', *Journal of Contemporary Drama in English*, 8 (1): 2–14.

Bauman, Z. and C. Bordoni (2014), *State of Crisis*, Cambridge: Polity Press.

Beck, U. (1992), *Risk Society: Towards a New Modernity*, trans. M. Ritter, London: Sage.

Berlant, L. (2011), *Cruel Optimism*, Durham: Duke University Press.

Berlant, L. (2016), 'The Commons: Infrastructure for Troubling Times', *Environment and Planning D: Society and Space*, 34 (3): 393–419.

Bond, E. (2020), 'Introduction: The Drama Species', in D. O'Hanlon (ed.), *Theatre in Times of Crisis: 20 Scenes for the Stage in Troubled Times*, v–xiv, London: Bloomsbury Methuen.

Bourdieu, P. (1998), *Acts of Resistance: Against the Tyranny of the Market*, trans. R. Nice, New York: The New Press.

Cazdyn, E. and I. Szeman (2011), *After Globalization*, Oxford: Wiley-Blackwell.

Clarke, J. (2010), 'Of Crises and Conjunctures: The Problem of the Present', *Journal of Communication Inquiry*, 34 (4): 337–54.

'crisis, n.', OED Online. December 2021. Oxford University Press. https://www.oed.com/view/Entry/44539?redirectedFrom=crisis (accessed 14 December 2021).

Curtis, N. (2013), *Idiotism: Capitalism and the Privatisation of Life*, London: Pluto Press.
Daddario, W. and T. Schmidt (2018), 'Introduction: Crisis and the Im/possibility of Thought', *Performance Philosophy*, 4 (1): 1–8.
Delanty, G. (2014), 'Introduction: Perspectives on Crisis and Critique in Europe Today', *European Journal of Social Theory*, 17 (3): 207–18.
Delgado, M. and C. Svich (eds) (2002), *Theatre in Crisis? Performance Manifestos for a New Century*, Manchester: Manchester University Press.
Diamond E., D. Varney and C. Amich (eds) (2017), *Performance, Feminism and Affect in Neoliberal Times*, London: Palgrave Macmillan.
Dolan, J. (2005), *Utopia in Performance: Finding Hope at the Theater*, Ann Arbor: University of Michigan Press.
Duggan, P. and L. Peschel (eds) (2016), *Performing (for) Survival: Theatre, Crisis, Extremity*, London: Palgrave Macmillan.
Ehrenberg, A. (2010), *The Weariness of the Self: Diagnosing the History of Depression in the Contemporary Age*, trans. E. Caouette, J. Homel, D. Homel, and D. Winkler, Montreal: McGill-Queen's University Press.
Fisher, M. (2009), *Capitalist Realism, Is There No Alternative?* London: Zero Books.
Fisher, M. (2016), *The Weird and the Eerie*, London: Repeater.
Fisher, T. and E. Katsouraki (eds) (2017), *Performing Antagonism: Theatre, Performance and Radical Democracy*, London: Palgrave Macmillan.
Fragkou, M. (2019), *Ecologies of Precarity in Twenty-First Century Theatre: Politics, Affect, Responsibility*, London: Bloomsbury Methuen.
Haiven, M. (2014), *Crises of Imagination, Crises of Power: Capitalism, Creativity and the Commons*, London: Zed Books.
Hall, S. and D. Massey (2010), 'Interpreting the Crisis', *Soundings*, 44: 57–71.
Harvey, D. (1989), *The Condition of Postmodernity: An Enquiry into the Origins of Cultural Change*, Oxford: Blackwell.
Harvey, D. (2005), *A Brief History of Neoliberalism*, Oxford: Oxford University Press.
Harvey, D. (2010), *The Enigma of Capital and the Crises of Capitalism*, Oxford: Oxford University Press.
Harvie, J. (2013), *Fair Play: Art, Performance and Neoliberalism*, Basingstoke: Palgrave Macmillan.
Haydon, A. (2013), 'Theatre in the 2000s', in D. Rebellato (ed.), *Modern British Playwriting 2000–2009*, 40–98, London: Bloomsbury Methuen.
Katsouraki, E. (2017), 'Epilogue: The "Trojan Horse" – Or, from Antagonism to the Politics of Resilience', in T. Fisher and E. Katsouraki (eds), *Performing Antagonism: Theatre, Performance and Radical Democracy*, 289–311, London: Palgrave Macmillan.
Klaić, D. (2002), 'The Crisis of Theatre? The Theatre of Crisis!' in M. Delgado and C. Svich (eds), *Theatre in Crisis? Performance Manifestos for a New Century*, 144–60, Manchester: Manchester University Press.

Klein, N. (2007), *The Shock Doctrine: The Rise of Disaster Capitalism*, New York: Metropolitan Books/Henry Holt.
Klein, N. (2014), *This Changes Everything: Capitalism vs the Climate*, New York: Simon and Schuster.
Lorey, I. (2015), *State of Insecurity: Government of the Precarious*, trans. A. Derieg, London: Verso.
Lost Dog (2020), *In a Nutshell*, 23 September. Available online: https://www.youtube.com/watch?v=CiMX1_bE7U8 (accessed 27 July 2021).
McGuigan, J. (2009), *Cool Capitalism*, London: Pluto Press.
McGuigan, J. (2016), *Neoliberal Culture*, London: Palgrave Macmillan.
Mouffe, C. (2000), *The Democratic Paradox*, London: Verso.
O'Hanlon, D. (2020), *Theatre in Times of Crisis: 20 Scenes for the Stage in Troubled Times*, London: Bloomsbury Methuen.
Okin, S. M. (1999), 'Is Multiculturalism Bad for Women?', in J. Cohen, M. Howard and M. C. Nussbaum (eds), *Is Multiculturalism Bad for Women? Susan Moller Okin with Respondents*, 7–26, Princeton: Princeton University Press.
Palladini, G. (2015), 'The Weimar Republic and Its Return: Unemployment, Revolution, or Europe in a State of Schuld', in M. Zaroulia and P. Hager (eds), *Performances of Capitalism, Crises and Resistance: Inside/Outside Europe*, 17–36, Basingstoke: Palgrave Macmillan.
Rancière, J. (1999), *Dis-Agreement: Politics and Philosophy*, trans. Julie Rose, Minneapolis: University of Minnesota Press.
Rebellato, D. (2017), 'Of an Apocalyptic Tone Recently Adopted in Theatre: British Drama, Violence and Writing', *Sillages Critiques*, 22. Available online: https://doi.org/10.4000/sillagescritiques.4798 (accessed 20 July 2021).
Steinbock, E., B. Ieven and M. de Valck (eds) (2021), *Art and Activism in the Age of Systemic Crisis: Aesthetic Resilience*, New York: Routledge.
Tomlin, L. (2019), *Political Dramaturgies and Theatre Spectatorship: Provocations for Change*, London: Bloomsbury Methuen.
Walby, S. (2015), *Crisis*, Cambridge: Polity Press.
Williams, R. (1977), *Marxism and Literature*, Oxford: Oxford University Press.
Zaroulia, M. and P. Hager (2015), 'Introduction: Europe, Crises, Performance', in M. Zaroulia and P. Hager (eds), *Performances of Capitalism, Crises and Resistance: Inside/Outside Europe*, 1–13, Basingstoke: Palgrave Macmillan.

Part One

Corporealites

2

Ageing as crisis on the twenty-first-century British stage

Siân Adiseshiah

In this chapter I analyse the intersection of crisis and ageing and the implications of this encounter, as addressed in recent theatre in the UK. The language of crisis, crisis understood both in one sense as a singular, discrete event, and in another as a pervasive, enduring catastrophe, permeates narratives of contemporary life in multifarious aspects. The considerable increase in life expectancy in the recent period, and the growth in the proportion of older people as part of the general population, is very evidently a striking social phenomenon deserving of attention. Since at least the late nineteenth century, this phenomenon, however, has been figured as a problem, and the negative evaluation of old age only intensified in the twentieth century (Chase 2009). In the contemporary period, the equation of old age with risk rather than opportunity has been presented in public discourse as a natural response to significant increases in longevity in the West (Gilleard and Higgs 2011). The concomitant resource implications, particularly since the 2008 financial crash and the Covid-19 pandemic of 2020 (which is ongoing at the time of writing), of living longer, have served to strengthen the articulation of ageing as consonant with narratives of crisis.

While contemporary theatre has responded to the phenomenon of ageing and, or as, crisis in a number of powerful ways, attention to this intersection has not yet been addressed in theatre scholarship.[1] The subjects of ageing, old age, longevity and generational politics have provoked some welcome full-length interventions from within theatre studies in the recent period, and augmenting these are scholarly articles that press the importance of

---

[1] Contemporary playwrights have demonstrated a keen interest in dramatizing ageing, old age and generational politics over the past two decades. For example, see Lavery (2001), tucker green (2005), Blythe (2006), Morgan (2011), Price (2011), Morgan (2012), Churchill (2015), Stephens (2017), and Edgar (2018).

foregrounding old age in our engagement with theatre.[2] Yet despite the frequent framing of old age as crisis in public discourse, there is no scholarly work that explores this particularly potent and provocative alignment in the context of theatre. This chapter addresses this gap by scrutinizing the ways in which crisis and old age have become increasingly associated, and by considering how two contemporary plays – Caryl Churchill's *Escaped Alone* (2016) and Lucy Kirkwood's *The Children* (2016) – intervene in this configuration. Doing this helps to make visible the coarticulation of old age and crisis, endeavours to disentangle this pernicious alignment, and begins to discover the potential for alternative narratives of both crisis and ageing.

While much drama in the contemporary period demonstrates interest in ageing, old age, longevity and generational politics, Kirkwood's *The Children* and Churchill's *Escaped Alone* are two plays where narratives of both crisis and ageing are explicitly centred and both plays acknowledge an increasing conceptual interconnectedness of crisis and ageing in the twenty-first century. I discuss *The Children* and *Escaped Alone* together because while they have a striking amount in common, they seem to arrive at divergent conclusions about ageing and crisis, the former reproducing, the latter repudiating, this conceptual interconnectedness. Both written by women, these plays premiered in the main auditorium at the Royal Court Theatre, London, in the same politically tumultuous year – 2016 (the year of the UK European Union membership referendum and the election of Donald Trump as President of the United States) – with the same director, James MacDonald, and same designer, Miriam Buether; they are both post-apocalyptic dramas rendered through private, domestic scenes; both plays feature a musical interlude: a dance in one, a song in the other; both Royal Court productions were staged with boxy, hyper-naturalistic three-wall sets (a kitchen in one, a garden in the other); the actor, Deborah Findlay, appeared in both productions (as Hazel in *The Children* and Sally in *Escaped Alone*); and, crucially for this chapter, they both prioritize ageing, old age, longevity and generational identity: the characters are in their 60s, 70s and older and older age is explicitly foregrounded as essential to both works. For all these similarities, however, they configure the intersection of crisis and ageing differently, and this difference has significant political effects. First, I introduce the ways in which I am thinking about these terms and their intersection.

---

[2] For full-length discussions on ageing and old age from Theatre Studies perspectives, see Basting (1998), Lipscomb and Marshall (2010), Mangan (2013) and McCormick (2017). Shorter responses to this theme include: Harpin (2012), Fuchs (2014), Moore (2014), Fuchs (2016), Moore (2017), Harvie (2018) and Moore (2019).

Crisis

Vicky Angelaki frames her enquiry into the staging of crisis in twenty-first-century theatre with reference to two *OED* definitions: one originating from the Latinized form of the Greek word *krisis* referring to the moment in the development of a disease when recovery or death are the only outcomes; the other refers to a turning point in a state of affairs where the immediate requirement is for a decisive change for better or worse (2017: 2). With emphasis on change for the worse, the sociologist Sylvia Walby defines crisis as 'an event that has the potential to cause a large *detrimental* change to the social system' (2015: 14; emphasis added) but she also considers a 'lack of proportionality between cause and consequence' (14) to be a defining characteristic; key for Walby in conceptualizing crisis is the proposition that 'something potentially having large, long-term consequences is the result of something small happening in a short period of time' (19). With reference to late nineteenth-century capitalism, Stuart Hall and Bill Schwarz view crises as occurring 'when the social formation can no longer be reproduced on the basis of the pre-existing system of social relations' (1985: 9). The notion of a structural breach is taken up again thirty years later by Hall, this time with Doreen Massey and Michael Rustin, who focus on the radical transformative possibilities incited by the arrival of crisis; they refer to '[t]he present economic crisis' as 'a moment of potential rupture', an opportunity for far-reaching systemic change (2015: 13).

An opposing conception of crisis is the notion of the contemporary moment (the post-9/11, post-financial crash contemporary) as in some form of *perpetual* or *permanent* crisis – or what Lauren Berlant calls 'crisis ordinariness' – where people are compelled to 'adapt to an unfolding change', 'a process embedded in the ordinary that unfolds in stories about navigating what's overwhelming' (2011: 10). Thus, rather than conceiving of crisis as triggering a call for a decision or a change in direction, crisis in Berlant's sense means precisely the opposite: indecision, stagnation or the congealing of (an already) bad situation, and the requirement to adapt, or make the necessary adjustments, in order to be able to bear a seemingly endless state of precarious existence in a post-historical present. The possibility of material change imagined in earlier incarnations of crisis is thus replaced by technocratic forms of crisis management, where crises afford business opportunities, which result in the perpetuation of the status quo, or the normalization of worsening conditions. This conception of crisis is without a horizon beyond further processes of crisis recovery, which bring with them only more of the same – what Walter Benjamin called the catastrophe of the perpetuation of the status quo ('[t]hat things are "status quo" *is* the catastrophe' (1999: 473; original emphasis). Crisis management works to conceal the cracks from where a decisive break from present circumstances might be advanced.

The dominance of the second of these two very different conceptualizations of crisis and its permeation of a structure of feeling in the contemporary post-2008 moment has led to a shift in the signification of crisis, which has prompted Willem Schinkel to declare that there is now a 'crisis of crisis' (2015: 38). No longer evoking its original Greek focus on a turning point or its referral in more recent usages to historical rupture, its meaning has moved to connote 'a perpetuation of what is' and refers to a 'condition marked by post-historical permanence' (38). At the same time, we should note that this shift is unstable; the very investment in crisis narratives implies (a potentially radicalizable) knowledge of the meagreness of the present. Naming crisis – even if it is deployed normatively to describe ordinary, everyday life (as opposed to a singular, discrete event) – is simultaneously to mark present human (and non-human) life as attenuated, insufficient and dejected. The challenge for political theatre – a theatre seeking alternative narratives of social relations – is how to revive (or newly instigate) representations of crises that enable political agency, representations that configure the destructive fallout of crises as simultaneously producing the potential to bring into view breaks with the catastrophe of the status quo.

Ageing/longevity/old age

Ageing has long been seen as a personal crisis. Susan Sontag describes ageing as 'a movable doom. It is a crisis that never exhausts itself, because the anxiety is never really used up. Being a crisis of the imagination rather than of "real life," it has the habit of repeating itself again and again' (1972: 33). The crisis of ageing is represented in popular discourse as a source of comedy, shame, embarrassment and humiliation: old age is undesirable and undesired, and ageing an undignified process of unalterable degeneration. Within this tragic narrative emerges the much-repeated complaint of invisibility. Betty Friedan writes of '[t]he blackout of images of women or men visible over sixty-five, engaged in any vital or productive adult activity, and their replacement by the "problem" of age, [which] is our society's very definition of age. Age is perceived only as decline or deterioration from youth' (1993: 8). Gerontologist Margaret Gullette refers to age as the 'different difference': unlike gender or critical race studies, 'writing about age is not taken as an intellectual or theoretical interest ... rather, it can only be a brave sign of recognition of one's own advancing age' (2004: 111). The intersection of older age with gender constitutes further limitations on ageing women, who, as Sontag observed in her essay, 'The Double Standards of Aging', are more afflicted by ageing than men, an experience she sees as 'an ordeal of the imagination – a moral disease, a social pathology' (1972: 38).

Yet despite the endurance of the notion that old age is an appalling state inherently threatened by mortality, more recently a complicating set of ideas and contestations associated with later life have emerged. As the period of healthy life after retirement has significantly expanded and successive cohorts entering retirement have been doing so with increasing resources, a more affirming image of post-work older age has been refigured in terms of the 'third age', a period of later life organized 'around the themes of self-realisation and the pursuit of personal interests' (Higgs and Gilleard 2014: 12). In the context of an abundance of new consumption choices offered by an array of anti-ageing products, body modification processes, later life health and exercise practices and regimes, and organized travel and leisure pursuits, media depictions of vibrant, glamorous actors, pop stars, DJs, models, and marathon runners in their 60s, 70s, 80s and older, interrupt the more familiar figure of the older ordinary person in decline. Appropriation of cultural practices usually associated with youth by those in later life (performatively interpellated as the new or young old) is permitted as a praiseworthy transgression, a vital expression of dynamic agency that reifies notions of individual will, self-conscious life-building, social mobility and self-scripting.

This recent development undermines the homogenization of old people as a category – a (shifting) demographic of five or six decades – and contests the pervasion of gerontophobic images that align post-work older age with biological and social senescence and decrepitude. Yet, as Higgs and Gilleard contend, the third age is distinctive for 'its active exclusion of "agedness" from the discourse of later life' (12). The repression of notions of frailty, vulnerability or dependency from third-age representations has the effect of deferring agedness, deep old age or *real* old age (the old old) to the 'fourth age', a cultural space or social imaginary within which agency and personhood are replaced with frailty and permanent dependency. Thus, while the diversification of images of older age to include representations of old people as vibrant, strong, active and autonomous, helps to convey a richer, more pluralistic narrative of the experience of ageing, it achieves this by reproducing gerontophobic conceptions of later life: what these images tell us is that older people who live active lives are exhibiting characteristics of *youth* – not old age – and are endorsed for doing so. To reconfigure this (neoliberal) discourse is to discover alternative narratives of frailty, dependence and care; it is to attribute importance to dependent, frail lives: to see these lives as not just liveable, but valuable. Both plays discussed here are keen to validate older lives; however, while *Escaped Alone* brings into question normative attributions of value to different phases of the life course, *The Children* leaves ageist structures intact.

The Children

Older people's claims on the future, their culpability for the state of the world and their obligations to younger generations are primary concerns in Kirkwood's *The Children*. The play focuses on three characters, a couple – Hazel and Robin – and their ex-colleague, Rose, who, it transpires, has had an affair with Robin. The stage directions stipulate that all three are '*in their sixties*' (Kirkwood 2016: 2), and more specific age references are revealed further on in the play when Hazel mentions that she's sixty-seven (53) and Rose that she's sixty-five (59). They are retired, having worked as physicists at a nuclear plant on the East coast. This is a post-apocalyptic narrative: an earthquake has caused a spillage from the nuclear power station and much of the local environment is highly toxic and out of bounds, and there are extended power cuts and food shortages. However, the play does not present estranged dystopian landscapes depicted in works such as Cormac McCarthy's *The Road* (2006) or Emily St John Mandel's *Station Eleven* (2014); as Michael Billington notes in his review of the Royal Court production, what we see is a 'precarious normality' set in a familiar-looking cottage kitchen, within which all the action takes place (2016). The challenge of the play lies not in the cognitive estrangement of the dystopian setting but in the ethical-political dilemma posed by Rose, who invites Hazel and Robin to join her and a crew of over-65s to return to the plant in order to clean and fix it, and relieve the existing staff who are in their twenties and thirties.

This is an exemplar of the disproportion in scale of cause and effect that Walby outlines in her definition of crisis; a minor earthquake has caused a spillage in the nuclear plant, which has devastated the region for generations to come. However, while the crisis is attributed to a discrete event, the structure of feeling in the play is Berlant's 'crisis ordinariness' (2011: 10): the sense of an endemic, pervasive catastrophe stretching far into the future. Rose's arrival at the cottage interrupts what feels like an extended, post-historical present where Hazel and Robin have adjusted to the crisis and revised their routines and expectations of what constitutes liveability. Hazel is particularly adept at crisis management, as evidenced with her '*domestic hand*', '[w]*ild flowers in milk bottles*' (4), efficient administration of the 'scheduled blackouts' (11), not using electricity 'more than we absolutely have to' (14), keeping healthy, eating yoghurt and practising yoga. Hazel performs these rituals with care – with zest even – a carriage that demonstrates the pleasure she feels at her own adroit response to this permanent crisis.

Contrary to stereotypes of lifeless, old people, Hazel and Robin inhabit the present in active and vital ways – appearing as relevant, vibrant, fleshly, libidinal and complex. On three separate occasions in the play, Hazel utters the mantra, 'if you're not going to grow, don't live' (16). This form of affirmation of older life celebrates third-age notions of the autonomous, multifaceted, vigorous, post-work subject. However, Hazel's alignment of (the right to) life with growth is at once a deeply ableist conception of liveability, and, at the same time, an investment in a neoliberal logic of progress for evaluating human existence, a logic that has ironically contributed to environmental devastation. In this way, the deferral of old age in third-age celebrations of active forms of living is present in Hazel's prizing of youthfulness as the ideal; 'I AM NOT OLD' (53), Hazel retorts to Rose when the latter encourages her to consider returning to the plant to relieve the younger workers ('you've both already had long and full lives' (53)).

There is an erotic energy in circulation in the cottage, which is a welcome disaggregation of sexual expression and youthfulness. The amatory encounters between Robin and Hazel, and Robin and Rose, performed by the actors in the Royal Court production in playful, but validating ways, belie the normative depiction of old age as asexual or abjectly sexual. However, this gesture of marking old age as erotically capacitated is undermined by Robin's declaration to Rose that the thing he desired most but could not have was sex with Fiona, the nubile, large-breasted, *young* milk maid, who made a play for him, but fell asleep sucking her thumb in his lap before his Viagra kicked in. The Fiona story confirms Sontag's polemic about the double standards of gendered old age, where older women are held to much higher and narrower standards of attractiveness than older men, which impacts significantly on the sexual dispositions and opportunities of both genders. While sexual desire is a meaningful part of the lives of these baby boomers, we are informed – through the Fiona story – that the ultimate arousal for an older man is actually a 'girl' with 'mesmerising' breasts (45). Through this clichéd fantasy of the heterosexual male gaze, sexualized girlhood is presented as peak femininity to which the ageing woman can never return.

Hazel's intensive efforts to defer old age are interwoven with her teleological reading of death, death as the inescapable and terrifying conclusion of old age: '[h]ow can anybody consciously moving towards death, I mean by their own design, possibly be happy? People of our age have to resist – you *have* to resist, Rose' (15; original emphasis). In contrast, Robin describes his body as 'rented meat' (69), points out that 'we've decided that natural decay is unnatural' (70) and declares in frustration to Hazel that he would 'quite like to die at some point' (69). Robin's perspective on ageing and death thus constitutes a counterpoint to Hazel's, one supplemented by the play's gentle parody of the self-congratulatory, third-age agenda Hazel promotes:

> [y]ou have a choice, don't you, exactly, at our age which is that you slow down, melt into your slippers, start ordering front-fastening bras out of Sunday supplements or you make a committed choice to keep moving you know because you have to think: This is not the end of our lives but a new and exciting chapter. (16)

The revelation that Rose has had (or still has) breast cancer and the knowledge that Robin has been fatally affected by radiation (as he coughs up blood towards the end of the play) betrays the fiction of the independent, vigorous, active ageing subject that underpins Hazel's philosophy of ageing.

The Children thus sets in motion two competing scripts of ageing: firstly, a third age, active ageing narrative associated with Hazel, which promotes an agentic, lively self, unhindered by physical limitations or dependency; secondly, a depiction that attaches ageing to a discourse of decline, poor health and death, exemplified by Robin and Rose, where ageing and decline are coarticulated, and decline is incrementally a decrease in value in terms of what it signifies to be fully human. Through a lively and sympathetic construction of Hazel's character, the play, in part, entertains a conception of active ageing: Hazel's vitality, humour, self-sufficiency, and care-giving are compelling and likeable traits, traits appreciated by Robin, Rose and the audience alike. However, the play simultaneously undermines this conception by placing these in a structure of pointlessness. Hazel's dynamism is particularly expressed through crisis management strategies, and ultimately the play makes evident the futility of these. The stage directions state that '[t]he land beneath [the cottage] *is being eroded*' (4), this erosion observable only when an apple rolls down the table because the kitchen is at a slight tilt. The physical disintegration of the land beneath Hazel's and Robin's home is the void at the centre of the crisis, a void masked by the various forms of problem management that Hazel so expertly performs. It is the logic of Rose's mission – along with its underpinning equation of ageing with decline and its investment in a politics of generational responsibility – that the play finally facilitates.

Crucially for my argument, *The Children*'s reproduction of both the narrative of ageing as decline and the proposition of competing generational interests becomes entangled in the play with conceptions of crisis. Rose's interruption of the regime of adjustments to which Hazel and Robin have learned to adapt, and her expectation that they return to the power station to 'restore control' (47), suggests that the critical potential of crisis might be rescued – crisis as a turning point that leads to a decisive break – and brings with it a glimpse of new possibilities. The heroics of these baby boomers are simultaneously a self-sacrificial act of atonement that makes way for reconciliation and new beginnings. A corollary of this, however, is that old age and environmental crisis are coproduced as threats to be overcome. The only way for these older people to act decisively in response to this crisis – a crisis they are deemed to have caused – is to give up their claims to a future, this sacrifice validated as valiantly selfless but socially and morally essential. Perhaps more disturbingly, it is possible to interpret the play as suggesting that despite this generational self-sacrifice nothing will fundamentally change beyond the premature deaths of Rose and her team. Rather astonishingly, Rose says '[p]ersonally I think fusion is still our best hope' (34), this appearing to suggest that the apparatus of nuclear power may not be dismantled after this particular crisis. What seems at first to be a decisive response to the crisis, might, in fact, be another form of crisis management, which will inevitably be followed by more of the same.

The most perceptible political intervention the play advances emanates from its investment in the narrative of generational responsibility. Rose says, '[t]hese … *young people* these *children*, basically, actually with their whole lives ahead and it's not fair it's not right it seems *wrong*. Doesn't it? Because we built it, didn't we?' (58; original emphasis). The play is freighted with an ethics of generational obligation, accountability and guilt, which seems in tune with what Jen Harvie has described as 'adversarial ageism', where the growth in the proportion of old people is identified as a crisis, old people are demonized for being 'avaricious and burdensome' and generations are pitted against each other (2018: 332), the most famous proponent of this perspective being the Conservative Party member and former MP David Willetts (2010). Ultimately, *The Children* maps the crisis narrative of contemporary environmental politics onto ageing, old age and generational conflict, and in the process intimates the expendability of the old to the maintenance of the (catastrophe of the) status quo.

Escaped Alone

Escaped Alone features four characters, who are all women in their seventies: in fact, the stage directions insist that '[*t*]*hey are all at least seventy*' (Churchill 2016: 4). The play juxtaposes oddly hyper-naturalistic scenes in Sally's pretty back garden with richly surreal, apocalyptic monologues, spoken by the character, Mrs Jarrett, who, in the Royal Court production, stepped outside of the garden and directly addressed the audience on seven separate occasions, reporting on catastrophic events that had already taken place. The contrast between these past-tense monologues and the present-tense garden scenes of familiar, age-normative behaviour (the women chat and drink tea in the garden) makes visible a striking temporal disjunction at work in the play, a disjunction that disrupts what Elizabeth Freeman calls chrononormativity.

Chrononormativity refers to the way in which time is curated to facilitate the maximum accumulation of profit. Freeman describes chrononormative time as being constituted by the 'interlocking temporal schemes necessary for genealogies of descent and for the mundane workings of everyday life' (2010: xxiii). Chrononormative time is synonymous with dominant perceptions of temporality – what we might also call hegemonic time – a structure of time in service to capital, which in turn, as Sarah Sharma writes, 'caters to the clock that meters the life and lifestyle of some of its workers and consumers', while 'others are left to calibrate themselves to serve the dominant temporality' (2014: 139). The inescapability of chrononormativity is also a masking of what Ernst Bloch calls 'nonsynchronism', a state where '[n]ot all people exist in the same Now. They do so only externally, by virtue of the fact that they may all be seen today. But that does not mean that they are living at the same time with others' (1977: 22). There are similarities between nonsynchronism and what Johannes Fabian has called a 'denial of coevalness' (1983: 32). To be coeval is to form part of the same temporality with others – to exist in the same historical community. Within the context of anthropology Fabian has used the notion of denying coevalness to understand anthropology's othering of the human objects of its gaze. Denying coevalness is a way of seeing that views marginalized communities as living in different historical moments, which reinforces colonial binaristic thinking: primitivistic/progressive, static/dynamic and backward/advanced. The denial of coevalness and Bloch's notion of nonsynchronism are the corollaries of chrononormativity: that time constructed in such a way as to function as the most efficient conduit for the movement of capital inevitably marks other modes of temporality, or subjects outside of chrononormativity, as temporally backward, obdurate or deviant.

Escaped Alone's disturbance of conventional time is thus simultaneously a challenge to neoliberal logics: the play refuses familiar temporal patterns that invisibly host the flow of capital. There are multiple layers of temporality in *Escaped Alone*: the stage directions state that the time of the play is: '*Summer afternoon. A number of afternoons but the action is continuous*' (4). The conflation of several afternoons, where nothing happens except for conversation between old women, produces the sense of time suspended; Lisa Baraitser analyses suspended time in terms of 'felt experiences of time *not passing*' that are 'affectively dull or obdurate temporalities' (2017: 2;

original emphasis) and she calls for engagement with 'time that is lived as radically immoveable, experiences of time that are not just slow, sluggish, or even interminable in the sense of Heidegger's account of boredom, but are radically suspended' (4). This slow or stuck time of the play – static conversation over several afternoons – is discontinuous with the time of the audience – the play usually runs for approximately 50 minutes – and this discontinuity reflects Lynne Segal's observation that 'time seems to speed up as we age' (2014: 184). This difference in generational experiences of time locates age cohorts as out of sync with each other. This temporal dislocation – a recalling of Bloch's nonsynchronism – is marked in some of the women's memories of 'shillings and pence' (7) and what 'used to be the fish and chip shop' (9), memories that interrupt the here and now of the present with an historical elsewhere of the past. The separation of Churchill's characters in a different timescape from the audience's is a radical disjunction that forms a central part of the materiality of the play.

The dynamic, non-naturalistic deployment of temporality in *Escaped Alone* contrasts with the linear, naturalistic use of time in *The Children*, where in the latter the internal time of the play largely maps onto the time the audience spends watching it. An additional contrast between the plays is the depiction of older age. With the exception of Mrs Jarrett, the women in the Royal Court production of *Escaped Alone* stay seated throughout the play – even during the song in part six (The Crystals' 'Da Doo Ron Ron' in the Royal Court production). None of the women actively participates in third-age self-making: there is no mention of yoga or any other form of exercise; nothing about good, healthy diet; no talk of clubs or activities; no mention of travel or holidays; and no reference to sexual desire. In the earlier sections of the play they discuss the past, family members, everyday living (shopping, going to the dentist) and television programmes. In part four, they venture into more technical, philosophical and political subject matter, such as very large numbers ('and then of course you get a googol and a googolplex' (18)), what it is politically acceptable to joke about, and the experience of time accelerating as they age. In part five, they share utopian desires (flying, the ability to speak every language, invisibility). In part seven they return to age-conventional topics of experiences of retirement, doctors appointments, hip replacements, hairdresser visits; and in part eight they speak again about family members. These conversations are interspersed with extended moments of paused action, where spotlighted characters share their anxieties and phobias through monologues about cats (Sally), agoraphobia (Lena) and spouse killing/prison (Vi). Mrs Jarrett's version of this is her repetition of the phrase 'terrible rage' twenty-five times (42). These women do not reflect third-age conceptions of older age. Sharing memories of the past, discussing physical ailments, exchanging stories of family members, and passing long periods of time sitting and talking do not exemplify typical characteristics of energetic, entrepreneurial third-agers. Fourth-age attributes of weakness, slowness and neediness are observed by the women but without the concomitant hollowing out of human value. These attributes feature prominently but are not defining. In place of yoghurt and yoga are disquisitions on philosophy and science. These, perhaps, appear absurd, but this absurdity works productively to expose and loosen the semantic continuity between old woman and social irrelevance.

Towards the end of the play, there is a revelation that Sally thinks she may have lied in the witness box to protect Vi against the charge of murdering her husband (Vi was convicted of manslaughter): 'I didn't tell it quite how it was because... I took into account what he was like' (34). Vi is initially affronted: 'you think I'm a murderer?' (34) and Sally replies: 'I don't care if you are... so long ago... look I'm sorry' (35). The scene concludes as follows:

Sally   I don't even know what I said any more

Mrs J   what did you see?

Sally   certainly don't know what I saw any more

Vi   you think I'm a murderer

Sally   maybe you were I don't know do you think you're a murderer

Vi   no

Sally   okay so maybe you weren't

Vi   I don't remember either

Mrs J   you don't remember what you

Vi   no it's gone

Sally   there you are then. (35)

Here is a fusion of memory loss – senescence if you like – with feminist love and solidarity, further layered with an anarchic disregard for (patriarchal) law, which in turn produces a narrative of old age as replete with emotional significance, generosity, and humour, and importantly one that does not reify youthfulness.

Against what Cynthia Rich describes as the 'twice unseen' condition of old women – 'unseen because they are old, unseen because they are women' (1984: 84) – the audience of *Escaped Alone* encounters these old women but is simultaneously alerted to their social invisibility, their unseen-ness detectible through their temporal separation. There is, however, a transitory moment of temporal coalescence in the speech that formed a hashtag in tweets about the play: Mrs Jarrett's 'terrible rage' speech (42). The effect of that monologue lies in its profoundly powerful expression of common feeling in this extended period of crisis (terrible rage as a response to this terrible age, age referring to both epoch and life course). This potent phrase is provocative in its negation of the affective or spiritual consolation so common to many post-apocalyptic narratives, and while refusing a singular meaning, it resonates with the age-focused reading I offer in this chapter. In May Sarton's novel, *As We Are Now*, about a 76-year-old former maths teacher abandoned in a care home, the protagonist Caro Spencer writes in her diary, '[p]eople expect serenity of the old. That is the stereotype, the mask we are expected to put on.... My anger, because I am old, is considered a sign of madness or senility' (1985: 81). Significantly, in Churchill's play, Mrs Jarrett's rage does not communicate as madness or senility. Mrs Jarrett's 'terrible rage' speech is a charged moment of interruption, perhaps akin to what Sara Ahmed calls 'a feminist snap': 'a snap is one moment of a longer history of being affected by what you come up against' (2017: 190). The speech could also be read as an example of Elinor Fuchs's notion of 'estragement', a coinage that removes the 'n' from Brechtian estrangement (*Verfremdung*) to produce an amalgam of 'strange' (or 'estrange') and 'age': '[i]n an age-conscious *Verfremdung* scene the ageing figures may see as if for the first time' (2014: 77). Mrs Jarrett's snap or moment of estragement is centripetal in its disruption of familiar narrative and dramatic structures – there is no climax, dénouement, closure, appeasement or atonement in the play.

As the only character not designated by a first name, the naming of Mrs Jarrett invites attention. There is an evocation of Cynthia Jarrett, an African Caribbean woman – frequently referred to in the press as 'Mrs Jarrett' – who infamously died of a heart attack during a controversial police search of her home after the arrest of her son in relation to what the police regarded as a suspicious car tax disc, an event that was one of the precipitators of the Broadwater Farm riots in Tottenham in 1985. In place of a tragic precipitator of riots on an estate in North London, *Escaped Alone*'s Mrs Jarrett appears as a reporter of surreal crises of apocalyptic proportions ('[v]illages were buried... Babies were born and quickly became blind.... Survivors were now solitary and went insane at different rates' (8). She is a clairvoyant figure in the sense that Peter Pál Pelbart conceives: as seeing 'something that exceeds her, that overflows him; a phenomenon that has nothing to do with fantasy. The object of clairvoyance is reality itself, a dimension of reality where its empirical contours are extrapolated in order to better grasp its potential, entirely real albeit not yet unfolded' (2015: 2). Mrs Jarrett is the Derridean stranger who arrives without invitation; she is the trespasser, a transgressor of space and time. She is constituted through a symbolic navigation of ontological and epistemological discourses, a navigation that articulates (female) old age as aligned with both philosophical truths and worldly knowledge.

Dislodged from *The Children*'s positioning of it as the necessary sacrifice for a redeemed future (or more likely for a continuation of the status quo), *Escaped Alone* articulates old age as essential to responding to the challenges of crisis. Neither declining in human value nor sacrificed to a youthful ideal, female old age in *Escaped Alone* is presented as trivial, static, nostalgic and needy, as well as profound, tender, witty and knowledgeable, a presentation that in turn assigns value to the full range of human faculties and frailties. The performance of Mrs Jarrett – as played by Linda Bassett with an Estuary English accent and loose leggings – offered another form of (classed) dissonance as the aggrandized Cassandra figure from Greek myth evoked by the character's role in the play chafed against normative expectations of the post-menopausal woman, the woman whose 'growing erotic invisibility' (Segal 2014: 26) renders her rapidly uninteresting to the public gaze. The ex-lollipop lady, a mother, who has had a hip replacement, derails the canonical trajectory of both the voices of prophecy and the visitors returning from utopian lands: such as the Portuguese explorer, Raphael Hythloday from More's *Utopia*, or the aristocrat Julian West in Edward Bellamy's 1888 novel *Looking Backward*. The radical feminist utopias of the 1960s and 1970s replaced bourgeois white male heroes with female protagonists, occasionally working class, and even less frequently of colour (Joanna Russ's *The Female Man* and Marge Piercy's *Woman on the Edge of Time*), but never with *old* protagonists. In this way, the centrality of female old age in a contemporary post-apocalyptic narrative staging of crisis is a bold surprise, a genre-shifting undertaking.

Experiencing ageing as personal crisis in the way that Sontag describes and as exemplified in *The Children* does not appear as a trope in *Escaped Alone*. While *The Children* maps ageing as personal calamity onto a crisis narrative of environmental apocalypse, *Escaped Alone* refuses the connection between ageing and crisis: it regards the two as philosophically distinct. Instead, the play brings into productive confrontation the relation of old age (female old age in particular) and narratives of crisis. The play does not offer an aesthetic or ideological resolution to contemporary crises: spectators are left kindled, needled, roused and nagged by a coruscating theatrical intervention. The play's loosening and rearrangement of conventional semantic connections in discourses on ageing and crises has the potential to revitalize the political functionality of both crisis and old age, and to mark old age, and female old age in particular, as of consequence in the key narratives of our time. The play gestures towards the resignification of crisis as a catastrophic phenomenon of the contemporary in need of a collective response. It achieves this through a radical manipulation of temporalities and spatial relations, where chronological, historical and mythical time flood the space of the present and breach the connections between ageing and crisis. While ageing and crisis are coproduced in *The Children*, in *Escaped Alone* this coproduction is disaggregated: old women are positioned as the lens through which crisis is examined; they are both the protagonists and narrators of the crisis narrative, but they do not form the basis of its constitution.

References

Ahmed, S. (2017), *Living a Feminist Life*, Durham: Duke University Press.
Angelaki, V. (2017), *Social and Political Theatre in 21st-Century Britain: Staging Crisis*, London: Bloomsbury Methuen.
Baraitser, L. (2017), *Enduring Time*, London: Bloomsbury Methuen.
Basting, A. (1998), *The Stages of Age: Performing Age in Contemporary American Culture*, Ann Arbor: University of Michigan Press.
Benjamin, W. (1999), *The Arcades Project*, Cambridge: Harvard University Press.
Berlant, L. (2011), *Cruel Optimism*, Durham: Duke University Press.
Billington, M. (2016), 'Review of *The Children*', *Guardian*, 25 November. Available online: https://www.theguardian.com/stage/2016/nov/25/children-review-lucy-kirkwood-royal-court (accessed 22 June 2019).
Bloch, E. (1977), 'Nonsynchronism and the Obligation to Its Dialectics', *New German Critique*, 11 (spring): 22–38.
Blythe, A. (2006), *Cruising*, London: Nick Hern.
Chase, K. (2009), *The Victorians and Old Age*, Oxford: Oxford University Press.
Churchill, C. (2015), *Here We Go*, London: Nick Hern.
Churchill, C. (2016), *Escaped Alone*, London: Nick Hern.
Edgar, D. (2018), *Trying It On*, London: Nick Hern.
Fabian, J. (1983), *Time and the Other: How Anthropology Makes Its Object*, New York: Columbia University Press.
Freeman, E. (2010), *Time Binds: Queer Temporalities, Queer Histories*, Durham: Duke University Press.

Friedan, B. (1993), *The Fountain of Age*, London: Jonathan Cape.
Fuchs, E. (2014), 'Estrangement: Towards an "Age Theory" Theatre Criticism', *Performance Research*, 19 (3): 69–77.
Fuchs, E. (2016), 'Rehearsing Age', *Modern Drama*, 59 (2): 143–54.
Gilleard, C. and P. Higgs (2011), 'Ageing Abjection and Embodiment in the Fourth Age', *Journal of Aging Studies*, 25 (2): 135–42.
Gullette, M. (2004), *Aged by Culture*, Chicago: University of Chicago Press.
Hall, S. and B. Schwarz (1985), 'State and Society, 1880–1930', in M. Langan and B. Schwarz (eds), *Crises in the British State 1880–1930*, 7–32, London: Hutchinson.
Hall, S., D. Massey and M. Rustin (2015), 'After Neoliberalism: Analysing the Present', in S. Hall, D. Massey and M. Rustin (eds), *After Neoliberalism: The Kilburn Manifesto*, 3–19, London: Lawrence and Wishart.
Harpin, A. (2012), 'The Lives of Our Mad Mothers: Aging and Contemporary Performance', *Women and Performance: A Journal of Feminist Theory*, 22 (1): 67–87.
Harvie, J. (2018), 'Boom! Adversarial Ageism, Chrononormativity, and the Anthropocene', *Contemporary Theatre Review*, 28 (3): 332–44.
Higgs, P. and C. Gilleard (2014), 'Frailty, Abjection and the "Othering" of the Fourth Age', *Health Sociology Review*, 23 (1): 10–19.
Kirkwood, L. (2016), *The Children*, London: Nick Hern.
Lavery, B. (2001), *A Wedding Story*, London: Faber and Faber.
Lipscomb V. B. and L. Marshall (2010), *Staging Age: The Performance of Age in Theatre, Dance and Film*, New York: Palgrave.
Mangan, M. (2013), *Staging Ageing: Theatre, Performance and the Narrative of Decline*, London: Intellect.
McCormick, S. (2017), *Applied Theatre: Creative Ageing*, London: Bloomsbury Methuen.
Moore, B. (2014), 'Depth Significance and Absence: Age Effects in New British Theatre', *Age, Culture, Humanities*, 1 (1): 163–95.
Moore, B. (2017), 'The Age Performances of Peggy Shaw: Intersection, Interoception and Interruption', in C. McGlynn, M. O'Neil and M. Schrage-Früh (eds), *Ageing Women in Literature and Visual Culture: Reflections, Refractions, Reimaginings*, 73–92, London: Palgrave.
Moore, B. (2019), '"It Did Get Rid of the 'These People Are Old People' Thing in My Brain": Challenging the Otherness of Old Age through One-to-One Performance', *ArtsPraxis*, 5 (2): 185–201.
Morgan, A. (2011), *Lovesong*, London: Oberon.
Morgan, A. (2012), *27*, London: Oberon.
Pelbart, P. P. (2015), 'What Is the Contemporary?', *Afterall Journal*, 39: 2.
Price, T. (2011), *Salt Root and Roe*, London: Methuen.
Rich, C. (1984), *Look Me in the Eye: Old Women, Aging and Ageism*, London: The Women's Press.
Sarton, M. (1985), *As We Are Now*, London: The Women's Press.

Schinkel, W. (2015), 'The Image of Crisis: Walter Benjamin and the Interpretation of "Crisis" in Modernity', *Thesis Eleven*, 127 (1): 36–51.
Segal, L. (2014), *Out of Time: The Pleasures and Perils of Ageing*, London: Verso.
Sharma, S. (2014), *In the Meantime: Temporality and Cultural Politics*, Durham: Duke University Press.
Sontag, S. (1972), 'The Double Standard of Aging', *The Saturday Review*, 23 September: 29–38. Available online: https://www.unz.com/print/SaturdayRev-1972sep23-00029 (accessed 8 July 2019).
Stephens, S. (2017), *Nuclear War*, London: Methuen.
tucker green, d. (2005), *Generations*, London: Nick Hern.
Walby, S. (2015), *Crisis*, Cambridge: Polity.
Willetts, D. (2010), *The Pinch: How the Baby Boomers Took Their Children's Future – and Why They Should Give It Back*, London: Atlantic Books.

3

Creative contexts and crises of care: Ella Hickson's *The Writer*

Vicky Angelaki

At the current moment in British playwriting, the work of Ella Hickson stands out for its experimentation, innovation and sociopolitical astuteness. What is particularly impressive regarding Hickson's output and her overall impact, considered contextually within the younger generation of British playwrights, is the expansiveness of her canvas, meaning both her thematic oeuvre and her formal openness. Since her beginnings as a writer, Hickson has engaged with some of our most significant challenges in the contemporary period: the economy, gender inequality and labour/exploitation feature prominently among these. Hickson has experimented with different play formats: some of her work is what we might describe as full length, stretching beyond the two-hour mark, entering the territory that we might most typically associate with stage naturalism and realism. Some of her other work, on the contrary, is minimalist and concentrated on a specific moment in time, with which she engages sharply and precisely, not allowing the play to stretch into a longer expedition. Whichever the scenario, however, I would like to argue that especially since *Oil* (2016) onwards, Hickson's meaningful, substantial stage environments as cultivated by her texts and realized in particularly fortuitous productions have, to use an expression that is associated with the assertion of female presence in public discourses and spaces, and which signifies the right to a presence in the dialogue, visibility and influence/intervention, righteously taken up space.

In this chapter I specifically concentrate on Hickson's *The Writer*, staged at London's Almeida in 2018. *The Writer*, I propose, is a landmark play within Hickson's existing body of work because of its considerable contribution to formal innovation in contemporary playwriting, as well as its highly astute and extraordinarily topical engagement with the surrounding socio-artistic context. Specifically, I refer to transgressive behaviours against female artists within the predominantly male-managed creative industries broadly conceived. Taken together, these factors render the play a significant intervention, which ought to be recognized for its vision and boldness as much as for its clarity and lucidity. My analysis will go on to focus on the assertion of female presence in institutional spaces systemically associated with male authority as a way of both highlighting and undermining these stratifications and their failures, especially when it comes to exposing crises of care. In my view, then, *The Writer* is engaged both in the furthering of access and equality agendas, and in promoting the safeguarding and protection of the female artist against exploitative structures and norms.

Gender, creativity and capitalist norms

The Writer deals with one female artist's consistent and continuous attempts to establish herself as a creative voice with authority, while, at the same time, striving to negotiate the expectations and demands of others on her work. These demands are starkly gendered: from those in positions of power when it comes to commissioning and supporting her writing, to her domestic partner, who is, likewise, supportive of her work insofar as it serves his own agenda regarding their relationship. The professional and personal contexts have the potential of being equally exploitative, the play suggests. For Hickson's protagonist, the process of creation gradually begins to merge with a process of self-discovery, including a fluid sexuality. An openness in form – a lacuna in the text of the play – mirrors not only the writer's experimentation, but also her (re)discovery of the possibilities within herself. By the end of the play Hickson's protagonist appears to have asserted at least some of her power, and has, on the personal front, moved on to a homosexual relationship that seems to be more nuanced and fulfilling than the heterosexual cohabitation model that we saw her strive to escape earlier in the play. Whether such freedom can hold, however, remains inconclusive as the play reaches its finale. Perhaps it is inevitable, the text appears to suggest, that a degree of compromise – in art and in life – will always exist. Likewise, perhaps the power lies in acknowledging this fact and actively working, within the best of one's abilities, to upset gendered stratification from within. In that sense, *The Writer* is both dreamlike and conceptually expansive and, at the same time, thrives on the pragmatism that we encounter, especially in female characters, in much of Hickson's other work, both before and after the specific play.

While such thematic and formal concerns make it particularly tempting – and, also, to an extent accurate – to categorize *The Writer* as a prime example of theatre mindful of its context, in this case, the #MeToo and #TimesUp movements, the play also extends beyond these. In fact, as Hickson reveals, *The Writer* predates the revelations that created the avalanche of developments linked to the broader environment that enabled transgressive behaviours such as Harvey Weinstein's (Williams 2018). Beyond timing, though, it strikes me that the primary reason for which Hickson's play is irreducible to the specific context is that it serves not as a hollow vehicle for the rhetoric, but as a full-bodied work of representational art that assumes upon itself the weight of advancing a playwriting agenda that thrives on substantial – unsafe, even – experimentation. By this I mean that both Hickson and Blanche McIntyre, the director of the premiere production, create a textual and visual world that holds its own ground emphatically, rendering the play an event that, beyond topical, is also enduring. If Caryl Churchill's *Escaped Alone* (2016) concluded with the two words that are now enshrined in the contemporary playwriting canon – 'terrible rage' (2016: 42) – then Hickson, without in any sense being derivative, plunges into this very emotion to establish its causes, its consequences and its galvanizing force. As Hickson observes, 'It's a rage that is fearless: I genuinely have no fear about shouting that loud. I realised, I suppose, that people might start putting my plays on with slightly less resistance, and when you're in that position, you have a responsibility to say the difficult things' (qtd. in Williams 2018). Hickson, then, appears motivated by the kind of public-facing care that is firmly sociopolitically embedded to expose the very lack of institutional but, also, domestic care. The former has often plagued an entire industry and its treatment of female artists in various positions; the latter has systematically subsumed women in hierarchies tipped against them: even as the primary earners, or as accomplished professionals, at home their role has often been one of subservience.

Critics' views of *The Writer* were broadly positive with #MeToo understandably emerging as a consistent reference. Certain reviewers were particularly astute in picking up on the nuances of the play's disruption, making reference to 'the nature of gender and the need for the mythic in a society governed by fixed, male-determined rules' (Billington 2018); 'the difficulties faced by women trying to create something true to themselves as an artist, without giving in to the expectations of men, or the pressure to produce something safe and sellable' (Tripney 2018); 'art made by women – [that] is corrupted by the distorting prism of patriarchal capitalism' (Lukowski 2018); 'power structures both artistic and personal and how received ideas shaped by an inescapably patriarchal society infuse the two realms' (Mountford 2018). Such is also the nature of my concern here, specifically refracted through the angle of cruelty that dominant patriarchal structures force upon processes of selection, curation and dissemination. And while this is far from suggesting that there is no margin of difference within male leadership – it is surely a self-evident point that there is, and that there can be – Hickson's play rightly suggests that we have seen enough of how different industries operate to recognize the profound problematics that run through too great a number of professional, including, of course, creative, contexts – not least because of 'the increasingly pervasive idea of play as commercial product' (Thompson 2018).

In order to engage with such concerns within broader crisis research, I am particularly interested in establishing a dialogue between Hickson's play and the work of Sylvia Walby. The rationale for such analysis stems from Walby's gendered discourses on crisis, which provide me with an optimal framework for locating my own argumentation given the affinities between play text and sociological investigation. Patriarchy and capitalism, without facile conflations, rank amongst the most strongly emerging constants in her extensive and profoundly interdisciplinary body of work. Here, and considering the critical and theoretical remit of this volume, I particularly wish to concentrate on Walby's more recent texts *The Future of Feminism* (2011) and *Crisis* (2015), although it is important to begin with a grounding statement from her earlier book, *Patriarchy at Work* (1986). In this volume, Walby identifies a primary thread in her research as the imperative of demonstrating that women are 'significant actors in resisting their exploitation' (1986: 1).

I am especially drawn to the word 'actor' and its semantic layers, because it not only captures the sense of an agent, a person performing a certain (course of) action, but it also opens up to a more nuanced interpretation, whose possibilities Hickson's play undertakes a thorough investigation of on levels representational and meta-representational alike. *The Writer* begins with a ruse: what we are encouraged to think is the opening scene in the play, whereby a young, female spectator has a coincidental post-show conversation with the director (male, middle-aged) of the play she has just seen, is, in fact, a scene in a play within the play – the text that Hickson's eponymous Writer has scripted. The man's pretence is that he is keen to hear about this specific audience member's impressions of the show. It is clear that his persistence in keeping a difficult conversation going is making the young woman uncomfortable and she voices her extensive reservations regarding the show, as well as the male establishment's assumed capability of determining what a young woman might be interested in seeing in the theatre unequivocally. The absence of care as a major concern in the play emerges clearly through a veiled reference to Laura Wade's *Posh*. Without naming it, but with a description that allows little doubt, the young spectator uses it as an example of the theatre's inability to deliver any real change in the world, because the same establishment being staunchly criticized on the stage is so convinced of their own 'power' (Hickson 2018: 17) and the audience is so irretrievably embedded in '[t]he money, the systems, the secret longing to keep it all in place' (18) that there is, as with the privileged class, no care towards making a substantial difference that would alter the course of things.

As the conversation unfolds, even the director's offer to the woman to write a play for the theatre they find themselves in (one not too dissimilar from the Almeida in terms of how it, its Artistic Director or the local area are described) comes from the undisguised motivation of having something 'zeitgeisty' (21) not in the conviction that it might deliver change, but in the confidence that it will generate revenue. There is no care here: it is not the spectators' hearts and minds that are aimed for, it is their mere presence in – and therefore financial support of – the theatre. This is, arguably, the only common ground between the interlocutors; the fact implicitly acknowledged. It is a transaction, not a mission to change the world. And, yet, as the woman goes on to reveal a few moments later, her anger at the theatre's inability to intervene comes precisely from a recognition of the fact that 'theatre is sacred, should be – these spaces – communal and civic and made to heal us' (25). 'Heal' is a crucial word here, because it recognizes the fact that something has been broken that needs to be repaired; it is a term imperative for care, which, in the young person's not fully monetized, or capitalism-appropriated world, still resonates. Soon, the institutional structures that operate on the opposite of care, while claiming to be advancing the greater good – in this case, the theatre and its civic role – are exposed. It turns out that this woman and this man have met before: some years ago, when she was a student, he, as a successful practitioner, after meeting her at a drama festival where they were both speakers, attempted to use his power of promising to commission a play by her in order to elicit sex. It is shortly after this revelation that stage dynamics shifts and the Writer and Director enter, revealing that the Writer and Director we have been watching are in fact actors performing in the script under development (30). The scene now morphs into a feedback session, including audience plants. At the end, the Writer inquires of the Director, with some uncertainty, how things will proceed and he asks her to deliver the script soon. Her own agency as an 'actor' is thrust into doubt; she strives and delivers the work, but approval is external and elusive.

Hickson's startlingly sincere play, therefore, also strikes me as highly invested in establishing the semantic and practical implications of the term 'actor'. The fact that Hickson has written a play about theatre – but also film, and therefore, by extension, art – production more broadly brings a complex set of significations to the term 'actor'. In the text, we encounter, especially in the eponymous Writer character, but also in that of the female actor/the Writer's partner, women who are acting, as well as acting out, against patriarchal norms in contexts both scripted and unscripted – even though, often, Hickson makes it remarkably difficult for us to distinguish between the two. What these meta-selves have in common, though, is resistance: to male forms of storytelling; of programming artistic work; and of determining how creativity ought to fit the economy.

In her more recent monographs (as cited above), Walby has engaged with the complex presents of feminism, pursuing a resolutely intersectional approach. Walby's work predates Hickson's, capturing a shifting social context which she, at the same time, historicizes with a view to the future. Hickson's *The Writer* appears at a junction that marks the transition from histories of silent (or, if not silent, often tacitly enabled) oppression against female artists to a context of speaking – and, as above – acting out. Walby is not writing with theatre performance in mind, so to indicate that there is a shared sensibility between Walby and Hickson does not imply that the connection materializes on a specific disciplinary level. Rather, I suggest that both writers, within their respective domains, are engaged in interventionist social discourses that log inequality with an often – and rightly – polemical approach, a sobering, lucid perspective on the injustices. At the same time, both Hickson and Walby are, in my view, committed to the pursuit of a dialectic, invested in a future of possibility that is yet to be written but that, certainly, cannot disregard the past, or, for that matter, the present. Part of this effort concerns addressing the shortcomings that still linger, even those that may have been assumed resolved.

I have previously engaged with the concept of crisis elsewhere, with a concern towards indicating what I still very much subscribe to, namely, that the moment of crisis can also be fathomed as a turning point. On the one hand, it absolutely presents us with a challenge that we might deem insurmountable; life altering; perhaps even terminal. On the other hand, however, a moment of crisis can deliver a certain radical reckoning; a process of recalibration; a refocusing and reorganization that might lead to restructuring and even improvement of living conditions (Angelaki 2017). For the purposes of this chapter, I am particularly interested in how Walby frames crisis in the context of gender and access, a discussion to which the term 'male' or 'masculine monoculture' that Walby uses (2015) to describe the lack of egalitarian distribution in positions of power is especially relevant. In *The Writer* we witness one artist's endeavour to pierce through this 'male monoculture' as it is encountered in the theatre and film industries, not only in terms of a seat at the table (which is of course important in terms of presence and agency) but also in terms of what this has meant as far as the creation and proliferation of taste functions. In other words, Hickson's Writer is experiencing the mental, emotional and physical journey through a systemic crisis, at the end of which we hope that she will emerge more empowered, more influential, with a stronger chance to shift the rules of the creative discourse. The other side of this is that the Writer might not only survive the process creatively, but also thrive – that is, develop an increased understanding of her own capacities as an 'actor', from raising her visibility and resilience in the creative process to wielding more influence and power over it. At the same time, one hopes that this journey of perseverance through self-discovery and vice versa will not only serve at an individual level of personal growth – again, however significant this may be – but that it will also perform at the level of exposing the lack of care for the individual attempting a shift. It is in this way that resistance to processes of mainstreaming for economic gain, thereby becoming financially – and creatively – disadvantaged and disenfranchised can be sustained by the female subject in the longer run. Once more, the fact that financial crisis is gendered is a point that recurs in Walby's analysis; the levels of exposure are not equal.

The other potential gain is that the Writer's confrontation with the industry might yield a paradigm shift for greater care towards audiences. Through challenging rather than placating spectators and through creating a formally more ambitious and experimental theatre, for which, however, space will be made in mainstream venues, a longer-term change can be implemented. In that sense, spectators will be seen as more than profit margins and the relationship between theatre and audience will acquire greater depth beyond the utilitarian level. It is in that broader framework of care towards the public that Walby's comments as to 'the [in this context male, problematic] gendering of decision-making' and 'changes in gendered priorities' (2015: ch. 1) when it comes to policy formation and planning become particularly relevant. It is, also, that same battle that is fought throughout Hickson's play when it comes to the arts, to producing and to programming.

In assessing *The Writer*, we ought to keep in mind that it is written and produced: in the wake of one kind of crisis (the UK's recession, assuming we accept that the country now finds itself in a financially prosperous, or at least stable condition – this remains to be seen, not least in the aftermath of the Covid-19 pandemic); in the midst of another crisis (the waves of uncertainty stirred by the forever unfolding narrative of Brexit and the revelations of the #MeToo era); and in advance of a future crisis (if we acknowledge that for lack of sufficient care, a country is always exposed to the possibility, given the right set of circumstances, of a confrontation with its own inactions and problematic policies in allowing precariousness to proliferate, in not setting crucial gender and gender/earning quotas, and in not satisfactorily shielding itself from the probability of another recession – once more tied to the uncertainty of Brexit and the pandemic). It is, therefore, particularly important to consider to what extent *The Writer* is a play that exposes this lack of care in the contexts of a prosperous Western country (the UK) that theoretically has all the means at its disposal but it is still not managing to tackle workplace inequality, allowing this permanent crisis to proliferate, globally speaking, as applicable, not taking action drastic enough to confront the root of the problem even when the former models of male monoculture and gendered decision making have been tried and tested, their effectiveness questionable at best.

Locating *The Writer* within such a crisis framework, then, I find Walby's point here particularly astute:

> The crisis changed gendered relations. Women have lost jobs and suffered from the cuts in public services; but they have not been pushed back into the home. Despite loss of jobs and of public services, women are not leaving the labour market and production and returning to reproduction. The crisis has not re-familialized women despite cutbacks in state-provided services. The changes challenge conventional theoretical frameworks in which women are seen as moving between home and work, reproduction and production, or domestic and public spheres, according to improvement or deterioration in the economy.
>
> (2015: ch. 7)

Such concerns are given considerable space in *The Writer*, particularly in the segment that involves a domestic moment, where the Writer and her partner discuss an offer she has received to make her text (presumably the text we saw being workshopped in the opening of the play) into a film. He is excited, not least because of the financial benefits; she is against it, '[b]ecause the story I wrote, when I wrote it, was true. The thing I said was true. And if I turn it into a film the producers will break it and and smash it and twist it into this thing that isn't true and that will hurt' (43). Hickson's engagement with lack of care begins to deepen: this concerns the artistic product, but also its creator. Beyond the institutional lack of care, there is also the interpersonal one. The Writer's partner is desperate for her to capitalize on the opportunity for considerable profit – and from their conversation it is clear that she is, already, the primary earner. When she resists this pressure, he grows weary and passive aggressive, his enthusiasm fading quickly. She retorts: 'Were you hoping your investment was going to mature?' (44) exposing his lack of care towards her; his monetization of her as an individual with a unique skill for the purposes of his own comfort. The way in which this scene ends, too, as the Writer and her partner dissolve their relationship, coincides with the dissolution of the entire premise of their future – a partnership, a family – and of domesticity: the set of their home collapses on stage. As the scene closes, it gives way to the next stage in the Writer's process, her creativity emerging from the shackles unleashed. In other words, the feminist pushback continues; despite numerous attempts at neutralization and domestication, women, and, in the case of Hickson's play, the Writer, resist. Even if, as per toxic established systems, women are the most precarious players in capitalist economies, it is essential to recognize that, sometimes against the odds, the prevailing tendency, in work, in creativity and in one's relationship with oneself, is not to surrender to the inevitability of a crushing system.

In *The Future of Feminism*, Walby pursues such an approach so as to develop a framework that appreciates, as well as anticipates, the challenges of the coming years. There are many aspects of Walby's work here that render it impressive in its undertaking, while, at the same time, focused and optimistic, without appearing reductive. The rigour emerging from the book is refreshing, not least because a decade since its publication we can recognize amongst its many contributions its emphasis on the intersections between environmentalism and feminism. This is a field that has continued to grow considerably and, in whose nuances, Hickson also appears to be interested. Other than *Oil*, which pursues this thread as its primary point of focus, as I have also discussed elsewhere (Angelaki 2019), in Hickson's yet more recent plays this imperative reappears, as is the case with *The Writer*. The most fluid section of *The Writer*, which involves sexual explorations in an unsaturated landscape, where the Writer feels both her agency and her freedom, exemplifies how theatre might make a more conscious turn towards exploring the gendered experience of nature. Walby's adamant suggestion that feminism is still very much active and indeed a success story, but, also, a term that – far from outmoded – will continue to be relevant, is significant. The energy and vigour with which Hickson commits to her enquiry, while recognizing its challenges, as seen in *The Writer*, is entirely in conversation with Walby's work.

In the scene concerned, then, Hickson delivers, on both page and stage, one of the most experimental explorations of form and content that contemporary British playwriting has had to offer. As Romola Garai, who played the title role in the premiere production, observes, 'What feels very new about this play is it is making formal points and political arguments simultaneously, and those things can interact' (qtd. in Williams 2018). Interact they did – and although it is not entirely possible to capture this here exhaustively given the length and focus of this essay, I would like to provide an indicative account. In my spectatorial experience, at this stage in Hickson's play the line between conceptual exploration, narration, lucid dreaming, installation and theatrical performance became decisively blurred, giving way to a hybrid that is traditionally – though also short-sightedly – not associated with text-based theatre. Perhaps the best way of capturing the sensation that this scene imparted upon spectators, while acknowledging that not all members of the audience would have had the same reading, is that it provided a journey within the Writer's mind and desire, with no holds barred, or limitations: an attempt at tracing the unruliness of the *écriture féminine* and its corporeal expression.

Considering the text itself, this is how Hickson frames the scene:

[THE PROVOCATION: *What follows should be an attempt at staging female experience, the director should be aware of avoiding the inherently patriarchal nature of theatre:*
Female characters should do – they are not having things done to them. Bodies are for action, not titillation or decoration. There should be no looking. The protagonist should own the space.] (57)

The style could be reasonably described as stream of consciousness. In this, alternative forms of storytelling are interjected: photographs and songs. Hickson's narrative primarily concentrates on a woman's – presumably the Writer's – account of her saturated everyday experience, which produces a moment of challenge, which, in turn, generates a rebellion against gender-normativity/heterosexuality and a release. This materializes in the shape of a mental breakdown in the beginning of the scene, which fuses into a reflection on female sexuality. A journey opens up into a relationship with a female partner for the Writer that plays on themes of ancient myths, engaging with the story of Semele, who acts, here, as host and guide for the Writer. Soon enough, on the journey, the Writer meets a fellow traveller and together they explore the landscape and their respective desires. Having discussed the awkwardness of sexual encounters with men, Hickson's narrator now declares, 'For the first time in my life I feel like I'm in bed with an ally' (64). The statement is significant in a broader context of full exposure with a female partner, who, indeed, feels precisely so, rather than as an antagonist (unlike a male lover). But this idea of an ally runs deeper in Hickson: it concerns intercourse, companionship, but also structural layers of support versus demand. In society, it is the latter, rather than the former, that are dominant, Hickson's text suggests: 'Post-coitally, with her, I feel more whole. Not the semi-devastation that follows sex with men, the land-grab, the Blitzkrieg, the small strange impulse to cry. With her it was an aggregation' (64).

In the next scene, we are once more landed in dry pragmatism and in gendered negotiations of power between the Director and the Writer, where the segment we have just witnessed becomes part of the Writer's textual submission to the Director. He does not share her vision; there is no egalitarian exchange. The discourse, once more, shifts to profit: the Writer needs to prove to the Director that the investment in her is worthwhile – that her narrative will sell. There is no care towards the individual creator or towards the artistic product. They are both, equally, a means to an end, at the hands of a powerful male authority figure, who represents the inflexibility of the system. Arguably, it is the Writer's confrontation with the Director in this scene that delivers Hickson's message as to lack of care and institutionalized absence of safety at its most explicit:

> Artists have to feel safe. If you want them to make art. We have to feel – emotionally – safe. We – I, need to belong to something. The places you have to go – the things you have to feel and think are… going there – can get… dangerous. And you're so often alone and I've got no one and you do and… (72)

The above comment on the artist's exposure is, I would argue, profoundly gendered – in a context where the female artist tends to be both more closely associated with the product of her labour and, at the same time, to be given more limited access to modes of dissemination for this very labour, the statement bears considerable significance. I find Walby's *The Future of Feminism* nowhere more relevant to the case study of this chapter than when it boldly proposes:

> In the tension between feminism and the mainstream, does the feminist project become integrated in a way that assimilates it to the status quo, or does it colonise, hybridise or mutually adapt with and change the mainstream? This tension between feminism and the mainstream is potentially productive for both, although it can, in some circumstances, lead to the fading of feminism as a distinctive force.
>
> (2011: ch. 1)

The intervention that Hickson's writer makes, that is, is gendered by default. Especially following the creative enhancement that the Writer undergoes, the point is made to the audience all the more resolutely. Here, I argue that Walby's assertion regarding the concept of 'gender mainstreaming' can also help us better understand the issues at stake in *The Writer*: 'The most successful approach to gender mainstreaming involves maintaining a core of distinctive expertise and specialist politics while simultaneously dispersing such feminist expertise into all policy areas and into the work of normal policy actors. This dual approach to gender mainstreaming does produce tensions, but these can be productive' (2011: ch. 1). In *The Writer* we observe the very tensions arising from the processes that Walby describes here. Hickson's protagonist is on the inside track – she is not an outsider to the system, nor is she oblivious to playing to its pre-set rules. Still, she does experience a process of abjection, which, no less emotional and mental than it is visceral, gradually gives rise to consistent acts towards a form of revolution from within. The purpose is to radically reassess and reshape the mainstream. We are dealing with a system that is inflexible in its rules of success, a reality that is profoundly gendered given the different rules that apply to female and male artistic creators. As Garai observes, 'I have worked with female writers where their social need to look obliging and collaborative is higher, so their work goes through considerably more drafts… Having the courage to say "I'm not going to do any more" comes at a much higher social cost [for women]' (qtd. in Williams 2018). It is that precise lack of care that the Writer experiences on an intellectual and embodied level, whether towards herself, as her creativity is consistently prodded for monetization, or towards the product of her labour, which is forever reworked on the basis of male-gendered projections of success, as profoundly embedded within mainstream contexts of representational art.

Towards tentative conclusions: Care out of a crisis

The Writer forms part of the contemporary experimental tradition as also developed in the work of other playwrights who have led textual innovation, a process of reinventing forms that has, in its most powerful iterations, rightly placed the inadequate care structures towards the female actor in her manifold possibilities under a microscope. The production context of *The Writer* both facilitates and compels such an enquiry. In the 2016/17 theatre season (directly preceding the season in which *The Writer* was programmed) the Almeida gave a major revival to Martin Crimp's 1993 play *The Treatment*. *The Treatment* concentrates on a woman called Anne, who proposes her life's story as a film narrative to two Manhattan producers. Like vultures, they consume and absorb Anne as narrative and commercial potential, intellectually and creatively eviscerating her and, by the end, killing her off in the plot of her own life, both as an artist, metaphorically, and, tragically, also as a person, literally. I find it intriguing that Hickson's play follows this context in the Almeida, both in the sense of the theatre showing an increased engagement with contemporary social developments and dialogues (as above), which is significant, and in the sense of artistic traditions taking shape. Without in any way suggesting that Hickson is derivative of Crimp, as that would be profoundly inaccurate, I argue that it is fascinating to observe the directions in which Hickson is developing these extant discourses through her own work in 2018. Hickson, in no uncertain terms, crafts new forms so as to capture the imprisonment of female creativity within masculine institutional norms that restrict and suffocate – much in the way that Crimp's earlier plays, in terms of content and formal openness, had also explored and exposed. What Hickson's Writer and Crimp's Anne (whether in *The Treatment*, or in her multiple variables in *Attempts on Her Life*) have in common, is their ability to metamorphose: they can stand for different concepts, and ideas. The crisis escalates when, rather than being the agents in their own performance of multitudes (intimate and public), they are deprived of their agency as 'actors' and are relegated to being characters in the imaginations of others, whose over-emphatic agency superscribes its own narrative upon the female subject.

Here, it is purposeful to turn, once more, to Walby in *Crisis*:

> Gender is a social relationship rather than an essence. Gender has meaning as a social relationship between genders. Gender relations are a system of social relations, in the sense that they are self-reproducing. The practice of gender reproduces gender relations; and in this way is a system. A gender regime is a pattern of gender relations; and can take different forms.
>
> (2015: ch. 7)

This chapter has argued that Ella Hickson has shown a consistent and noteworthy engagement with the interrelated concepts of gender and care and the all too frequent contexts, personal, interpersonal and professional, where the latter is found to be lacking. It has proposed that such a lack of care has a unique capacity to saturate social relationships and to impact the individual's sense of safety and exposure (mental, emotional, sexual), as well as of fulfilment and satisfaction (personal, professional and material). In Hickson's work, exposing the fact that there is an observable lack of care that is wide ranging in contemporary British society amounts to no less than a crisis. I return here to my earlier suggestion that crisis might also provide an open moment and space for intervention: whether this might be populated by gestures towards change is, of course, the ultimate question.

The Writer communicates the potentialities of such openness through its experimentation and innovation in form. It does not, that is, present the path of options and prospects as closed up, but as alive with the viability of change and disruption to the proliferation of the problematic; its landmark scene, discussed earlier, is an embodied representation of this. Still, at the same time, Hickson is a realist, and, as this chapter has recognized, her work is highly attuned to the force of gravity. Hence, in the final part of the play, where the Writer finally appears to be working – and living – within a context of greater care and freedom, with a more responsive partner and a professional power that guarantees some increased agency, the play still creates an atmosphere of tentativeness. Certain compromises have been made to reach this state; the Writer is still not entirely fulfilled emotionally; her current relationship, which began as an opening up to freedom, appears to be imposing its own quiet restrictions. Even in this form of better companionship, the Writer strikes us as still burdened; still not fully at ease. This is Hickson's way, perhaps, of communicating that rather than an optimal solution, the most pragmatic expectation when it comes to society and women is the one that requires the least amount of surrender. I am again drawn to Walby's work, this time as part of the collectively authored volume *The Concept and Measurement of Violence against Women and Men*. 'Gender relations saturate, shape or inflect many aspects of violence; they are not only its context' (Walby et al. 2017: 31–2), the volume proposes. Such a heightened level of agency – institutionalized, too often invisible and unaccounted for – ought to be rendered present in our discourses and seen for its continued impact, this work suggests. Back in 2011, Hickson described her process as 'experimenting with a view to educating myself in the capacities of theatre' (qtd. in Banham 2011). It is a mission statement of sorts, which Hickson's writing has honoured with considerable consistency; and one that, as her name and plays have started to garner significant publicity, has appeared to be remarkably generous in terms of the shapes that this experimentation might assume. There is, ultimately, a recognition of the fact that all accomplishments are provisional and cannot be taken for granted that emerges from Hickson's work. For the playwright herself, there is a notably fearless exposure in the choice of topic and method. As Hickson's plays themselves suggest, all acts of intervention must continue unabated in order to deliver lasting rupture; complacency will always destroy what was, at first, insurgent. But if the actions are sustained, at the other end awaits the prospect for more honest theatre; and, perhaps, also, for a more caring social framework.

References

Angelaki, V. (2017), *Social and Political Theatre in 21st-Century Britain: Staging Crisis*, London: Bloomsbury Methuen.

Angelaki, V. (2019), *Theatre & Environment*, London: Red Globe Press.

Banham, R. (2011), 'Ella Hickson: A Playwright for Our Generation', *A Younger Theatre*, 23 March. Available online: https://www.ayoungertheatre.com/ella-hickson-precious-little-talent/ (accessed 24 January 2020).

Billington, M. (2018), 'The Writer Review – Romola Garai Blazes into the Battlefield of Desire', *Guardian*, 25 April. Available online: https://www.theguardian.com/stage/2018/apr/25/the-writer-review-almeida-romola-garai-sexual-revolution (accessed 24 January 2020).

Churchill, C. (2016), *Escaped Alone*, London: Nick Hern.

Crimp, M. (1997), *Attempts on Her Life*, London: Faber and Faber.

Crimp, M. (2017), *The Treatment*, London: Nick Hern.

Hickson, E. (2018), *The Writer*, London: Nick Hern.

Lukowski, A. (2018), '*The Writer* Review: Romola Garai Stars in This Thrillingly Meta Assault on the Theatre Establishment', *Time Out*, 25 April. Available online: https://www.timeout.com/london/theatre/the-writer-review (accessed 24 January 2020).

Mountford, F. (2018), '*The Writer* Review: Romola Garai Blazes in Defiant Attempt to Rewrite the Script', *Evening Standard*, 25 April. Available online: https://www.standard.co.uk/go/london/theatre/the-writer-review-romola-garai-blazes-in-defiant-attempt-to-rewrite-the-script-a3822836.html (accessed 24 January 2020).

Thompson, J. (2018), 'Ella Hickson: "I Always Want to Be in the Conversation with What's Being Made Now in Theatre"', *Evening Standard*, 17 April. Available online: https://www.standard.co.uk/go/london/arts/ella-hickson-i-always-want-to-be-in-the-conversation-with-whats-being-made-now-in-theatre-a3816371.html (accessed 24 January 2020).

Tripney, N. (2018), '*The Writer* Review at Almeida Theatre, London – "Formally Inventive and Vividly Written"', *The Stage*, 25 April. Available online: https://www.thestage.co.uk/reviews/2018/writer-review-almeida-theatre-romola-garai-london/ (accessed 24 January 2020).

Walby, S. (1986), *Patriarchy at Work*, Cambridge: Polity Press.

Walby, S. (2011), *The Future of Feminism* [Ebook], Cambridge: Polity Press.

Walby, S. (2015), *Crisis* [Ebook], Cambridge: Polity Press.

Walby, S. et al. (2017), *The Concept and Measurement of Violence against Women and Men*, Bristol: Policy Press.

Williams, H. (2018), '"Dismantle Capitalism and Overturn the Patriarchy": Why *The Writer* Is More than Just a #MeToo Play', *Independent*, 24 April. Available online: https://www.independent.co.uk/arts-entertainment/theatre-dance/features/writer-metoo-romola-garai-ella-hickson-blanche-mcinture-almeida-theatre-london-a8319561.html?/ (accessed 20 October 2020).

4

'I'm not afraid of being labelled a dirty boring feminist': Reproductive work, feminism and/in crisis at the Royal Court

Elisabeth Massana

Feminist discontent took to the streets and the public arena worldwide in late 2017 with the spread of the #MeToo movement and in early 2018 with the organization of several feminist strikes and marches on 8 March. Together with marching, as discussions of the #MeToo movement spread worldwide, many of us shared stories of being sexually assaulted or of having been subjected to physical or structural violence, the common denominator linking our experiences as women. Trying to make sense of this systemic violence against women I found comfort in Silvia Federici's history of the criminalized women of the seventeenth century who were killed for trying to have control over their own bodies. In *Caliban and the Witch* (2004), she argues that the feminized body – I opt for this trans-inclusive form rather than Federici's 'female body' following recent queer and transfeminist readings of her work (Long and Frost 2015: 101) – is the last border of capitalist accumulation, suggesting that the transition from a feudal to a capitalist system implied a rationalization of social reproduction and exploitation through the expropriation of feminized bodies, and concluding that capitalist development began with a war on women. Ultimately, her work 'demonstrates how the demonization of women's control over their reproductive capacity, and the subsequent violence unleashed against them, was absolutely necessary for global capitalism to emerge' (Carlin and Federici 2014: 1), showing that capitalist accumulation was possible because of the expropriation of the bodies of those who constitute the Other in our white hetero-patriarchal cisgender and able-bodied hierarchical world. The bodies expropriated therefore are feminized and racialized bodies: 'Caliban'

Elisabeth Massana's work was supported by the Spanish Ministry of Economy and Competitiveness (MINECO) and the European Regional Development Fund (ERDF) project 'British Theatre in the Twenty-First Century: Crisis, Affect, Community' (FFI2016-75443).

and 'the Witch', the colonized enslaved Other and women (Federici 2020). If Federici's work shows that men and women have a different history under capitalism, do they have a different history in relation to crisis?

With this question in mind, this chapter focuses on two recent plays which opened at the Royal Court under the artistic direction of Vicky Featherstone: Cordelia Lynn's *Lela & Co.* (2015) and Vivienne Franzmann's *Bodies* (2017). The choice of plays and venue is not coincidental. During the climax of the #MeToo movement, Vicky Featherstone, the first woman to be appointed artistic director of the Royal Court, became a prominent name due to her vocal condemnation of sexual harassment and her work towards drafting a sexual harassment protocol, which was subsequently made available to the wide theatrical community in the UK (Aitkenhead and Featherstone 2017). As a result, Featherstone was named most influential person in British theatre in early 2018 (Brown 2018), and when asked about her public role as a spokesperson for women's rights, she proudly stated that she was 'not afraid to be labelled a dirty boring feminist' (Enright 2018). If Featherstone had become *the* feminist artistic director in the midst of a crisis, it seemed relevant to look at how the Royal Court was responding to crisis from a feminist perspective.

The second impulse behind this chapter has to do with what Sarah Gorman, Geraldine Harris and Jen Harvie identified in the 2018 special issue of *Contemporary Theatre Review* on feminisms and performance as a 'significant resurgence and renewal of interest in feminism in Britain, the USA, and many other countries worldwide over the last five years' (2018: 278). This was exemplified by women taking to the streets in various countries, as well as by the public revelations of sexual harassment in social media after the Harvey Weinstein scandal, amongst others. In the British context in particular, Elaine Aston has explained the 'unleashing of feminist energies' as a response to the austerity policies implemented by Cameron's coalition government (2018: 301).[1] As Prudence Chamberlain states, 'The movements against austerity actually contributed and fed into a new wave of feminism, creating a culture of protest and resistance that seemed to have diminished in previous years. The politicisation of the nation, only amplified by the MP expenses scandal and savage cuts to public services, added energy to the start of the feminist wave' (2017: 3). As an active participant in both feminist strikes in Barcelona – which were part of the context of

---

[1] In the 2010 general election, the first to take place after the outbreak of the 2008 economic crisis, the British electorate voted in a hung parliament that resulted in the formation of a coalition government led by Conservative David Cameron, with Liberal Democrat Nick Clegg as deputy prime minister.

feminist discontent mentioned at the beginning of this chapter – and as I assembled, discussed, prepared for the strike and marched, I realized that there was one element in the call to strike that was particularly difficult, or a special source of conflict, for many, and that was the 'strike of care'. Feminist strikers announced that '[o]n March 8 we cross our arms interrupt[ing] all productive and reproductive activity' (Arruzza, Bhattacharya and Fraser 2019: 2). Reproductive work, as will be seen in the analysis of the plays, needs to be understood as 'the complex of activities and services that reproduce human beings as well as the commodity labour power, starting with childcare, housework, sex work and elder care, both in the form of waged and unwaged labour' (Barbagallo and Federici 2012: 1). Yet, the interruption of reproductive work in the context of a strike was the most difficult to achieve: traditionally invisible and, as a consequence, not considered proper work, it exceeded the logics of the strike.

This invisibility of reproductive work finds its origins in the division of work that marks the transition from a feudal to a capitalist system (Mies 1998; Federici 2004) and, I wish to suggest, continues to be invisible under the crisis-rhetoric. As shall be seen, both plays analysed here shed light on this division of work by pointing to the links between reproductive work and systemic violence against women in capitalism. The chapter therefore explores how these two plays engage with women in (contexts of) crisis by asking to what extent the plays contribute to a critique of the capitalist control of the feminized body, and/or to a gendered perspective on the multiple crises the plays engage with. My contention is that both texts engage with Federici's claim by showing how the control of the feminized body and the systemic violence against it are fundamental for the system to survive. Additionally, I propose that, through specific dramaturgical strategies, both plays contribute towards the collapse of definitions of crisis that establish a clear chronology. In short, the purpose of the chapter is twofold, to challenge post-2008 definitions of crisis by asking whether the narrative of the 2008 crisis can be sustained if we look at it from a feminist perspective, and to look at how the plays challenge chronologies of crisis.

Feminism and crisis

If, as Sara Ahmed proposes, 'to live a feminist life is to make everything into something that is questionable' (2017: 2), the first thing I propose we question is how crisis has been narrated. Post-2008 definitions of crisis focus on the capacity to enact an intervention into the very discourse of crisis (Walby 2015: 2), while demonstrating how by naming something as a crisis action can be taken, policies can be implemented. At the same time, these definitions contribute towards sustaining the centrality of an abstract universal (masculine) subject affected by crisis (Butler and Athanasiou 2013; Federici 2020). As Cinzia Arruzza, Tithi Bhattacharya and Nancy Fraser state, '[i]n "normal" times, the system's crisis tendencies remain more or less latent, afflicting "only" those populations deemed disposable and powerless' (2019: 66). This is explored in their post-2008 crisis short manifesto for a feminism for the 99 per cent, where they establish a conversation with both neoliberal feminism and the recent feminist strikes to contend that while 'liberal feminism supplies the perfect alibi for neoliberalism' (12), the feminism behind the strikes '[redefines] what counts as "work" and who counts as a "worker", [and] it rejects capitalism's structural undervaluation of women's labour – both paid and unpaid' (8–9). The crisis this feminism challenges is a crisis of society as a whole, 'a crisis of *capitalism* – and in particular, of the viciously predatory form of capitalism we inhabit today: globalizing, financialized, neoliberal' (16; emphasis original). Crisis therefore, they suggest, is an intrinsic element of capitalism, which generates these crises periodically (16–17). In their words:

> This type of process, whereby general crisis leads to societal reorganization, has played out several times in modern history – largely to capital's benefit. Seeking to restore profitability, its champions have reinvented capitalism time and again – reconfiguring not only the official economy, but also politics, social reproduction, and our relation to nonhuman nature. In so doing, they have reorganized not only class exploitation, but also gender and racial oppression, often appropriating rebellious energies (including feminist energies) for projects that overwhelmingly benefit the 1 percent.
>
> (19)

Attending to this periodical reappearance of crisis, Judith Butler and Athena Athanasiou approach crisis as a 'truth regime', a discourse that 'become[s] a way to governmentally produce and manage (rather than deter) the crisis… a perennial state of exception that turns into a rule and common sense' (2013: 149); most importantly, they suggest that 'the discourse of "crisis" is already a way to "manage" the crisis' (150). As Marilena Zaroulia, drawing on Jacques Rancière, has stated, crisis can be identified as a pathology that serves to obscure that 'the very system that the crisis threatens is pathological – in short, the system is always in crisis' (2018: 181). As seen, crisis has been explained as a pathology that can be cured, an excess that can be regulated, in essence, an excuse to implement harsh austerity policies, increase violent border control and securitization, and call on individual responsibility for people's lack of financial security on the one hand, while redirecting public resources to the rescue of financial and political institutions, and ultimately ensuring the survival of our economic system: capitalism. However, this narrative of crisis, as the discussion of the plays will suggest, silences the lived experience of the disposable and powerless, those always-already in crisis.

The first words we hear from Lela, the main character of Lynn's *Lela & Co.*, are the following:

> When I was born the women greeted me with singing. Not my mother, obviously, she was flat out on her back like a felled tree, which seems fair enough given the circumstances, but my grandmother sang me to sleep that first time, and the maiden aunts did their bit till my mother was back to herself again and could join the task of lullabying. That's a woman's responsibility, see? And when my grandmother died my mother and the aunts sang her into oblivion because that's a woman's responsibility too, to sing the songs, the early songs and the late songs, the songs of sleeping and the songs of mourning. That's how it works here, women wake you up and they put you to sleep, they bring you to life and then they ease you into death. Men handle the bits in between.
>
> (2015: 3)

We could briefly summarize *Lela & Co.* as the tale of a girl trying to narrate her story. Throughout the play, which opened at the Royal Court Jerwood Theatre Upstairs in 2015 and was directed by Jude Christian, the monologue delivered by the character of Lela is constantly being interrupted by the many voices of the men in her life – all of whom were played by the same actor – who contradict, overpower and ultimately negate her experience, transforming her struggle to narrate her story into a battle for survival and existence. In a story that is framed by a struggle to be heard, her narrative, as seen in the quote above, is inserted into a particular tradition of storytelling, which is that of the oral narratives of her female ancestors who sang the songs of birth and the songs of death, who maintained tradition and managed life and reproduction, but who were silenced in between. As the play advances, however, we will witness not only how she is constantly silenced by men, but also how her place as a storyteller and keeper of tradition is also denied by the other female members of her family. Throughout her monologue, during which she will be framed as an unreliable narrator by the men in her life, we learn that Lela lives in a village in the mountains neighbouring a country at war. When she is fifteen, she will meet her husband through her brother-in-law, and will move across the border with him (presumably after being bought, or after a transaction of some sort between husband and brother-in-law) where she will be abused physically and psychologically and ultimately trafficked into prostitution so that her husband can earn a living. Lela will be transformed into a business enterprise until she finally manages to escape and return home, only to be forced to silence her experience so as not to shame her family. Their complicit silence and refusal to listen to her story is explained by her as 'a way, a very way, a very human way of not hearing and not seeing, no not even seeing' (48). She offers a summary of her story that highlights what was told and what was left unsaid from it:

> so I live now every day I live each day and so my sister cared for me though she did not care for me and so my brother-in-law was good though he was not good and so my husband is dead though he is not dead living now he is yes and so I had no child though I had a child once and so I was loved though I was not loved and happy I am me and my little soldier and my little girl happy yes forever and ever. (48)

The juxtaposition of her experiences of pain, violence and neglect by her family with the folk-tale happy ending version that accompanies them highlights the tension between her lived experience and its narrative, as well as between her struggle to find a voice and the complicit silence of those around her.

Franzmann's *Bodies*, also performed at the Jerwood Theatre Upstairs and also directed by Jude Christian, focuses on the story of Clem, a white middle-class professional woman, and her husband Josh, who desperate for a baby have engaged in an international transaction with a Russian donor and an Indian surrogate, Lakshmi, to finally have a child. The play opens with a dialogue between Clem and Daughter, her sixteen-year-old offspring, where they chat about kale crisps and trans fats. The apparent naturalism of the scene is challenged when Clem asks Daughter, 'Which school do you go to?' (2017: 9), which leads to a conversation about Daughter's life and routines which Clem, her mother, is curiously unaware of. The following scene, where Clem and Josh are in a waiting room in a fertility clinic in India, helps us understand that Daughter has not been born yet; when and if she does, she will do so thanks to Lakshmi, the surrogate. Clem's estranged and complex relationship with her socialist dad, who has motor neurone disease, and his carer Oni, a black woman who understands the father better than Clem, together with her ethical conundrums in front of the surrogacy, ultimately transform the play into an exploration of white guilt and a dissection of white middle-class privilege. This allows us to question not only the relationship between capitalism, multiple crises and the female body, but also the relationships of solidarity and sorority amongst women.

In the course of the play, Franzmann explores the complex world of commercial surrogacy, highlighting what Sophie Lewis defines in *Full Surrogacy Now: Feminism against Family* as the horror of neoliberal surrogacy in which 'marginalized, often racialized proletarians (who aren't encouraged to reproduce themselves) are encouraged by the market to behave as self-managing contractors of their own bodily organs in the perpetuation of rich people's existence, the realization of their dreams' (2019: 16). Lewis highlights as well the lack of voice given to surrogates in discussions around the legitimacy and need to regulate or ban surrogacy (55), which Franzmann's *Bodies* reproduces by having the unborn teenage daughter become Lakshmi's surrogate voice for most of the play. Daughter will even be the one who manifests, and transmits to Clem, the lack of agency presupposed of surrogates when surrogacy is made illegal in India in scene thirteen. In trying to convey both her feelings as an unborn child, and Lakshmi's, Daughter states: 'Is it because they think surrogates are victims? That they can't make decisions about how to use their own bodies without government intervention' (90), paradoxically highlighting Lakshmi's bodily agency but taking over her voice. Lakshmi's story being told second-hand by a surrogate voice, which denies the character her verbal agency, as well as Lela's quest to narrate a story in *Lela & Co.*, and the forceful way in which her experience is negated, can be linked to the initial question that drives this chapter. What kind of stories have we told ourselves about the crisis, who has told those stories, and what kind of voices have been silenced by authoritative narratives such as those of the men in Lela's life, or by the surrogate voice narrating Lakshmi's?

Giving voice to the silenced histories of women and their relationship with crisis and capitalism, Federici stresses that for capitalism to emerge, feminized bodies had to be expropriated, turning them into 'machines for the production of labour power' (Carlin and Federici 2014: 1). As she argues, there is a strong link between dismantling community and communitarian life through the expropriation of common land, the demonization of members of these communities – especially feminized bodies – via campaigns of witch-hunting and economic and social privatization (Federici 2008: 23). The expropriation of the female body is amplified almost to the point of parody in *Lela & Co*. In the play, her trafficking into prostitution is announced in what resembles a cable TV advertisement, followed by a long and detailed list of the rules and regulations of the business enterprise 'Lela and Co. Limited', which include: 'full discretion on the part of clients and employees to be maintained at all times', 'full payment on the part of the client... prior to services rendered' or 'respect to the property of Lela & Co. Limited' (32), which as Lela explains consists in:

> **Lela**   No cutting or burning, no bruising beyond normal wear and tear, no excessive beating or slapping beyond normal use, no more than two clients to make use of the services of Lela & Co. Limited simultaneously at any one time, no foreign objects outside of the norm to be inserted into the orifices of/
>
> **Husband**   The company vacuum cleaner/
>
> **Lela**   with particular penalties laid down for metal and glass, including but not limited to: bottles, poles, gun barrels and knives (32)

In *Bodies*, Lakshmi's body is literally expropriated by her role as a surrogate mother, with no say over it during her pregnancy. When she tries to escape to get an abortion, she is restrained and forced to carry the pregnancy to term. This, however, is once more not voiced by her, but by Clem:

> **Clem**   The clinic found her before she could do anything else. They tied her hands and feet and threw her in the car and took her back to the centre. They put her back in the dorm with the other women who won't go near her, because she's full of bad luck and they all know it. But it's still in her. It's scraping her uterus, drinking her blood, gulping her food, swelling her up with its wings, its beak scratching at her soft insides, tap-tap-tapping on her organs. She punches her womb every night. They have to restrain her, tie her arms to the side of the bed because she'll kill it if she can. (112)

In the play, however, surrogacy, and the externalization of reproductive work does not only fall on Lakshmi. Both Oni and Lakshmi carry the burden of Clem's family's reproductive work while being unable to care for their own families. Considering this, surrogacy in *Bodies* resembles Lewis's argument by which

> 'Surrogate', more than 'reproductive' or 'feminized', might be a word that proves useful... in bringing together the millions of precarious and/or migrant workers labouring today as cleaners, nannies, butlers, assistants, cooks and sexual assistants in First World homes, whose service is figured as dirtied by commerce, in contrast to the supposedly

'free' or 'natural' love-acts of an angelic white bourgeois femininity it in fact makes possible.

(2019: 56)

Clem's love-acts therefore, as both a mother and a daughter, are made possible via Lakshmi and Oni's bodies and their own estrangement from love-acts towards their own families, illustrating Lewis's point that surrogacy work makes possible bourgeois femininity, a notion that is established very early in the play. The initial discussion between Clem and Daughter about kale crisps (3) quickly situates the action in a context of middle-class affluence. This context, in turn, is reinforced by conversations between Clem and her husband Josh where he mocks her for her working-class background – a social position she has since risen from. Josh's establishment of a separation between their bourgeois present and Clem's working-class past is stressed again when he refers to her father as having 'the socialist stare', as well as to his 'union mates' who would 'shrivel [John's] bollocks to acorns' (14) in disapproval for his choices. In the meantime, Lakshmi is in a reproductive clinic away from her children. At first, we are told that the children are with her husband, 'Their father. Back home in their village' (32), a situation that resembles Oni's, whose husband and daughter are also back home (31). In the case of Lakshmi, however, we will learn that there is no father to take care of her children:

Clem The agency said –

Daughter That was a lie.

…

Clem There must be relatives or –

Lakshmi No.

Clem The community. Other villagers who –

Lakshmi There is no one.

Daughter She's left her son and her daughter alone. (105–6)

The lack of solidarity between Clem and the two women who function as surrogates for her love-acts resembles that between Lela and the women in her family, specially her sister. After Lela escapes the confinement imposed by her husband and the abuse she is subjected to both by him and by the clients of his prostitution business, she walks for days to go back home. Upon arrival, having survived war, prostitution and the death of her own daughter due to malnutrition, she meets her brother-in-law and sister Elle, who refuses to look at her: 'And she won't look at me. And then I knew. Knew what she knew. Knew what she had always known, how with her designer glasses no longer fake. And she hasn't looked at me since' (Lynn 2015: 47). What her sister knew, and the reason she refuses to meet Lela's gaze, is that Lela was being abused by her husband. Similarly, the rest of women in Lela's life embrace an analogous kind of silence, an oppressive silence for Lela, who tells us:

> So I live now. And I live in silence and I do not speak of many things and we do not speak of many things and the aunts sit in the chair and look sideways and suck in their cheeks and say 'Mm-mm-mmmm', but those aren't words and so they're safe, yes safe, there is safety for everyone in numbers and in numbers numerous more numerous than little Lela all alone they have decided silence. (48)

This division and lack of solidarity between women that we find in both plays is reminiscent of the division of women that, according to Federici (2004), was one of the many consequences of witch-hunting. As she explains, witch-hunting introduced a new social and ethical code which would have deep consequences for women in capitalism, amid them the confinement in a position that would frown upon sorority and solidarity amongst them. In this light, if we consider Sylvia Walby's gendered perspective on crisis, specially how she locates gender imbalance only in the 'exclusion of women from economic and financial decision-making' (2015: 2) and 'in centralized political institutions in states' (7), we can see how she reproduces the neoliberal feminist idea that suggests that the presence of women in positions of power will generate a trickle-down effect that will ultimately benefit those less favoured, as exposed by Mies (1998: 76). The lack of solidarity between Lela and the women in her family, as well as the one between the privileged middle-class Clem and the surrogates Lakshmi and Oni, suggests otherwise.

Throughout both plays, moreover, we witness how these women, upon whom reproductive work falls, are subjected to constant acts of violence such as the imprisonment and obstetric coercion of Lakshmi in *Bodies*, or Lela's constant abuse, which starts with her husband raping her before forcing her to become a prostitute:

> At which point he took me by the hair and smashed my face into the wall so I was discombobulated and then he turned me over and raped me until I stopped screaming. And then another one came in and did the same. And then another. My husband had a lot of friends. He's a popular man.
>
> (Lynn 2015: 26)

As Lisa Fitzpatrick states, in *Lela & Co.* 'the violence exceeds the violence of rape' becoming an 'ontological violence that seeks to utterly destroy the body of its target', a violence that 'aims to destroy the uniqueness of the body, tearing at its constitutive vulnerability' (2018: 215). This kind of sexual violence against women is seen by Rita Laura Segato as the expression of a deep symbolic structure intrinsic to patriarchal societies and capitalist development (2013: 19), in a similar argument to that of Federici (2004) and the relationship she establishes between violence and reproductive work. Read in the context of the plays, this shows us that Lela, Lakshmi and Oni's stories exemplify how feminized bodies become those upon which this work falls, and how these bodies are prone to being victims and survivors of violence, both prerogatives for the survival of capitalism.

The collapse of the crisis chronology

The 2008 economic crisis and its ramifications have been defined as a cascade (Walby 2015: 1), a conjuncture (Hall and Massey 2010: 57) or a rupture (Bauman and Bordoni 2014: 10), all images that suggest a disruption of the normal or a turning point which nonetheless seems to hint at the possibility of a better future, 'a transition which is necessary to growth, as a prelude to an improvement in a different status, a decisive step forward' (Bauman and Bordoni 2014: 3). However, these definitions are problematic in that they establish a very particular temporality manifested in what I have called a *chronology of crisis*, divided into a pre-crisis, a moment of crisis (the turning point) and a hopeful post-crisis. With the help of the plays under discussion, I wish to suggest that by revising crisis from a feminist perspective the aforementioned chronology of crisis collapses. This suggestion challenges understandings of crisis, and in particular the post-2008 crisis, as change or as a turning point (Angelaki 2017: 2), as this obscures the fact that this change or turning point is defined by a system that is already built upon the existence of subjects always already in crisis: feminized and racialized bodies, colonized subjects, queer and gender non-conforming people, disabled bodies and all those who do not conform to the norm.

As noted by Chamberlain (2017), timekeeping has been rendered problematic for both feminism and queer theory, suggesting that time needs to be read against a linear understanding so as not to reproduce the very same normativity that excludes marginalized subjects. This includes embracing the messiness of temporal overlaps, looking backwards instead of forwards so as to imagine non-normative futures and accepting the discomfort of deviant timekeeping and a resistance to chrononormativity (Freeman 2010: 3; Chamberlain 2017: 48). Approaching crisis from a feminist perspective contributes towards exposing the temporal otherness of the feminized body as it is excluded from the crisis narrative. The feminized body is always already in crisis, and this is a prerequisite for the capitalist system to function.

In terms of the theatrical aesthetics of crisis, as Vicky Angelaki states, in times of crisis, and in the particular context of the post-2008 crisis:

> social and political performance becomes redefined, moving further away from social realism and into a territory where formal experimentation and sensory richness are no longer seen as tropes of alternative stages but as methodologies that, in twenty-first century British theatre, have infiltrated the mainstream. This marks a significant turn in contemporary theatre-making of the crisis era.
>
> (2017: 4)

Besides offering a feminized approach to definitions of crisis on the basis of what constitutes labour and which bodies are responsible for not only productive but reproductive work, through their staging, both *Lela & Co.* and *Bodies* also contribute towards challenging – and potentially collapsing – what I have previously defined as a chronology of crisis, by opening the possibility for alternative temporalities through experimenting with dramaturgical strategies.

Lela & Co. does not have any markers of time or space – we do not know when the play is set, or where – which contributes to problematizing the idea of crisis as linked to a specific turning point for the female subject. Additionally, the play explores 'the complexity of [the] embodied experience of survival' (Fitzpatrick 2018: 220) through 'sensory dissonance' (214), which in the staging is materialized in the use of darkness and smell. In the production at the Royal Court Jerwood Theatre Upstairs, spectators were informed that part of the play would be performed in the dark. For about forty minutes the whole room was in complete darkness while Lela explained the most violent and jarring experiences she had been through. These *imagined* forty minutes, they could be more, or maybe less, as it was difficult to have a clear grasp of how long we were in the dark for, contributed to an experience of disorientation that, in the context of establishing a clear crisis chronology, made it more difficult to pinpoint events or experiences to a specific moment in time. What was happening to Lela could take place anywhere, anytime and to any woman.

In addition to this use of darkness, *Lela & Co.* experimented with sensory richness and dissonance through the use of smell. During the play a candy floss machine was used on stage and several pink candy floss sticks were given to members of the audience. The sweet smell lingered in the small room for a long time during the performance, almost crashing against the hardness and seriousness of what spectators were being told. The usual happy and childlike memories associated with candy floss were severely disrupted by the juxtaposition of the sweet smell and the crude story. As spectators left the auditorium, after learning of Lela's return home and imposed silence by the members of her family, they were given a little bag of candy floss to take home. The act of taking the bag of candy, of removing an element from the play, contributed towards extending the time of the play beyond the confines of the duration of the performance. Time could no longer be contained, and neither could the violence Lela had been subjected to, which exceeded her own body and her own experience.

In the case of *Bodies*, the setting presented a set of different structures or frames that resembled containers which mirrored Clem's wishes to compartmentalize the different areas of her life: her wishes to become a mother, her socialist father who needs intensive care and the life of the surrogate. Despite her intentions to compartmentalize and rationalize, the setting could not contain the different aspects of Clem's life separate, neither in the space of the performance, nor in time. On the one hand, the presence of an imaginary teenage daughter who would become the voice of Lakshmi, the surrogate mother, and her transition through the different containers on set, disrupted both time and space. Daughter is the only character – who belongs to the world of the imagination, to a future that is not yet, and that maybe never will be – who connects with Lakshmi and who listens to her voice, possibly suggesting that the only way forward for feminism, and possibly for the world, is to transcend the space that separates us, the borders that separate and contribute towards inequality and exploitation. On the other hand, during the performance Lakshmi could be seen painting the walls yellow rather erratically. This paint would then be seen dropping in and from different places of the set, signalling once more to the impossibility to contain Lakshmi's experiences in a particular time and place.

These strategies contribute to the establishment of affective contact with women throughout the history of patriarchy and capitalism. I refer here to what Caroline Dinshaw defines as 'the possibility of touching across time, collapsing time through affective contact between marginalized people now and then', which according to her has the capacity to 'form communities across time' (Dinshaw et al. 2007: 178). Both plays refuse, to a greater or lesser extent, to contain the experiences of reproductive work and violence of these women in a particular point of time in history. Read against the understanding of crisis as a turning-point, these stories, and the way they were performed, contribute towards collapsing the chronology of crisis.

The aftermath of crisis

Thinking about the post-2008 crisis through the lens of feminism and the history of women under capitalism shows us how the turn from the feudal system to capitalism confined feminized bodies to a perpetual state of crisis manifested in women being responsible for and relegated to unrecognized reproductive work. This paradigm change led in turn to the expropriation of their bodies, which are perpetually subjugated to a state of violence. Explored both thematically and through their dramaturgical strategies, both *Lela & Co.* and *Bodies* show the effects of this distribution of work and the violence that emerges from it. Moreover, both plays enact an intervention in the discourse of crisis, particularly in the way in which crisis has been presented in a clear chronology that allows for the implementation of policies that will lead to a hopeful aftermath that, however, is neither promising nor freeing for those marginalized subjects perpetually in a state of crisis.

References

Ahmed, S. (2017), *Living a Feminist Life*, Durham and London: Duke University Press.

Aitkenhead, D. and V. Featherstone (2017), 'The Royal Court's Vicky Featherstone: "We All Knew about Sexual Harassment. We. All. Knew"', *Guardian*, 4 November. Available online: https://www.theguardian.com/stage/2017/nov/04/royal-court-vicky-featherstone-we-all-knew-about-sexual-harassment (accessed 9 April 2019).

Angelaki, V. (2017), *Social and Political Theatre in 21st-Century Britain: Staging Crisis*, London: Bloomsbury Methuen.

Arruzza, C., T. Bhattacharya and N. Fraser (2019), *Feminism for the 99%: A Manifesto*, London: Verso.

Aston, E. (2018), 'Enter Stage Left: "Recognition", "Redistribution", and the A-Affect', *Contemporary Theatre Review*, 28 (3): 299–309.

Barbagallo, C. and S. Federici (2012), 'Introduction', *The Commoner*, 15: 1–21.

Bauman, Z. and C. Bordoni (2014), *State of Crisis*, Cambridge: Polity Press.

Brown, M. (2018), 'Vicky Featherstone Named Most Influential Person in British Theatre', *Guardian*, 4 January. Available online: https://www.theguardian.com/stage/2018/jan/04/vicky-featherstone-named-most-influential-person-in-british-theatre (accessed 9 April 2019).

Butler, J. and A. Athanasiou (2013), *Dispossession: The Performative in the Political*, Cambridge: Polity Press.

Carlin, M. and S. Federici (2014), 'The Exploitation of Women, Social Reproduction, and the Struggle against Global Capital', *Theory and Event*, 17 (3): 1–6.

Chamberlain, P. (2017), *The Feminist Fourth Wave: Affective Temporality*, New York: Palgrave.

Dinshaw, C., L. Edelman, R. A. Ferguson, C. Freccero, E. Freeman, J. Halberstam, A. Jagose, C. Nealon, N. Tan Hoang (2007), 'Theorizing Queer Temporalities: A Roundtable Discussion', *GLQ: A Journal of Lesbian and Gay Studies*, 13 (2–3): 177–95.

Enright, L. (2018), 'Vicky Featherstone: "I'm Not Afraid of Being Labelled a Dirty Boring Feminist"', *Pool*, 8 January. Available online: https://www.the-pool.com/work/pool-pioneers/2018/10/Vicky-Featherstone/ (accessed 10 December 2018).

Federici, S. (2004), *Caliban and the Witch: Women, the Body and Primitive Accumulation*, New York: Autonomedia.

Federici, S. (2008), *Witches, Witch-Hunting, and Women*, Oakland: PM Press.

Federici, S. (2020), *Beyond the Periphery of the Skin: Rethinking, Remaking, and Reclaiming the Body in Contemporary Capitalism*, Oakland: PM Press.

Fitzpatrick, L. (2018), *Rape on the Contemporary Stage*, London: Palgrave Macmillan.

Franzmann, V. (2017), *Bodies*, London: Nick Hern.

Freeman, E. (2010), *Time Binds: Queer Temporalities, Queer Histories*, Durham and London: Duke University Press.

Gorman, S., G. Harris and J. Harvie (2018), 'Feminisms Now', *Contemporary Theatre Review*, 28 (3): 278–84.

Hall, S. and D. Massey (2010), 'Interpreting the Crisis', *Soundings*, 44: 57–71.

Lewis, S. (2019), *Full Surrogacy Now: Feminism against Family*, London: Verso.

Long, E. and J. Frost (2015), 'Notes on the Erotic in the Capitalist Mode of Production', *Lies: A Journal of Materialist Feminism*, 2: 99–112.

Lynn, C. (2015), *Lela & Co.*, London: Nick Hern.

Mies, M. (1998), *Patriarchy and Accumulation on a World Scale*, London: Zed Books.
Segato, R. L. (2013), *La escritura en el cuerpo. De las mujeres asesinadas en Ciudad Juárez*, Buenos Aires: Tinta Limón Ediciones.
Walby, S. (2015), *Crisis*, Cambridge: Polity Press.
Zaroulia, M. (2018), 'Performing That Which Exceeds Us: Aesthetics of Sincerity and Obscenity during "the Refugee Crisis"', *Research in Drama Education: The Journal of Applied Theatre and Performance*, 23 (2): 179–92.

Part Two

Collective action

5

'We need to make the world we live in': Crisis and utopia in Jack Thorne's *Hope* and Lung's *E15*

Enric Monforte

In *Acts of Resistance: Against the Tyranny of the Market*, Pierre Bourdieu critiques neoliberalism as a 'utopia (becoming a reality) of unlimited exploitation', that through 'a *programme of methodical destruction of collectives*' installs an 'individualist micro-economic model' as the ideal system, despite its catastrophic social costs (1998: 95–6, 98; original emphasis). This 'new market-forces conjuncture' (Hall and Massey 2010: 66) has dramatically impacted life in the West in recent decades. In the UK, it has been characterized by the dismantling of the Welfare State of the post-war period by the Conservative governments since 1979, led by Margaret Thatcher and John Major, through policies such as fostering individual profit, the privatization of public services and national industries, the reduction of public spending and a deregulation of financial markets. And subsequent UK governments, both New Labour and Conservative, have both consolidated and advanced Britain's market-oriented political identity.

Reacting to these conditions Jack Thorne's *Hope* (2014) and Lung's *E15* (2015) document the effects of the economic crisis on vulnerable groups in contemporary neoliberal Britain. Despite their different modes of representation, the predominantly socially realistic *Hope* and the verbatim *E15* depict a system of power that subjects defenceless individuals to extreme precarity. Both focus on the erosion of communities, which are understood as necessary – albeit fragile and fragmented – spaces of belonging that may eventually foster agency and lead to local and global political action. Significantly, they present optimistic, affirmative notes, which connect them

---

Enric Monforte's work was supported by the Spanish Ministry of Economy and Competitiveness (MINECO) and the European Regional Development Fund (ERDF) project 'British Theatre in the Twenty-First Century: Crisis, Affect, Community' (FFI2016-75443).

to the utopian potential of theatre as a space of resistance from which to challenge the neoliberal status quo.

While it has been argued that 'crisis is the normal condition of capitalism' (Delanty 2014: 214), the global crisis of 2007/8 jolted confidence in an unfettered neoliberal utopia. Sylvia Walby identifies four interconnected phases in this crisis, common to many countries in Europe and North America: a 'banking, credit and financial crisis', a 'deep economic recession', 'attempts to reduce government budget deficits by cutting public expenditure' and 'a political crisis that might become a democratic crisis' (2015: 2–3). This has given way to what Pankaj Mishra (2016) has termed an 'age of anger' and 'irrationalism', a consequence of the effects of neoliberalism and global capitalism, in turn the result of the failure of the ideals of Enlightenment rationalism and nineteenth-century utilitarianism. Such failure, together with the inability to act in the best interests of individuals and society, may ultimately endanger the stability of democracy (2016).

Bearing the above in mind, and thinking about theatrical responses to such anger, in this chapter I follow Stuart Hall's understanding of crises as 'moments of potential change' (Hall and Massey 2010: 57), 'break', or as '"ruptural fusion[s]"' (60), and his belief in the necessity of 'counter-intervention' (65). I also consider Bourdieu's notion of 'forces of *resistance*' aimed at the creation of a 'social order ... oriented towards *rational pursuit of collectively defined and approved ends*', and the 'defence of the *public interest*' (1998: 103–5; original emphasis). Applying Hall's and Bourdieu's ideas to Thorne's *Hope* and Lung's *E15*, I argue that such moments of crisis could be seen as opportunities to 'counter-intervene', to resist, to rebuild vulnerable collectives and precarious communities.

Death by a thousand cuts: *Hope* and rethinking Labour

Hope, which opened at the Royal Court Theatre Downstairs in November 2014 directed by John Tiffany, presents the ethical and political dilemmas of a dedicated group of ethnically diverse Labour councillors in an unnamed English working-class, impoverished constituency as they deal with the devastating effects of the 2007/8 crisis on their community. The consequent precarity produced by crisis austerity policies – the third phase mentioned by Walby – is a central feature of the play. Thorne assembles a varied cast of characters all marked by intrinsic vulnerability who face the task of justifying and implementing further cuts to local public services. Hilary, the leader of the council, is a middle-aged woman who lives an ascetic life in extremely humble lodgings, wholeheartedly devoted to her work and to the idea of caring for society by serving the community. Mark, the deputy leader, is a middle-aged Scotsman and recovering alcoholic who has a strong belief in the redemptive power of politics: 'Being political – being a political person – saved me' (Thorne 2014: 76). Julie, who, in her thirties, has moved back to her father's home hesitates over committing to a relationship with Mark. George, Julie's father, is an embittered former Labour leader who has lost faith in the world as a consequence of the crisis of social democracy and its co-option by neoliberal thought, but who still longs for recuperation of Labour as a 'critical site' or 'nodal point' in British politics (Hall and Massey 2010: 70). For George the lack of mass protest in the face of the recession signals a crippling absence of belief in the Labour movement and an acceptance of the conditions shaped by neoliberalism (Thorne 2014: 66–7). Sarwan also clings to the erstwhile role of Labour of helping the dispossessed and makes a plea for the return of the one-time soul of the party: 'We're the Labour Party. Together. United. We'll never be defeated' (57). Finally, the idealistic and somewhat naïve Lata, on her part, entered politics prompted by her mother's lack of opportunities, which she states in a moving speech: 'My mother wasn't a strong woman. My father was – occasionally quite brutal with her. She let him. She let the world happen to her. I think we need to make the world we live in' (59). The idea of 'making the world' (60), of taking action and responsibility and showing agency, is central to the play, as this is precisely what the characters end up doing at the end, in a counter-intervention of resistance when they oppose the party establishment, thus hinting at other, more inclusive ways of governance.

After three years of unrelenting cuts following the dictates of the Conservative and Liberal Democrat coalition government led by David Cameron, the councillors are required to still carry out even more substantial ones, with devastating impact on local government services. After considering other options, such as increasing the council tax; closing the city farm, public toilets, museum and library; halving the swimming pool budget, and reducing street lighting (16–19), the Budget Steering Group approaches the areas liable to yield more savings: 'Elderly care. Disabled care. Sure Start Centres' (19),[1] especially focusing on the first two. This resonates with Walby's notion of the crisis as gendered (2015: 10–11),

---

[1] Sure Start children's centres where launched in 1999 under the Labour government of Tony Blair and were intended to 'provide integrated care and services for young children and their families, with a particular focus on closing the achievement gap for children from disadvantaged backgrounds' (Bouchal and Norris [n.d.]: 2; see also Department for Education 2013). Between 2011 and 2017 two-thirds of the centres' funding was reduced as a consequence of austerity cuts, also resulting in the closing down of up to 1,000 centres out of the 3,600 that existed in the period 2009–10, their thriving moment (Butler 2019).

due to the gender demographic of those working in the caring professions and those most reliant on their support. The prospective closures prompt a virulent reaction from Gina, Mark's ex-wife and head of a Day Centre facing closure, who immediately launches a successful grassroots campaign against the closing. The party national leadership becomes troubled by the possible negative repercussions on a forthcoming election and threatens to replace the council, which leads Hilary to decide to close a number of Sure Start Centres instead. Two of those centres are in a 'largely Pakistani and Bangladeshi area' (50), whose inhabitants are partly diverted to another centre in an area with a strong presence of the far-right, populist English Defence League (EDL). The resulting clashes in the community lead to a Pakistani man being stabbed to death in an area where street lighting had been cut. In recognition of the impossibility of their position, the council finally refuses to make a budget – the counter-intervention of resistance above mentioned – but the government ends up carrying out far worse cuts than the ones initially considered. The play closes with a reflection on the meaning of public service in times of crisis. After the councillors are disempowered by the party they address the audience:

> **Lata** *looks forward.*
>
> **Lata** How can I help?
>
> **Sarwan** *takes a breath and then looks forward.*
>
> **Sarwan** How can I help?
>
> **Julie** *looks at* **Sarwan** *and then looks forward.*
>
> **Julie** How can I help?
>
> **Hilary** How can I help?
>
> **Mark** How can I help? (96)

The ending of the play offers a tentatively hopeful look into the future on the part of the politically defeated but nevertheless ethically empowered councillors. This is seen through the reflection on the meaning of public service and the paramount importance of helping and cohabiting with others as the only possible way out. As councillors address the audience and offer their support – a question recurrently asked to their constituents through the play – they state with clarity the original aim of their task as public servers and citizens, thus offering themselves wholeheartedly to the public they serve with the aim of saving them and, in doing so, perhaps also saving themselves. This highly poetic concluding moment stresses their own vulnerability and precariousness and, at the same time, enables them to establish connections between themselves.

Hope contains elements of the state-of-the-nation tradition of the 1970s and 1980s yet changes and subverts it, a pattern Chris Megson has identified in some recent plays, and which he sees as directly related to the effects of globalization (2018: 43–5). The subversion of the paradigm is to be seen in two ways. On the one hand, through a transition that begins with the local, follows on to the national, goes beyond it and finally reaches towards the global, theorized by Jill Dolan (2005), Siân Adiseshiah and Louise LePage (2016) or Dan Rebellato (2018), amongst others, and which Lyn Gardner describes as 'state of the world plays' (qtd. in Megson 2018: 44). On the other, by reaching different, less gloomy outcomes, by 'affirming... solidarity and hope – what Anders Lustgarten names Radical Optimism – as prerequisites for... social transformation' (Megson 2018: 45), instead of a clearly defined, ready-made ideological message delivered to the audience.

Hope, I contend, could be read as an example of a cosmopolitan, state-of-the-world global model. The play offers a reflection of the situation in the UK since the onset of the financial crisis of 2007/8 through the experiences of the precarious community of councillors in their impoverished town. The movement towards the global could be seen through the direct effects globalization has had upon a specific British context, which at the same time unites the plight of the characters of the play, and the less affluent citizens they represent, to the one experienced by their counterparts elsewhere at a worldwide level. In this way, *Hope* would move beyond the confines of a specific national identity and hint instead towards a shared, global (ethico-political) commonality based on vulnerability and precarity. Importantly, the way in which this is done shifts from pessimism to a moderate, melancholy-tinged optimism, perhaps related to the wish to return to more genuine social democratic forms of government.

Dramaturgically, director John Tiffany's rendering of *Hope* effects this critique of the neoliberal ethos in what appears to be a predominantly socially realistic style interspersed with some experimental, alienating traits. These include extreme fragmentation – there are forty-six short scenes arranged in five acts; having characters stay on stage after finishing their participation in a given scene; giving the play an open ending – thus avoiding formal closure and challenging teleology – or breaking the fourth wall at the end of the play, when characters address their final lines to the audience. To these can be added the further breaking of the realistic flow at some points through the inclusion of other defamiliarizing, self-referential moments. Thus, the performers enact physical routines – doing an imitation of wire-walking perhaps as a metaphor of their situation; doing push-ups, stretches or warming-up boxing routines; lying on a piano or on a desk; advancing on their knees, or hiding – which are totally unrelated to the lines their characters say about how to prioritize the cuts or what the function of a council is. This dissociation between words and action is emblematic of the paradoxes and compromises of the neoliberal utopian context in which Thorne's characters find themselves.

However, perhaps the most relevant dramaturgical aspect of the Royal Court production is the fact that Tiffany and designer Tom Scutt incorporated a portable proscenium-arch dais within the stage space where parts of the dramatic action take place. This device introduces a metatheatrical, defamiliarizing dimension that significantly adds layers of meaning to the play. *Hope* opens with Mark, the main character, standing on this raised stage in front of a drawn blue curtain where, with the help of Julie, he rehearses the speech which will disclose the policy on the cuts that the councillors will have to put into practice. At the end of the scene both characters push the raised stage back upstage, revealing the empty space where the action of the play is mostly going to unfold, described as '*a 1920s-era council office. The sort of place that has beautiful lead-lined glass windows and ugly 1970s furniture*' (4). The stage on stage, then, works as a kind of frame for the whole play and will be used intermittently until the last act, when it will become central one more time. It functions as a pivotal dramaturgical strategy that emphasizes the councillors' roles as mediators and performers who are themselves also at the mercy of the system, in this case represented by the party establishment (Zaroulia, forthcoming). As seen, both identities will be challenged at the end, when the councillors decide to play the roles chosen by themselves and stop performing those given to them by the party.

Rebuilding communities in *E15*

E15 was created by Lung, a British touring theatre company with headquarters in Barnsley, in the north of England, written by Helen Monks and Matt Woodhead, and directed by the latter. The play was commissioned by Battersea Arts Centre in London and supported by The Civic in Barnsley.[2] It premiered at the Gilded Balloon, part of the Edinburgh festival fringe in 2015, and has toured extensively since then. *E15* is a verbatim play that

---

[2] This is the production I saw at the Battersea Arts Centre in March 2017 and to which I refer in the chapter.

dramatizes the effects of the housing crisis in London through the Focus E15 Campaign, 'one of the biggest national housing campaigns in history' (Lung 2016: vii), started by a group of twenty-nine young single mothers in 2013 in Newham, London. Yet again, Walby's recognition of the gendered dimension of neoliberal crisis is pertinent as the play spotlights a group of particularly vulnerable women, subjected to both gender and class oppression. Following Lung's particular interest in '[m]aking theatre by communities, for communities and with communities' (iv), the play was the result of more than 175 hours of interviews made over a six-month period with 'housing campaigners, journalists, politicians' and the mothers themselves (viii), which the writers then put into dramatic form. As Monks and Woodhead state in the introduction to the playtext, '64,000 families are moved out of London every year. Currently, in London, 1 in every 25 children is homeless. Homelessness in London has increased by 30% in the last year. But this is not something that is just happening in the capital – it's nationwide' (viii).

E15 tells the story of Jasmin, Sam and Sapriya, young single mothers in their early twenties. Jasmin was thrown out of her parents' place when her father discovered that the child she was expecting would not be white. Sam became homeless when escaping an abusive partner, and then became pregnant. Sapriya escaped Nigeria to avoid an arranged marriage with a much older man and then was also thrown out of her sister's place in London when she discovered her pregnancy. They are all referred to the Mother and Baby Unit at Focus E15, 'a hostel that gives supportive housing for 210 young and vulnerable people in East London' (49). There, they meet Jordan, a homeless teenager whom the council placed at the hostel. Conflict arises in the play when all residents in the Mother and Baby Unit are handed eviction notices by East Thames Housing Office, the association that runs the hostel. This is in turn due to the freezing of the funding they receive from Newham council – run by Labour – and part of a general plan of cuts and privatization of services involved in the regeneration and gentrification of the area which started with the preparations for the 2012 London Olympics. With the eviction notices, they also lose other important services, such as 'support workers' or 'counselling services' (51–2). The council argues that an inevitable reduction of housing benefit and soaring London rents makes it advisable for the women to move away from Newham and into private accommodation in places as far away as Manchester or Birmingham (vii). As a consequence, they decide to get organized and start a campaign.

The emphasis on the notion of community at the centre of Lung's theatrical practice is reflected in Jasmin's words on the necessity of 'speaking to [her] neighbour' (52): 'I think Sam was the thing that kept me going. She made me realize it's not just me, it's not just me and my child, it's my neighbour, it's my neighbour's neighbour and it's their children too' (53). Thus, they start by contacting all the other residents at the hostel – their literal neighbours – and then by putting up a weekly stall in Stratford Broadway in order to get public support. Donna, an older, radical political activist campaigning against another round of evictions in consequence of the application of the 'bedroom tax' (59) helps them get organized and build the campaign.[3] After repeatedly trying to speak to the Mayor of Newham to no avail, the mothers and their supporters start marching and occupying spaces, like the East Thames Housing Office or the Bridge House Housing Office. They collect signatures, rent a double-decker bus and visit City Hall to symbolically present them to London Mayor Boris Johnson. Eventually, they occupy four flats in The Carpenters Estate, a long-time empty estate ready to be sold, in a festive, collective action that strengthens their sense of community:

Jasmin   We looked down at the people of Newham and we knew, it was time to reclaim what was ours.

Sam   Everyone poured into the house.

Jasmin   Every single person on their way in got a kiss and a cuddle.

Sam   We were like,/'Welcome to your new home.'

Jasmin   'Welcome to your new home.'

…

Jasmin   And for the next two weeks it became a home for the whole community.… It was the first time any of us felt, properly, like we'd found a home. And it was a home we'd built together. (77–8)

---

[3] The 'Removal of the Spare Room Subsidy' (Department for Work and Pensions 2015) was implemented on 1 April 2013 under the Welfare Reform Act 2012. It 'entailed a reduction in HB [housing benefit] for working-age social tenants whose properties have more bedrooms than they are considered to need' (21). It was established that couples, children under ten and children under sixteen of the same sex living in social housing should share a room (two people per room) (22). Having one spare room implied a reduction of benefit of 14 per cent, which became 25 per cent in the case of two or more spare rooms (22). The measure was intended 'to increase mobility within the social housing sector leading to more effective use of the housing stock with households in more suitable sized accommodation, reducing waiting lists for social housing' (109). It was highly criticized by the Labour Party, which coined the name 'bedroom tax'. See also Butler and Siddique (2016).

As a result, the council finally agrees to their demands and opens forty homes in the estate for homeless people. Eventually, the mothers are offered accommodation in Newham, even though expensive and on 'short term contracts' (86), so they continue with their 'ongoing' campaign against homelessness, helping the people of Newham (86). At the same time, evictions at Focus E15 continue. The play ends with a strident call for action: 'Do something'; 'Educate, agitate, organize' (87). Simultaneously, Sam provides a somewhat gloomier note, alluding to a sombre future with the women left alone, each fighting future evictions on their own, the sense of community gradually disappearing:

> Yeah but now like we're separated. We're not as tight-knit as we was before. Just like even though our campaign's hugely grown, it's happening to me. My tenancy's run out. My year's up. Right now it's like shit, I'm in the shit again. And it's like ah, fuck... And at least when it was twenty-nine of us, we were all in it together. Like, it wasn't just me going through it. (88)

The juxtaposition of the highly energetic final moments of the play with Sam's bleaker picture emphasizes the necessity to keep fighting and the utmost importance of maintaining a robust sense of community as the only way to resist and survive the pressures of the neoliberal utopia, which the young mothers experience once again in their present dystopian solitude. The Focus E15 Campaign is still ongoing and in 2020 increasingly concerned with the effects of Covid-19 on the most vulnerable inhabitants of Newham.

Dramaturgically, the play is built in twelve fragmentary scenes or blocks of action, all taking place in Stratford, London. The scenes follow a chronological order, with the main action being interrupted on three different occasions through the insertion of didactic bubbles illustrating case studies from the original interviews related to evictions, the housing crisis and homelessness, that echo and reinforce the fictional characters' experiences. In performance, the bubbles were staged as one continuous flow. In bubble one, which takes place towards the beginning of the play, once the characters have been introduced and handed in eviction letters, three cases are presented of women and children from minority ethnic backgrounds who recount their experiences of eviction from their council flats. Bubble two is placed towards the centre of the play, once the women have started campaigning and after one of the residents in the hostel kills himself. It shows a shadow housing minister, a worker at the Citizens Advice Bureau, a housing charity employee and a civil servant discussing the housing crisis. Possible causes of the problem such as 'buy to let mortgages', 'right to buy' and the 'bedroom tax' are identified (68). These measures perpetuate the power of landlords and the widening gap between social classes. The position of Labour in the issue is also questioned. Finally, in bubble three, placed after the climactic moment of The Carpenters Estate occupation, a homeless man delivers a monologue about living on the streets. This was quite a powerful moment in the Battersea Arts Centre production, as the character spoke from within the audience and the actor looked like any other spectator, underscoring the ubiquity of precarity.

The walls of the performing space were covered with banners and posters bearing political slogans, with others also written on the floor of the acting space in chalk and pictures of the women and other victims of evictions hung across the bare space as 'a photographic manifesto of the personal lives being systematically oppressed and stigmatized by the British political establishment' (76). Other dramaturgical strategies to be found throughout the play also underlined a defamiliarizing, self-referential quality, as when actors repeatedly addressed the audience directly, 're-enact[ed]' particular situations (45), played different roles, talked through microphones or uttered some lines together, in a choral way. What characterized the production was an energetic, enthusiastic feeling (Gardner 2016; Calhoun 2017; Hitchings 2017). Audiences were given leaflets by the performers as they entered the auditorium, in a loud, festive environment, with balloons being passed on as people occupied their seats. Once the performance gathered momentum, that initial feeling gave way to moments of anger, but also of joy and euphoria, hope and optimism, especially in the last part of the play, during the occupation and the closing call to action. Audiences were asked to sign for the E15 campaign as they left the auditorium. The play thus draws on the aesthetic heritage of agit-prop theatre through its rejection of theatrical illusion, absence of scenery, use of direct address, one-dimensional characters, conceptual simplification and concision in the depiction of social issues (Innes 1992: 5, 72–3, 179–80). It also shows its intention of reaching out to audiences, of mobilizing and enlightening them through the use of humour and the creation of an affective atmosphere leading to a climactic finale. At the same time, this is done with 'real sophistication in its delivery' (Gardner 2016). The experience of watching *E15* reflected the effects of what Marissia Fragkou defines as 'performances of precarity' that have the capacity to turn audiences into 'political actors' (2019: 6) and emphasize 'interdependency and relationality' (7), as well as 'responsibility vis-à-vis the life of the Other' (8). To Vicky Angelaki, importantly, the feeling of community triggered by plays like this stresses not only theatre spectatorship, but also citizenship (2017: 4), thus productively linking them to a wider reflection on our responsibility as citizens in times of crisis.

As in the case of *Hope*, *E15* contains elements of the state-of-the-nation tradition, encapsulated in the narration of the ordeal of the young mothers as a microcosm of the situation of the wider nation and, in doing so, it offers a powerful critique of the present status of neoliberal Britain. At the same time, the play might also be read as a state-of-the-world play that starts at the local level – Newham – moves on to the national and could also be extrapolated to the global by reflecting on how the housing crisis in the UK is also the effect of powerful economic policies taking place worldwide with disastrous consequences for all those joining the increasingly bigger ranks of the dispossessed. Donna's final speech could be taken in this direction. After stating how the women are the victims of 'Newham Council, the government and the global system', she makes a questioning reference to the 'end of history':

> Francis Fukuyama – eat your fucking heart out. You said history has ended. History has not ended. History is actively being shaped and moulded by these brave mothers and other like them. Just as the world acts on us, we too can act on the world and effect change. (87)

Donna's words questioning Fukuyama's defence of the economic and sociopolitical policies at work in contemporary Western liberal democracies give the play global resonances and highlight how local acts of resistance can undermine the metanarrative of neoliberal globalization as utopia. To this, crucially, elements of hope, optimism and solidarity are underlined all through the play as sites of resistance and intervention.

Utopian performatives

Jill Dolan has suggestively written on theatre as a place where hope and utopia are worked out in order to foster a much-needed recuperation and revitalization of more radical forms of humanism and democracy (2005). She argues for a challenging reconstruction of humanism that, by being 'contextual, situational, and specific' instead of 'totalizing' will become 'multiple, respecting the complexities and ambiguities of identity while it works out ways for people to share and feel things in common, like the need for survival and for love, for compassion, and for hope' (22). According to Dolan, performances that stage utopian moments crucially 'lead to both affective and effective feelings and expressions of hope and love ... for other people, for a more abstracted notion of "community"' (2), what she, following Victor Turner, calls *communitas*. This happens mainly through 'utopian performatives', which 'describe small but profound moments in which performance calls the attention of the audience in a way that lifts everyone slightly above the present, into a hopeful feeling of what the world might be like if every moment of our lives were as emotionally voluminous, generous, aesthetically striking, and intersubjectively intense' (5). Theatre becomes the space 'to embody and... enact the affective possibilities of "doings" that gesture toward a much better world' (6). Utopia is then seen 'as processual, as an index to the possible, to the "what if", rather than a more restrictive, finite image', and it is this take that 'allows performance a hopeful cast' (13), a movement from the 'as is' to the 'what if' (21).

Both *Hope* and *E15* offer instances of utopian performatives that foster the creation of a local and global consciousness in the audience and promote a more inclusive notion of community. These moments might also be seen as tools towards a reconsideration of the present and the future and are imbued with the potential to effectively counteract the workings of what Bourdieu calls the neoliberal utopia and its endless operation.

In *Hope*, a powerful utopian moment takes place nearly at the end of the play. The scene between Mark and Gina's teenage son, Jake, and George is set in a park in a late afternoon/early evening. In the Royal Court production, the scene is performed on the raised dais, observed by the remaining cast who sit either on the raised stage or on the main playing area. The blue curtain opens. Jake sits, reading Dickens's *Great Expectations*, as the actor playing George enters with one chair, places it next to Jake and, once in character, enquires after the book. To a disenchanted George, the novel is 'about how the future makes a fool out of you' (94), but to Jake 'it's about how shit it is trying to be like everyone else. And I think it's about trying – I think it's about how trying is good. But hard' (94). To Jake's amazement, George, who is in his '*mid-seventies*' (4), offers him marijuana,

> Because I've had a hard life but I look at you and know you'll never have it as good as I did... I think you could do with a happier world... I'm smoking because I am proud fucking fuck-up. (95)

And Jake reacts: 'It is possible though, just so you know, it's possible I will have a better life than you. It's possible the world will be better. More equal. Better. Just so you know' (95). Trying becomes a way out, a way of saving oneself – something essential for Jake (24) – but also a necessary requisite in order to save one another: 'You've got to, right? I mean, it's sort of pointless, isn't it? Not trying? I mean, the world's sort of pointless – if you don't try' (96). Significantly, the metatheatrical space of the raised stage signals the potentiality of theatre as a place where ethico-political interventions may be effected. The scene provides the spectator with a plethora of additional meanings as the implications of the different types of theatre space converge at this point in the use of the park, a place with heterotopic connotations, that shelters both the bullied adolescent and the scarred, disenchanted councillor. In a beautiful moment between the youngest and oldest characters of the play, the importance of affirmation, idealism, responsibility and solidarity is emphasized.

E15 presents a compelling example through the story of Alex, the homeless man who, in bubble three, delivers a monologue about life in the streets. He recounts how, with the money he earned by doing some temporary work at Christmas, he invited some other homeless men to a restaurant:

> To see these lads I took out, the lads I know, they get fed on the streets but it's not the best food and this was a classy meal.
> You could see the enjoyment. It made my day. I was buzzing off it. I still do when I think about it.
> That's what it's about innit? Share the wealth. (81–2)

The scenes described above, emphasizing the importance of trying to change the world through the values of community and sharing as opposed to the individual ethos of neoliberalism, work as all-powerful performatives that hint at the utopian moment as full of possibility, as a doing, as processual. At the same time, they extend the 'intersubjective vulnerability' between the characters to that between stage and spectator through the creation of powerful 'gestures of feeling' (Dolan 2005: 31). They fulfil the aim stated by Dolan: the vindication of *communitas* and the revitalization of a more diverse humanism 'through performative gestures of utopic hope' (2005: 32) for the defenceless councillors and the working-class citizens they represent in *Hope* and for the underclass peoples of *E15*. This is the starting point, the movement that will take place from the 'as is' to a utopian 'what if' that is implied in the acknowledgement of the intrinsic intersubjective vulnerability between the characters, between spectators and actors, and finally between spectators themselves both in the theatre and as global spectators. And it is in those 'doings' that hope and a sense of a global community might emerge. The performative thus becomes a counter-intervention on the part of active political actors that takes place in the theatre – the place where '"other" spaces of crisis and resistance' are imagined (Zaroulia and Hager 2015: 8). As such, it stresses the necessity of public service and care and prompts interdependency and relationality, as well as presenting a longing for a social form of capitalism that confronts the selfish individualism at the basis of neoliberalism.

Necessary optimism?

Hope and *E15* reflect on the effects of the economic crisis in the UK and look for ways to respond. Following Hall's notion of crises as prompting change and his belief in 'counter-intervention' and Bourdieu's idea of 'forces of resistance', the chapter has elaborated on how such moments could be used to generate ethico-political counter-interventions in society aimed at rebuilding the most vulnerable, fractured communities of citizens in present times. The plays envisage ways of changing a reality informed by economic austerity and global neoliberalism through the use of utopian performatives that introduce optimistic, hopeful, affirmative notes. This is related to the notion of theatre as a place where a contestation of the status quo can be found. Importantly, all this takes place in a movement from the local to the global, via the national. Ultimately, *Hope* and *E15* strive for the creation of more egalitarian, cosmopolitan communities based on public service and care, as they interpellate spectators to actively make the world we inhabit, however adverse the circumstances in an age of anger also marked, at the time the plays were performed, by the impending Brexit vote and subsequent Conservative landslide victory.

References

Adiseshiah, S. and L. LePage (2016), 'Introduction: What Happens Now', in S. Adiseshiah and L. LePage (eds), *Twenty-First Century Drama: What Happens Now*, 1–13, London: Palgrave Macmillan.

Angelaki, V. (2017), *Social and Political Theatre in 21st-Century Britain: Staging Crisis*, London: Bloomsbury Methuen.

Bouchal, P. and E. Norris (n.d.), *Implementing Sure Start Children's Centres*, Institute for Government. Available online: https://www.instituteforgovernment.org.uk/sites/default/files/publications/Implementing%20Sure%20Start%20Childrens%20Centres%20-%20final_0.pdf (accessed 17 November 2020).

Bourdieu, P. (1998), *Acts of Resistance: Against the Tyranny of the Market*, trans. R. Nice, New York: The New Press.

Butler, P. (2019), 'Sure Start Programme Saved the NHS Millions of Pounds, Study Finds', *Guardian*, 4 June. Available online: https://www.theguardian.com/society/2019/jun/04/sure-start-saved-nhs-millions (accessed 17 November 2020).

Butler, P. and H. Siddique (2016), 'The Bedroom Tax Explained', *Guardian*, 27 January. Available online: https://www.theguardian.com/society/2016/jan/27/the-bedroom-tax-explained (accessed 16 November 2020).

Calhoun, D. (2017), 'Review of *E15*', *Theatre Record*, 37: 284.

Delanty, G. (2014), 'Introduction: Perspectives on Crisis and Critique in Europe Today', *European Journal of Social Theory*, 17 (3): 207–18.

Department for Education (2013), *Sure Start Children's Centres Statutory Guidance: For Local Authorities, Commissioners of Local Health Services and Jobcentre Plus*. Available online: https://assets.publishing.service.gov.uk/government/uploads/system/uploads/attachment_data/file/678913/childrens_centre_stat_guidance_april-2013.pdf (accessed 17 November 2020).

Department for Work and Pensions (2015), *Evaluation of Removal of the Spare Room Subsidy*, Research Report no. 913. The Cambridge Centre for Housing and Planning Research and Ipsos MORI. Available online: https://assets.publishing.service.gov.uk/government/uploads/system/uploads/attachment_data/file/506407/rsrs-evaluation.pdf (accessed 17 November 2020).

Dolan, J. (2005), *Utopia in Performance: Finding Hope at the Theater*, Ann Arbor: University of Michigan Press.

Focus E15 (2020), *Focus E15 Campaign: Social Housing Not Social Cleansing!* Available online: https://focuse15.org/ (accessed 9 September 2020).

Fragkou, M. (2019), *Ecologies of Precarity in Twenty-First Century Theatre: Politics, Affect, Responsibility*, London: Bloomsbury Methuen.

Gardner, Lyn (2016), '*E15* at Edinburgh Festival Review – Young Mums Speak Out in Newham Protest Play', *Guardian*, 5 August. Available online: https://www.theguardian.com/stage/2016/aug/05/e15-edinburgh-festival-2016-review-newham-protest-focus-e15-campaign (accessed 9 September 2020).

Hall, S. and D. Massey (2010), 'Interpreting the Crisis', *Soundings*, 44: 57–71.

Hitchings, H. (2017), 'Review of *E15*', *Theatre Record*, 37: 284.

Innes, C. (1992), *Modern British Drama: 1890–1990*, Cambridge: Cambridge University Press.

Lung (2016), *The 56 & E15*, London: Oberon.

Megson, C. (2018), '"Can I Tell You about It?": England, Austerity and "Radical Optimism" in the Theatre of Anders Lustgarten', *Journal of Contemporary Drama in English*, 6 (1): 40–54.

Mishra, P. (2016), 'Welcome to the *Age of Anger*', *Guardian*, 8 December. Available online: https://www.theguardian.com/politics/2016/dec/08/welcome-age-anger-brexit-trump (accessed 10 May 2020).

Monks, H. and M. Woodhead (2016), 'Introduction', in Lung, *The 56 & E15*, vi–viii, London: Oberon.

Rebellato, D. (2018), 'Nation and Negation (Terrible Rage)', *Journal of Contemporary Drama in English*, 6 (1): 15–39.

Thorne, J. (2014), *Hope*, London: Nick Hern.

Walby, S. (2015), *Crisis*, Cambridge: Polity Press.

Zaroulia, M. (forthcoming), 'Money and Capitalism', in V. Angelaki and D. Rebellato (eds), *The Cambridge Companion to British Playwriting since 1945*, Cambridge: Cambridge University Press.

Zaroulia, M. and P. Hager (2015), 'Introduction: Europe, Crises, Performance', in M. Zaroulia and P. Hager (eds), *Performances of Capitalism, Crises and Resistance: Inside/Outside Europe*, 1–13, Basingstoke: Palgrave Macmillan.

6
Peopling the theatre in a time of crisis

Sarah Bartley

Representation becomes imperative in times of crisis; concurrently, such periods can be marked by a threat to the functions of democratic, cultural and political participation. In this chapter, I explore the distinctive practices of Camden People's Theatre (established 1994) and Brighton People's Theatre (founded in 2015) to reflect on the utility of people's theatres in discrete moments of social, political and artistic crisis in the UK. Throughout the twentieth and twenty-first century people's theatres have been variously defined as: collective attempts to represent a public and their experiences onstage; radical engagements of a non-theatre going public; forums to put *the people* (rather than professional performers) onstage; and a redistribution of cultural capital from a perceived centre to a more dispersed regional landscape. Here, I particularly consider what characterizes contemporary people's theatres and their relationship to social and political turmoil. The economic crises of 1990 and 2008 have shaped life in the UK over the past thirty years and these two moments of acute crisis act as buoys marking the terrain of my analysis. Through an examination of the creative practices of these two companies and the contexts in which they emerged, I establish the distinctive practices of people's theatres as a mode of making that responds to conditions of crisis.

Reflecting on the global financial meltdown in 2008, Lauren Berlant asserted that such a crisis 'congeals decades of class bifurcation, downward mobility, and environmental, political, and social brittleness' (2011: 11). Throughout the 1980s the Conservative government rapidly grew the economy through removing regulation, increasing competition, privatizing state-owned industries, reforming labour laws and stimulating consumer spending through low interest rates and low-income taxation. This resulted in an overextension of the economy and a mirage of consumer wealth that was abruptly shattered through sharply rising inflation as businesses failed to keep pace with significant demand, that was itself built on instability. In 1990 higher interest rates were imposed in a bid to control inflation and, concurrently, the pound sterling joined the European Exchange Rate

Mechanism (ERM). A precursor to the euro, the ERM tied participating currencies to the value of the deutschmark in an effort to stabilize European markets and encourage trade among nations. This only served to intensify the economic crisis in the UK as the terms meant there was little capacity to cut interest rates at the point the country's economy entered into recession. On 16 September 1992, the UK crashed out of the ERM, following a battle to retain sterling's parity against the deutschmark and a rush of traders selling the pound on foreign stock exchanges; this day became known as 'Black Wednesday', costing the UK Treasury £3.3 billion (Tempest 2005).[1] The high interest rates that ensued had a severe impact on the UK housing market and a doubling in the level of unemployment led to a large fall in domestic spending (Jenkins 2010: 34–5).

Following the recession of the early 1990s, the UK experienced a prolonged period of economic growth. However, undeterred from the boom and bust of the 1980s and 1990s, this period was marked by accelerating financial deregulation, a growth in inequality and increased borrowing. The collapse of US investment bank Lehman Brothers Holdings on 15 September 2008 brought about through the bank's overreliance on subprime mortgages, sent unprecedented shockwaves through the global financial system. Across the world, stock markets plummeted. In the UK RBS, Lloyds and HBOS had to be bailed out with taxpayers' money to the tune of £137 billion leading to a substantial increase in the national debt (Mor 2018: 3), a return to high unemployment and a destabilization of the housing market. The consequences of 2008 continue to be felt more than a decade later through government-imposed austerity policies which have served to accelerate the neglect and oppression of already under-resourced communities across the UK.

In this chapter, I take up Berlant's concept of 'crisis ordinariness', wherein she recognizes 'the ordinary as an impasse shaped by crisis in which people find themselves developing skills for adjusting to newly proliferating pressures to scramble for modes of living on' (2011: 8). Here, I foreground these two specific moments of macro-economic crisis to acknowledge the present as structured by a propagation of systemic crises and I assert the potential of the people's theatre to offer ways 'of living on' under such conditions. Berlant advocates for recognizing how the affects of such conditions are made manifest in emergent genres and aesthetic forms (2011: 4); I posit that the recuperation of people's theatres in the contemporary UK might constitute

---

[1] The reputational and economic damage of Black Wednesday is still keenly felt in the UK, with some political commentators drawing a line between the fallout of this financial disaster and the country's vote to leave the European Union. See Keegan, Marsh and Roberts (2017).

a formal response to the negative affects of crisis. Specifically, how the practices of collectivity and solidarity alongside the popular, experimental and playful forms instigated by Brighton People's Theatre and Camden People's Theatre respond to the affective conditions of anxiety, divisiveness, anger and isolation, which have proliferated in the fallout of 1992 and 2008.

Naming the people

Based in the repurposed site of the Lord Palmerston pub, Camden People's Theatre (CPT) was founded in 1994 by a collective of practitioners including Sheridan Bramwell, Shaun Glanville, Lynne Kendrick, Penelope Prodromou and Tony Gardner. Over the company's 26-year history their proximity to the term people's theatre has fluctuated. The term itself, a people's theatre, encompasses a plurality of practices and alludes to a range of contextually located cultural and political interventions.[2] Tracing CPT's relationship to the term offers insight into the complexity and diversity of practices such a moniker invokes. As one of the founders Shaun Glanville shared,

> We had massive discussions about the naming. I think the idea of calling ourselves a people's theatre was partly about the kind of theatre that we wanted to make and who we wanted to make it for and with.... It was also to do with drawing on European models of... *volkstheater*. It was also that feeling of wanting to be rooted within a community and acknowledging the communities within that geographical area and trying to bring them in.
>
> (2020)

Glanville alludes to the way in which identifying as a people's theatre implicitly demands that the relationship of people to artistic practice is centred. Concurrently, a people's theatre indicates a particular connection to democratic modes of representation and collaborative working practices with which CPT wanted to align. Glanville also articulates the naming of the theatre as bound up with European models of *volkstheater*; a form which Alison Phipps identifies as encompassing both 'the impulse towards the traditional and expressing a sense of belonging' and 'radical tendencies, politically and critically reflecting upon the life of everyday people and urging action' (1999: 632). The people's theatre is therefore both rooted in

---

[2] I have examined various definitions, international and local examples of practice elsewhere in Sarah Bartley (2021).

the community and acting politically for and as a community; it seeks to assert a particular set of ideological, social and artistic aims. That is not to say there is no history of practices aligned with people's theatre in the UK; the socialist Unity Theatres and Citizens Theatres of the twentieth century were similarly underpinned by a desire to make social and political theatre for and by working-class people. CPT intended to foster experimental and non-hierarchical arts practices, to build relationships and embed themselves within the local communities, and to make politically relevant and urgent work (Glanville 2020).

There are two dominant conceptualizations of the people's theatre: as a unifying force that seeks to create relationships across different social groups; or as a practice which specifically seeks to engage the disenfranchised and support their public representation. Bérénice Hamidi Kim, in drawing a history of people's theatres in France, asserts that 'the notion that "all receive dramatic communion in the auditorium" was shattered by the realisation that there existed a "non-public", a category that became the emblem of economic, social and cultural exclusion' (2009: 73). The illegibility of the non-public provoked the emergence of people's theatres that sought to advocate and represent the experiences of this disenfranchised group. The history of CPT weaves both these ideologies – theatre for all and theatre for the dispossessed – into their practice; marking the potential for a more nuanced understanding of the people's theatre in the crisis ordinariness of the present, as a way to unite multiple groups of disenfranchised peoples.

When CPT arrived in Camden in the 1990s, the borough constituted (and still does) one of the most economically, ethnically and culturally diverse areas of London and the UK. The Hampstead Road had become a locus of intense racial tension between the predominantly white British and Irish residents of Somers Town and the first- and second-generation Bangladeshi population who largely resided in the Regents Park Estate. The relationship between these communities deteriorated following a number of high-profile incidents of racialized violence.[3] Moving into the building on the corner of Drummond Street and the Hampstead Road, Camden People's Theatre took up residence in the middle of this geographical and cultural conflict. Initially, sharing their building with the Drummond Street Asian Youth Association, CPT built strong relationships with the Asian community in Euston. Concurrently, CPT made work on both neighbouring estates, working with young people across communities, initially separately on targeted projects

---

[3] See Goulbourne (2001) for an in-depth discussion of the broader racial politics that surrounded this tension and its reporting.

and then together in the building to make performances. In the early 2000s the company ran Estate Side Stories, Camden Summer University and Youth Theatre projects that brought these groups together (CPT 2000 and 2001). This points to the potential of the people's theatre as a form to engage multiple publics and, in doing so, it recognizes all participants as *people of this place*, holding a space in which conflicting groups might see themselves as people of *the same place*.

Thinking about the more recent history of CPT, current Director Brian Logan shared that on joining the company in 2011 (as a co-Director along with Jenny Paton) the interviewing board suggested people's theatre might be removed from the company's name, noting that '[a]lthough 2011 is relatively recent it feels like a different epoch. It was a time when names like Camden People's Theatre were deeply unfashionable, it just sounded like some totally retrograde syndicalist union. We were encouraged to rebrand and start afresh with a different name' (2020). As Logan comments, the landscape for contemporary people's theatres has changed substantially. Indeed, a wave of contemporary people's theatres has subsequently sprung up in the UK in the intervening decade: Sheffield People's Theatre (2012), Brighton People's Theatre (2015), Leeds People's Theatre (2018) and Paisley People's Theatre Project (2019). That there has been a groundswell of companies working under this banner during a period of economic austerity speaks to the potential of the form within a context of economic and social crisis. Thinking back to the decision to retain the name in 2011 Logan articulates the provocation offered: 'Obviously when CPT had been founded, they didn't call themselves that by accident and it meant something to them then' (2020). In the early years of the twenty-first century, against the backdrop of a period of relative social stability and persistent economic growth in the UK, there was a gradual drifting away from articulating CPT's identity as a people's theatre, with the space being emphasized instead as a home for emerging experimental artists. Reading this shift through the relationship of performance to crisis, arguably identifies the possibility of a cultural turn to the people in times of turmoil. Indeed, in 2011 the effects of the economic crash were intensifying subsequent to the outgoing Labour government bailout of the UK banking sector and the newly established Conservative government's implementation of an economic programme of austerity. Concurrently, the incoming artistic team in 2011 set about negotiating a return to the original aims and agendas indicated by the people's theatre title, reflecting on what such a return might look like in contemporary Britain.

Nine years later, in 2020, CPT is predominantly perceived as a venue, an incubator for emerging companies and new work, and also continues to produce its own in-house productions. How does this aspect of the company's identity, as a producing venue and space of artistic development, expand understandings of the people's theatre and their relationship to crisis? CPT predominantly operates a festival-led approach to programming; staging up to four curated festivals each year that respond to a politically or socially urgent theme. Indicative examples include: *Calm Down Dear* (2013–), an annual curation of feminist performance; *Whose London Is It Anyway?* (2016), an interrogation of gentrification in the city; *No Direction Home* (2018), performances located around displacement, migration and refuge; and *Common People* (2018–), a collection of works on class and austerity. The programming at CPT stages and reflects the anxieties and fears of this period of protracted crisis. It is this responsiveness and political engagement with contemporary crises that reasserts the theatre as a *people's* theatre; it speaks directly to the experiences of the theatre's audience, while continuing to diversify that audience.

The festivals give one model for the marriage of popular and experimental performance modes that are cultivated at CPT. Logan states,

> If you accept… that normal people are alienated from theatre and high culture the thing they're alienated from is not the interesting types of performance that happen at CPT, it's people swanning around in gowns looking into the middle distance in French windows. It felt to me that the type of theatre maker we work with at CPT had enormous potential to build bridges between the work we make and people from non-theatre going constituencies. … how can we make popular and experimental really enforce each other; and, how can we honour the term people's theatre while still mainlining new forms of performance?
>
> (2020)

Supporting people not otherwise engaged with performance to encounter and deploy forms that sit within experimental practices demonstrates the potential for popular and experimental to intersect. It ensures community practices are not siloed, rather the engagement of people is bound up with their exposure to the exciting and experimental forms CPT develops and foregrounds. In particular, the socially and politically engaged festivals curated at CPT address the immediate experiences of people living in the contemporary moment and so extend a more urgent invitation to audiences into the theatre. Brighton People's Theatre offer a similarly broad range of encounters with practice to their members, as I discuss below, utilizing modes drawn from various artistic forms and models of grassroots community organizing. This approach of supporting an engagement with a more diverse range of forms is illustrative of the artistic practices of people's theatres in the

UK at the outset of the twenty-first century; and, arguably, participates in the ongoing innovation of practices within community performance.

Such is CPT's importance to the wider landscape of performance in the UK, that theatre critic Lyn Gardner has argued: 'British theatre would be less rich without its flagship theatres, but it would be completely stymied without the tiny, under-resourced venues such as CPT which are such a critical part of the theatre ecology' (2018). Shunt, Fevered Sleep, Ridiculusmus, Rachel Mars, Jamal Harewood, Milk Presents, Kelly Green, Sh!t Theatre, Emma Frankland, Barrel Organ and Nouveau Riche are just a few of those who have collaborated with the venue while early in their careers. In addition to providing spaces for this kind of performance in central London, CPT run several artist development opportunities: Starting Blocks, where five artists undertake a collaborative ten-week residency at CPT to create a piece of new work; Home Run, a £5,000 commission and in-kind support from the venue to develop a new project from work-in-progress to a full production; and an Associate Artists scheme which offers a £1,350 bursary and provides companies space to develop aspects of their practice with no set output (CPT 2020). In 2020 the central aspect of the theatre's identity is located around its position as a small but mighty DIY performance space in central London, which cultivates exciting new work from a diverse pool of emerging artists and community collaborations at an affordable price for audiences. Far from contrary to its identity as a *people's* theatre, the artists' support programmes that CPT offer enable a more representative range of artists to establish themselves as performance makers. Peopling the theatre is also about making material interventions that offer artists from diverse backgrounds the means to flourish in an increasingly elitist industry. Through critically engaged programming practices and the material support of emerging and underrepresented artists CPT's history of proximity to the terminology of the people's theatre expands the possibilities for this practice in the contemporary UK landscape.

Established in 2015, Brighton People's Theatre work across their city, engaging residents in theatre making workshops, playreading groups, and artistic programming and curation for the Brighton Festival. The creative team at BPT is made up of freelance artists who collectively equate to one full-time staff member; yet they have managed to engage over a hundred residents of Brighton, many of whom had not previously participated in cultural activities. Speaking on the naming of BPT, artistic Director Naomi Alexander notes the company was going to be called The 92%,

> in response to the Warwick Commission finding that it was the most white, most wealthy, most well-educated 8% of the population who

access the arts most frequently.... I'm aware that there is a growing movement of people's theatres in the UK and I'm interested in aligning with that... in terms of putting the means of production into the hands of the 92% of people who don't normally go to or make theatre. It's not necessarily about making political shows. The act of making theatre in this way is political.

(qtd. in Alexander and Hughes 2017: 177)

While Alexander eventually chose to name the company Brighton People's Theatre, in order to situate their work within both the longer historical lineage and the contemporary movement of people's theatres, the concept of the 92 per cent remains threaded throughout their practice. Published in 2015, The Warwick Commission into Cultural Value found that engagement in funded cultural activity was skewed (meaning the most privileged were benefitting disproportionately from public subsidy of the arts) and there was a significant lack of diversity in the cultural workforce in terms of race, disability and class. Responding to this context, Alexander's articulation of the politics of practices of creation resonates with the early principles of CPT, in a commitment to a way of working that, in its practices of making, is imbued with a set of inclusive and radical values.[4] For BPT this is made manifest in a focus on redistributing the means of production to those who have been otherwise excluded from cultural creation, to both resist the ways in which the arts sector mimics the elitist division of resources pervasive under capitalist societies and also contribute to broader social systems seeking to illuminate and reverse this inequality (Alexander 2017). David Bradby and John McCormick note there is a huge range of practices that identify under the banner of a people's theatre but 'it is easier to identify their common enemy than their common aims... all have been united in their impatience with existing theatrical forms, audiences, buildings, techniques' (1978: 11). This characteristic discontentment is evident in BPT's disruption of the elitist and exclusive nature of cultural life in the UK; and, CPT's rejection of dominant modes of making theatre and material interventions into the development of emerging artists.

Thinking about the work of these two companies alongside the crises that preceded their formation illuminates the responsivity potential of the people's

---

[4] The founding of BPT also strongly resonates with John McGrath founding of 7:84 in 1971, who derived their company name from a 1966 *Economist* statistic that 7 per cent of the nation owned 84 per cent of the country's wealth. Similar to the BPT, 7:84 was committed to making theatre of, and for, the people in non-hierarchical and collaborative ways.

theatre to the body-politic. CPT offer an anti-individual mode of making through collective devising that contested the dominance of the individual literary models in UK theatre at that time. Read against a backdrop of fifteen years of acute individualism and a catastrophic attempt to participate in the European Exchange Rate Mechanism, this asserts the role of the people's theatre form to reimagine modes of collectivity that were flourishing in European politics (with the formation of the European Union in 1993) and cultural practices (in models of collaborative performance making) but were struggling within the UK. In this instance then, the people's theatre response to the crisis of the early 1990s was both formal and ideological. By 2015, the UK had already experienced five years of austerity policies and individualist rhetoric that sought to blame the nation's economic and social pain on the poorest and most marginalized members of the population. The re-election of the Conservative party (with a large majority) that same year confirmed the success of their persistent ideological attack on the scapegoated figures of, among others, the welfare claimant and the migrant. Once more, facing such rampant individualism and exploitation, the need to redistribute the means of cultural production was increasingly urgent. The particular approach of BPT was therefore overtly supportive of its community, specifically those most clearly encountering the brutality of austerity. In the contested terrain of the demonization of the poor, the model of the people's theatre that emerged in the twenty-first century was to redistribute representational resources to those who were being damagingly misrepresented and weaponized by mainstream public rhetoric.

Histories and temporalities

In the UK, and globally, people's theatres have had close historical association with the political left and, in many cases, arose from broader socialist projects or movements. CPT emerged from the London branch of Unity Theatre, a civic theatre rooted in socialist beginnings and part of a constellation of companies borne out of The Workers' Theatre Movement that flourished from the early nineteenth century. As Rupert Watts notes, the London based Unity Theatre founded in 1936 'lived through many crises... even the War could not dampen the enthusiasm which kept Unity alive for so long' (1993: 16). However, in 1975 the theatre burned down and there followed a hiatus of activity until the revitalized Unity Theatre was established at the site of the Old Lord Palmerston pub in the early 1990s. Engaging a number of younger performance practitioners and appointing Sheridan Bramwell as the production co-ordinator indicated a renewed appetite for radical theatre.

However, the experimental performance and collective devising processes of the emerging artists that would later gather under the banner of CPT proved incompatible with established figures within Unity Theatre. This arguably marked a significant shift in the artistic forms being deployed within the strata of people's, unity, citizens theatres. As Glanville notes,

> What they wanted, I think, was a return to the kind of very clearly socialist agitprop type of theatre that they had been producing previously.... what we were interested in was being – with a small p – political through our methodology and our way of working rather than through content messaging if you like.... we all came from a pretty much left-wing socialist kind of viewpoint but that manifested itself in a way of working which was collaborative, not script led, and very influenced by kind of body-based performance techniques.
>
> (2020)

In the 1990s, and now, the artistic practices and aesthetic modes of the people's theatre CPT engaged with were experimental and formally innovative. The collective sought to make non-text-based performance, centring on devising and body-based performance practices that emerged through collaborative working practices. This shift from the previous focus of Unity Theatre ultimately proved too drastic and the artists who would later establish CPT broke away from Unity Theatre after around eighteen months of collaboration following an incident where they were removed from the building on Hampstead Road. This collective of artists continued working independently around the West Camden and South Euston area, forming as their own independent company under the banner of CPT. When the lease for the Hampstead Road building came up to tender in 1994 Camden Council awarded the site to CPT, who remain based there twenty-six years later.

This rupture happened against the backdrop of a nation in the midst of a deep recession, with high unemployment and a housing crisis; a context that required the Left to reimagine what it might offer, both culturally and politically. After another gruelling Labour election loss in 1992, Tony Blair was elected leader of the Labour Party in 1994 and later would become UK Prime Minister in 1997. Blair's reimagination of the popular left in the political sphere would become more centrist, led by third way ideologies that espoused the potential of a marriage between free market economies alongside social justice and a range of social inclusion policies. Conversely, at CPT in the 1990s creative practice was deployed to expose people to democratic modes of making and genuine approaches to community engagement, making the promise of representation evident. The aesthetic modes of the people's theatre at CPT were/are experimental and formally innovative; they seek to cultivate new practices that represent and inhabit the experience of lived reality in the present moment. In a way that feels distinct from other practices of community and applied arts occurring during the New Labour period, that sought to align with, or overtly deliver, state sanctioned cultural and social agendas, at CPT artists were positioning themselves as co-creators with the non-professional community members they were working with. This positioning might be more easily located in the lineage of the alternative theatre movement of the 1960s, 1970s and 1980s rather than alongside the instrumentalization of community practices that was occurring in the late 1990s.

Collaborating with communities using the experimental forms that are threaded throughout the venue's artistry remains core to CPT. Their in-house productions, *This Is Private Property* (2016), *Fog Everywhere* (2017) and *Human Jam* (2019), specifically sought to make experimental devised work about themes that are urgent to their community – the housing crisis, air pollution in London and the High-Speed Rail 2 (HS2) project – with people in their locale who are non-professional artists. The HS2 project seeks to improve transport and connectivity across the UK, but also threatens to destroy much of the area surrounding CPT to build a new rail station.[5] Down the road from CPT at St James Gardens, in the biggest exhumation project in European history, 63,000 bodies are being moved from an eighteenth- and nineteenth-century burial site to make way for the new track. This forms the central conceit of *Human Jam*, which explores the disruption of the dead to reflect on the threat this project poses to the living residents of Drummond Street. *Human Jam* deploys a collage of performance approaches, a mode I am arguing is both central to contemporary practices of the people's theatre and core to socially committed artistic response to crisis. In *Human Jam* this collage consists of performance lectures, a community chorus, disruptions of the action with 'the real', direct address and political songs. The focus on the burial site itself invokes an intersection of multiple temporalities: verbally, as Logan talks us through his volunteering at the site retrieving and deciphering headstones; and then, by the appearance of eighteenth-century land rights activist Thomas Spence, the past is embodied on the stage.

---

[5] The HS2 national infrastructure project is estimated to cost £106 billion. It has attracted multiple protests due to the spiralling costs of the project, the ecological damage it causes and the displacement of residents and communities in urban areas.

Spence's materialization in the present highlights the HS2 project as having an agenda much broader than transport:

Logan   'The 25-year development plan involves the sale of £5-6bn worth of publicly owned land around the station, in which Lendlease will acquire a leasehold interest for up to 300 years'.

Spence   That doesn't even mention a railway. It's about land.

(CPT 2019: 16)

The removal of housing and businesses from West Euston and the exhumation of the bodies facilitate the transfer of public land into private hands. Introducing Spence functions to interrogate land grabs across three centuries, from his activism in the 1700s to the current resistance of the people of Camden in the present day; from the enforcement of Enclosure legislation in Early Modern England to contemporary models of gentrification.

Human Jam was made in collaboration with the community under threat from HS2, both as research collaborators and as cast members. Throughout, a community chorus interjects with co-created protest songs to articulate their position:

In the name of HS2
They're digging up the ground

In the name of HS2
People fight but what can they do
Come here and hold my hand
While they take our land (21)

The use of song collectively expresses the immediate threat to the community and articulates a yearning for unity in the face of this threat. The community chorus also give voice to one of Spence's own songs from the eighteenth century:

But thank them for nought if the Heavens they could let,
Few Joys there the Poor would e'er see,
For Rents they must toil and for Taxes to boot,
The Rights of the People for me. (25)

Reanimating Spence's song, articulating the same threat to the land and oppression of people through the community chorus draws a lineage between historic oppressions and the present privatization of public land. Eugène van Erven has argued that 'contemporary radical popular plays' are indebted to Brecht's epic theatre. While van Erven is making this point in the late 1980s, it holds resonance today that such works 'contain songs that serve a narrative and analytical purpose quite similar to Brecht's' (1988: 175). Drawing on the model of epic theatre, in *Human Jam* song is deployed to perform collective power and expose explicitly to the audience the damage that is being done to the Euston area. In such practices, CPT demonstrate the potential for the people's theatre to draw a community together but also to connect that community to its histories of struggle in order to provoke a resistance in the lived crises of the present.

From revolt to play

BPT's first production *Tighten Our Belts* (2016) emerged out of a collaboration with Brighton Unemployed Centre Families Project, where Alexander ran a series of creative workshops for service users at the centre examining themes of austerity in the city. Funded by Arts Council England, Alexander established a strong relationship with the Brighton Dome, which provided a range of in-kind support around access to rehearsal and performance space, as well as production staff and advertising (Alexander 2017). *Tighten Our Belts* depicted a cast of characters from across Brighton who had been impacted by the severity of austerity policies. The performers introduced themselves at the outset and dropped in and out of different roles, with the line between performer and character often blurred; this served to emphasize these stories as real situations, happening to real people, but avoided asserting that these were the performers' own stories. Similar to *Human Jam*, the production utilized a range of formal approaches from agitprop, movement pieces, third person monologues and political songs, together composing a number of vignettes providing snapshots of characters rather than a singular complete narrative.

Hamidi Kim identifies the potential for a people's theatre to function as 'a protest against the current political system and the ruling classes, [aimed] at widening existing social divisions so as to make them still more unbearable and to stir spectators to revolt' (2009: 74). *Tighten Our Belts* sought to represent the violence of austerity to a broader public, to make the cruelty of these policies 'still more unbearable'. Punctuating the performance were three versions of the eponymous protest song 'Tighten Our Belts'. Each version of the song exposed how the government had constructed the narrative that overinflated public spending in the UK was to blame for the 2008 economic crisis, and then how they used this narrative to justify their devastating austerity policies. The first song, from the perspective of the voter, ran thus:

> We voted for the Tories, cos the country's in a mess
> They're cutting public spending – guaranteed success.
> We need the people working – it's better than the dole
> Let's discourage all the shirking and climb out of this hole
>
> (BPT 2016: 3)

Again, there is a resonance with the use of music in epic theatre. Here the song reveals the public narrative of austerity, at its base appealing to the in-work poor and positioning them against those in need of social security support. This points to the way voters reflected the discourse of the Conservatives articulated in the 2010 election, when the UK was reeling from the global financial crisis. The second rendition articulates the position of Conservative politicians, identifying the way in which austerity policies were implemented by invoking the global economic crisis. The third and final song, from the perspective of the disenfranchised, offers a chorus of resistance:

> They said 'We're speaking for the workers – we're speaking for the poor'
> They said 'We speak for the disabled – we're speaking for them all'
> They spun us a good story – they said it was for the best
> But now it's seven years later – they've failed the austerity test
> We've had to tighten our belts
>
> > They made the cuts, the debts remain
> > But they slashed our dole anyway (tighten our belts)
> > They've only helped themselves
> >
> > And now we're still all in the hole
> > It was the bankers' hubris
> > That got us in this mess
> > The Government was ruthless
> >
> > And wanted more for less
> > But we know the solution
> > So try not to despair
> > Here comes the revolution (22)

The use of perspective through the three iterations of the song in the performance tracks an emerging resistance in response to a toxic discourse that emerged in the wake of the 2008 crisis. Both *Tighten Our Belts* and

Human Jam utilize choral protest songs as a dramaturgical device to articulate a collective resistance to crisis both in the content of the songs and in the act of coming together to sing as one. As Casey Dué has argued – in relation to readings of Aristophanes, Spike Lee and Beyoncé – the Classical performance practices of choral song and movement when deployed in contemporary culture continue to have the potential to affect the 'audience on both an emotional and cognitive level and incite social change' (2016: 24).

In January 2019 BPT relaunched their programme offering a range of theatre making workshops led by artists at a Brighton community centre and a playreading group held at the Theatre Royal. The company's new tagline is 'Come and Play'; an ethos that is seeking to invite people into play and enjoy cultural experiences. In line with this ethos, at the start of 2020 the company held their first People's Inspiration Meeting, an open invitation to all Brighton residents to contribute to the kind of work BPT is to make in the future. Run as a workshop, this meeting invited the people of Brighton to consider what form, thematic focus and location an urgent piece of theatre about contemporary Brighton might take (Costa 2020). Alexander's approach is now firmly dedicated to the importance of joy in this process, 'Focusing on the most challenging aspects of people's lives... doesn't feel congruent with our values as a company' (qtd. in Costa 2020). This marks a significant shift from BPT's work devising *Tighten Our Belts*, which very much interrogated the acute struggle of encountering austerity, and perhaps offers insight into the relationship of artistic practice to crisis. In the moment of producing *Tighten Our Belts* the most disenfranchised in the country were still reeling from the Welfare Reform Act of 2012, with further punitive social security reforms on the horizon in 2016. The people's theatre in this moment gave a platform for the people to expose the harsh inequalities of our collective society and to invoke revolt against them. At the outset of 2020, the inclination to cultural practices of play and joy speaks to an extended drought of these opportunities in the contemporary landscape of the UK: a decade of austerity, a deeply divisive exit from the European Union and a period of electoral instability with four fractious general elections in nine years and increasing appeals to populism on the left and the right. Such a landscape yearns for a different iteration of a people's theatre, one that does not necessarily overtly address the oversaturated political discourse, but instead seeks to undertake politics in its practices of inclusion, participation, collective imagination. In some ways, this shift in strategy resonates with those early practices of the people's theatre at CPT; in the times following the *moment* of crisis we might then understand the people's theatre to respond to a desire for non-hierarchical modes of theatre making and creating, a space in which to re-envision our collective future together. Such arts practices might seed models of active participation across communities that then encourage people to reclaim an active role in shaping public discourse.

Current crises

October 2020. We are in the midst of the coronavirus pandemic and a confluence of crises: health, economic, representational, cultural. We are encountering a health crisis that is exposing the inequalities in the social fabric of society, in both the UK and elsewhere. We are standing on the precipice of global economies potentially collapsing, leading to unprecedented levels of unemployment and financial depression. In the UK, after a protracted period where the cultural sector was given no financial support, the UK government announced a £1.57 billion bailout package for cultural, arts and heritage institutions in July 2020. At the time of writing, questions continue to be raised about the prioritization of institutions over artists, the uneven distribution of funding across regions in England and the particular vulnerability of smaller arts organizations to financial collapse. Throughout the crisis, BPT have been offering online (and offline via the post) theatre making activities and workshops to residents of Brighton, continuing to foster play and community connection, working towards a sharing of creative practice. CPT have been in dialogue with the community of artists they regularly collaborate with around the support they need; concurrently, they are collaborating with Food For All (a volunteer food distribution service) to run a foodbank out of their building. In August CPT also announced four commissions for artists exploring live performance in a time of social distancing; a socially distanced festival for local residents; and a further fifteen new commissions for artists working digitally, with an emphasis on supporting those from marginalized backgrounds. Out of this crisis, there is a movement emerging that seeks to rebuild culture on fairer terms, with greater inclusion, more embedded in the communities they serve.

It seems in this moment – when we are witnessing increased collective action in the arts and in wider public life, alongside a growing awareness of the intensification of social inequalities following a decade of austerity – there is an appetite for the kinds of practice that the people's theatre might offer: practices that undertake a more inclusive offer to communities; that create in collaborative ways utilizing a collage of experimental and popular forms; that are embedded in a place and seek to respond to/with the people occupying their locale. A people's theatre gives voice to communities when their representation is under threat and it calls them into a collective. A turn to the people in artistic practice is an all-encompassing creative invitation which, in line with the historic roots of the practice, seeks to engage with the most marginalized or economically under resourced. Such practices meet crisis through a collage of performance forms and structures of collective making that endeavour to both unify a people and invoke a revolt.

References

Alexander, N. (2017), Interview with Sarah Bartley, 10 March.

Alexander, N. and J. Hughes (2017), 'A People's Theatre for Brighton – An Interview with Naomi Alexander', *Research in Drama Education: The Journal of Applied Theatre and Performance*, 22 (1): 172–81.

Bartley, S. (2021), 'UK People's Theatres: Performing Civic Functions in a Time of Austerity', *Research in Drama Education: The Journal of Applied Theatre and Performance*, 26 (1): 171–86.

Berlant, L. (2011), *Cruel Optimism*, Durham and London: Duke University Press.

Bradby, D. and J. MacCormick (1978), *People's Theatre*, London: Taylor & Francis.

Brighton People's Theatre (2016), *Tighten Our Belts*, unpublished script.

Camden People's Theatre (2000), Report and Financial Statements for the Year Ended 31 March 1999, *Companies House*, 10 January. Available online: https://find-and-update.company-information.service.gov.uk/company/03256616/filing-history?page=4 (accessed 12 June 2020).

Camden People's Theatre (2001), Report and Financial Statements for the Year Ended 31 March 2000, *Companies House*, 15 January. Available online: https://find-and-update.company-information.service.gov.uk/company/03256616/filing-history?page=4 (accessed 12 June 2020).

Camden People's Theatre (2019), *Human Jam*, unpublished manuscript.

Camden People's Theatre (2020), 'Artist Development Opportunities', *Camden People's Theatre*. Available online: https://www.cptheatre.co.uk/get-involved/artists/artist-development-opportunities/ (accessed 10 May 2020).

Costa, M. (2020), 'Our First Ever People's Inspiration Meeting', *Brighton People's Theatre*. Available online: https://brightonpeoplestheatre.org/2020/01/12/513/ (accessed 5 May 2020).

Dué, C. (2016), 'Get in Formation, This Is an Emergency: The Politics of Choral Song and Dance in Aristophanes' *Lysistrata* and Spike Lee's *Chi-raq*', *Arion: A Journal of Humanities and the Classics*, 24 (1): 21–54.

Gardner, L. (2018), 'Camden People's Theatre: Rackety and Radical', *StageDoorApp*, 18 December. Available online: https://stagedoorapp.com/lyn-gardner/camden-peoples-theatre-rackety-and-radical?ia=18 (accessed 11 June 2020).

Glanville, S. (2020), Interview with Sarah Bartley, 30 May.

Goulbourne, H. (2001), *Race and Ethnicity: Solidarities and Communities*, London: Routledge.

Hamidi Kim, B. (2009), 'The Théâtre Du Soleil's Trajectory from "People's Theatre" to "Citizen Theatre": Involvement or Renunciation?', in S. C. Haedicke, D. Heddon and E. J. Westlake (eds), *Political Performances: Theory and Practice*, 71–96, Amsterdam: Rodopi.

Jenkins, J. (2010), 'The Labour Market in the 1980s, 1990s and 2008/09 Recessions', *Economic & Labour Market Review*, 4 (8): 29–36.

Keegan, W., D. Marsh and R. Roberts (2017), *Six Days in September: Black Wednesday, Brexit and the Making of Europe*, London: OMFIF Press.

Logan, B. (2020), Interview with Sarah Bartley, June 4.

Mor, F. (2018), 'Bank Rescues of 2007–09: Outcomes and Cost', House of Commons Library, Briefing Paper Number 5748, 8 October.

Phipps, A. (1999), '*Volkstheater*', in J. Sandford (ed.), *Encyclopedia of Contemporary German Culture*, 631–2, London: Routledge.

Tempest, M. (2005), 'Treasury Papers Reveal Cost of Black Wednesday', *Guardian*, 9 February. Available online: https://www.theguardian.com/politics/2005/feb/09/freedomofinformation.uk1 (accessed 10 July 2020).

van Erven, E. (1988), *Radical People's Theatre*, Bloomington: Indiana University Press.

Watts, R. (1993), 'Looking Forward with New Unity', *Stage*, 3 December: 16.

Part Three

Nationscapes

7

Fields in England: Contemporary English drama and the countryside

David Pattie

Deep England

Ben Wheatley's 2013 film *A Field in England* follows a group of deserters from the English Civil War, as their attempts to recover treasure buried by an alchemist in the middle of a perfectly ordinary field descend into surreal violence. From this bald description, it might seem as though the film is an apposite summation of the state of England in the twenty-first century. A group of men, predominantly white and English, digging into the pristine rural soil for buried treasure, and descending into bloody violence seems an uncanny prefiguring of our current political crisis. But there is more to the film than a horrifically extended metaphor *avant la lettre* for Brexit. It chimes with a relatively recent development in British (or, more properly, English) popular culture, one that is linked closely to a change in the internal politics of the British Isles. David Matless, in an introduction to the 2016 edition of his 1998 text *Landscape and Englishness*, noted that in the interim period texts about Englishness had become 'a minor publishing phenomenon'

> launched by Jeremy Paxman's *The English* in 1999. The too-many-to-mention Englishness books include Robert Colls's *The Identity of England* (2002), Krishan Kumar's *The Making of English National Identity* (2003), and Andy Medhurst's telling study of English comedy, *A National Joke* (2007). Reissues of earlier analyses have followed, including in 2009 Patrick Wright's *On Living in an Old Country* (1985) and *A Journey Through Ruins* (1991), and in 2014 Colls and Philip Dodd's edited collection *Englishness: Politics and Culture 1880–1920*.
>
> (12)

It is not that England has lacked a full set of cultural signifiers that could act at various points in England's history as indicators of the nation's existence. Rather, as the historian David Edgerton has recently argued, conceptions of Englishness in the first part of the twentieth century were bound up with the idea of the imperial state; as H. G. Wells put it, the English thought of themselves as a 'world people' (qtd. in Edgerton 2018: 11). After the end of the Second World War, the idea of Britishness was employed to reconcile the nations of the UK to their newer, post-imperial existence. This was sustainable, as long as two conditions obtained; firstly, if the proceeds of economic growth benefitted the countries of the UK more or less equally, and secondly, if nothing happened to call the constitutional arrangements under which Britain operated into question. From the 1980s onward, both of those conditions gradually ceased to apply. Firstly, economic inequality spiked in the 1980s and did not decline over the succeeding decades; moreover, the impact of growing inequality was not evenly spread – by the 2010s, London and the South East of England had pulled away, economically, from the rest of the UK. Secondly, in the late 1990s the Labour government signed the Good Friday Agreement (altering the constitutional relation between Northern Ireland and the UK state) and inaugurated devolved government in Scotland and Wales (and, in so doing, acknowledged the status of Wales, Scotland and Northern Ireland as integral parts of a federal group of nations, rather than as part of the supra-national British state).

The impact of these twin changes on England has been profound. What it has produced is what could be termed a crisis of Englishness; it is no longer possible to argue that English identity can be subsumed in Britishness, at the same time as, for much of the country, the evidence of national economic decline is part of the everyday reality of people's lives. Unsurprisingly, this crisis has manifested itself in a number of ways (the retrieval of the Cross of St George as a national symbol; the plethora of books on England and Englishness noted above; the increased cultural visibility of the English folk music tradition; and so on). In the theatre, one of the most interesting manifestations of this general sense of crisis has been a turn to texts set in the English countryside. Gemma Edwards (2020) notes that 'this renewed interest in rural places and rural lives has been widely attributed by theatre-makers and reviewers to the Brexit vote and, specifically, the rural/urban divide that it revealed' (72); she rightly points out, however, that the rural turn predates Brexit – and that, in fact, it has been a feature of English playwriting for much of the twenty-first century. The turn towards rural subjects, at a time when the idea of Englishness is perceived as under threat from forces both political and economic, is understandable, given the way in which English identity itself has been culturally configured. As commentators such as Paul Readman (2018) have argued, the English rural landscape has frequently been treated as the most immutable feature of all. Raymond Williams, in *The Country and the City* (1973) argued persuasively that the rural imaginary has always been intertwined with representations of English and British identity; as the real landscape disappears into relative economic irrelevance, an unreal landscape takes its place. We find the same paradoxical image of the countryside elsewhere. A decade later in 1985, Patrick Wright argued that the countryside of the rural south, in particular, is a crucial part of the formation of Deep England – a version of the nation that exists both in the unrecoverable past and in an eternal present, easily recoverable by those who wish to find it:

> Deep England can indeed be deeply moving to those whose particular experience is most directly in line with its privileged imagination. People of an upper middle-class formation can recognize not just their own totems and togetherness in these essential experiences, but also the philistinism of the urban working class as it stumbles out, blind and unknowing, into that countryside at weekends.
>
> (Wright [1985] 2009: 82)

The essential experience of unchanging Englishness, in other words, hides in plain sight, visible to some but not to others. But even if you are fortunate enough to have the wherewithal to experience it, Deep England is a curiously unfixed place. William Gilpin's early tourist account of Stonehenge published in *Observations on the Western Parts of England* (1798) is nothing more than a list of unanswerable questions: '[When] we arrived at the spot, it appeared astonishing beyond conception. A train of wondering ideas immediately crowded into the mind. Who brought these huge masses of rock together? Whence were they brought? For what purpose? By what machines were they drawn? Or by what mechanic powers erected?' (qtd. in Ousby 1990: 92). And J. B. Priestley, travelling through the countryside some one hundred and fifty years later, has a similar experience, of an England whose boundaries simply cannot be fixed:

> The sun was now breaking through a fine spread of cloud. Over on the left, mile after mile, went the line of the New Forest, and its sombre crest of foliage had the same, solid, heavily shadowed look that you notice in the work of the old landscape artists. It lay there, half in gloom, half smiling, this forest I had never entered, like a piece of time that no clock of ours could tick away.
>
> (Priestley [1934] 1984: 26–7)

Deep England's presence, it seems, is always deferred, and it is always located elsewhere. The rural imaginary does not work in the service of a fixed idea of the unchanging essence of Englishness. The rural imaginary has an unstable relation to the real country; the rural imaginary is invisible to some; and for those who can see it, the meaning of the landscape disperses, vanishing even at the moment at which it is perceived.

One might say that, at moments like this, the English countryside is presented as eerie – a term, according to the cultural critic Mark Fisher, that indicates a place marked by both the failure of absence (because the precise location of England cannot be found in the hills and dales of a reified Wiltshire, or Shropshire, or Kent) and the failure of presence (because what is contained within the actual country does not fit with the imaginings of Gilpin or Priestley, or any other commentator looking to the landscape in an attempt to take the true measure of Englishness). For Fisher, the eerie is associated with moments of dislocating emptiness, or by moments where the apparently solid world reveals itself as unknowable: 'The eerie… is constituted by a *failure of absence* or by a *failure of presence*. The sensation of the eerie occurs either when there is something present where there should be nothing, or when there is nothing present when there should be something' (2016: 61; original emphasis). Fisher locates the eerie, at least partly, in a tradition of speculative, uncanny, and peculiarly English, fiction and drama which is set in a version of the English countryside that is as dispersed and as uncanny as Gilpin's Stonehenge or Priestley's New Forest (or, for that matter, Wheatley's *A Field in England*). In doing so, he suggests that there is an inherent eeriness in the idea of Deep England; and it is this eeriness – this sense of slippage, of absence and of a failure of presence – that I will trace in a series of plays that, in their various ways, call the idea of a fixed, unchanging Deep England into question. The rural landscape in Jez Butterworth's *The Night Heron* (2002), *The Winterling* (2006) and *Jerusalem* (2009), Mike Bartlett's *Albion* (2017), and Simon Longman's *Gundog* (2018) seems, either to displace itself, or to vanish in a mist of unresolved questions. If the English rural landscape suggests immemorial Englishness (and there is ample reason, in both English art and culture, to note the operation of this link – see Readman 2018), then immemorial England, as figured in these texts, becomes something unresolved, unknowable and fundamentally eerie; a part of the ongoing crisis of English identity, rather than a solution to that crisis.

A place for England

In Jez Butterworth's *The Night Heron*, the first thing we hear is a recorded voice, solemnly intoning some Biblical verses:

> **Voice** And the Lord God planted a garden eastward in Eden. And out of the ground made the Lord God to grow every tree that is pleasant to the

sight, and good for food; the tree of life also in the midst of the garden, and the tree of knowledge of good and evil. (Butterworth 2011a: 105)

The verses are commonplace (and as such, liable to appeal to Wattmore, the first character we see; a troubled would-be poet whose knowledge of scripture is rather superficial). But, at the play's beginning, they conjure up associations that are already part of the narrative of English exceptionalism – the idea that England, especially Southern, rural England, is Edenic (and that, by extension, the lucky inhabitants are in some way chosen by God). The idea of England as idyll contrasts sharply with the play's location (a run-down cabin in the Fens); and it also contrasts with the reality of the countryside itself, which is unstable and sometimes downright treacherous:

> **Griffin** There's a story in the *Bugle* too, one of them, the newcomers, birdwatcher it was, he's out last night on the marsh, he's lost the path. He's fallen into a suckpit, he's kicked and kicked and it's dragged him under. (107)

The bird the unfortunate twitcher has come to see is the night heron – a rare visitor to the Fens, whose nesting site and habits are difficult to capture (in part because the terrain in which it nests is unforgiving to the casual birdwatcher). The play follows Jess Wattmore, Griffin (who are both gardeners at the University of Cambridge) and Bolla Fogg, a woman who comes to share the cabin with them. The trio are perched on the outer edges of English life, both literally (the Fens are an inherently unstable landscape, treacherous in themselves and prone to the incursion of the rising sea) and metaphorically (they are figured as outsiders, in the already marginal community of the Fens). They might aspire to a secure place in the society that surrounds them, and they may ape some of the behaviours of high cultural Englishness (both Wattmore and Bolla are poets) but they will always be excluded; knowing this, they strike back (Wattmore, we learn, has assaulted and robbed a birdwatcher; Bolla kidnaps a student, because the student, she thinks, will know how to write poetry correctly). The security of a fixed identity is, for all three, tantalisingly out of reach; towards the end of the play, Bolla reads out a poem, in which she casts this precarity in apocalyptic terms, which are in themselves linked to a landscape:

> **Bolla** When Good Bolla wakes up the sun is shining,
> She doth look out the window and behold the golden sun
> But when Bad Bolla wakes up
> She doth see a black sun in a black sky ... (178)

However, the anthropomorphic landscape of Bolla's verse has no equal in the play's actual setting. The wide, flat, featureless landscape of the Fens is one in which the idea of absence seems to take on physical form. Landscape here is not encrusted with stories, in the way that the description of Deep England suggests; rather, it is, in Fisher's terms, eerie – a blank space on which stories can be inscribed. At the play's end, a birdwatcher, come to the Fens from Scandinavia, tries to account for the fact that the night heron is nowhere to be seen:

> **Man** How to explain… aahh, I don't know the word. I can't explain… Aaaahh. In short, he was lost. He will have fought to stay on course, but the winds are too strong. It is the winds, you know. The winds decide in advance… Nycticorax nycticorax. The native Indians called him the Night Angel. No. We have not seen him, no. But one day, perhaps. Maybe one day we will see him. (179)

It is hard to escape the echo of Beckett in these final lines; but whereas in *Waiting for Godot* final hope is vested in the (presumably) human figure of Godot, here, a very tenuous hope is located in the natural world – but the natural world itself is not subject to human agency. Absence can't be transformed into presence, just because the characters wish it.

In *The Night Heron*, the landscape is a *tabula rasa*; in *The Winterling*, it is a battlefield. The first thing we hear are guns firing over Dartmoor: the first thing we see is a man standing in a ruined, chaotic room, listening to planes flying low overhead. We soon learn that the implied conflict (Dartmoor is a location for military exercises) has become real, at least in relation to the moor's animals:

> **Draycott** They're gassing the badgers. It was on the radio. There's a mighty sett down Okement Foot. Been taking hens. Pheasants. All the way from here to Dolton. They got coughs too. Hacking coughs. The Government's had enough. They're sending a team in. Experts. (Butterworth 2011b: 186)

And, like the landscape in *The Night Heron*, it is treacherous to humans too:

> **West** Turn left at the hill, right at the sheep, you can't go wrong. You want to watch that track up. It's treacherous. Each spring, when the snow clears, they find three or four down there. It's ramblers mostly. Last ones they brung up was a couple of Welsh. Just married too. Skeletons they was. Huddled together. (190–1)

In this uncertain landscape, things go missing; a dog belonging to the central character has run off into the moor, and an Iron Age fort, whose location, we are told, is unmissable, somehow escapes the notice of several characters (the one person who sees it confidently declares that it is in the wrong place). Even when the moor makes its presence felt, it does so by withholding itself: '**Wally** All night we got these wild horses circling the tent. I never got a wink. All around us. Just... darkness. And snorting and... hooves' (205). The play extracts a great deal of comedy from these unaccountable absences and presences; but the cumulative effect of them is to create a landscape that seems unknowable and threatening. Towards the end of the first act, the character who has actually seen the fort is catechized as to its history, dimensions and use; at the end of the interrogation we learn that the stone circle on which the fort was built was used for sacrifice. The circle itself was created in the unimaginable past; the Iron Age fort dates from 600 BCE; the circle from 6000 BCE. If the characters' guess about the original use to which the circle was put is correct, then the dangers embedded in the landscape have been there for an almost unimaginable amount of time; and the reasons behind that violence have been lost – absent, when their presence would help the characters explain and assimilate the threatening landscape through which they move.

The Night Heron and *The Winterling* take place in a landscape marked by absence; the moor and the fen are places in which people, animals and buildings disappear. *Jerusalem*, on the other hand, takes place in a landscape in which, if anything, the signs of Englishness are far too evident. The play is, one could say, overdetermined by Englishness, all the way from the opening curtain (which, according to the stage directions, should be covered by a plethora of figures drawn from English folklore) to Boyle's closing invocation to all the Gods of England (which was met, in the original production, by the sound of giant footsteps). It is as though, rather than creating a countryside whose eeriness is based on absence, Butterworth has created one in which a sense of the uncanny comes from the all-too intrusive presence of folk and popular mythologies on a stage that seems as far removed from bucolic Deep England as it is possible to be. Byron's caravan, and the detritus around it, turns a location that is itself ripe with symbolism (the forest of Arden, Sherwood Forest, Shakespeare's forests, the enchanted woods in Spenser, et al.) into an edgeland – a marginal space between the urban and the rural. To find the gods of England alive in such a location is, to say the least, disorienting. As Anna Harpin (2011) notes, Byron is himself a conflation of English signifiers: his name is that of a romantic poet, his nickname that of a common farmyard bird; he is variously Puck, Falstaff, Jack in the Green, the Green Man, the Lord of Misrule, Prospero and any Shakespearian clown you might care to name. His speech (and Byron is a character defined more by rhetoric than anything else) draws on a plethora of competing signifiers of Englishness:

> **Johnny**   This, Wesley, is a historic day. For today I, Rooster Byron, and my brand of educationally subnormal outcasts shall swoop and raze your poxy village to dust. In a thousand years, Englanders shall awake this day and bow their heads and wonder at the genius, guts and guile of the Flintlock Rebellion. Davey Dean will be on a ten-pence coin. Lee Piper will be on a plinth in Trafalgar Square. Tanya Crawley and Pea Gibbons will have West End musicals written for them by Andrew Lloyd Webber and Sir Elton John. The Professor will be hailed in the same breath as Sir Isaac Newton and Charles Darwin, and after all that still no one will ever remember who the fuck was Ginger Yates. (Butterworth 2009: 53)

In speeches like this, Byron both invokes and subverts the tropes of Englishness; here, he swoops from cod Shakespeare ('Englanders shall awake this day ... ') to the commercial West End. Rhetoric like this is both comically heroic, and a desperate attempt at myth-creation – as though Byron knows that, no matter how impressive the sound of his voice might be, it is still used to describe a reality that can never match the myths he spins.

And yet, in the middle of this overwhelming tide of Englishness, there are moments where Byron seems to indicate something else – an absence, in the midst of all this presence. It is there, in the moments where his stories flood into each other:

> **Johnny**   I've seen a lot of strange things in this wood. I seen a plague of frogs. Of bees. Of bats. I seen a rainbow hit the earth and set fire to the ground. I seen the air go still and all sound stop and a golden stag clear this clearing. Fourteen-point antlers of solid gold. I heard an oak tree cry. I've heard beech singing hymns. I seen a man they buried in the churchyard Friday sitting under a beech eating an apple on Saturday morning. When the light goes, and I stare out into the trees, there's always pairs of eyes out there in the dark, watching. (102)

So much myth, piled up together, begins to suggest that the tales he tells himself have no common centre; there is no shared sense of the country and its meaning on which he can rely, and in its absence all he can do is to pile fragments of tales together, in an increasingly frantic attempt to create a coherent narrative within which he can place himself. Questioned by Phaedra, the outgoing May Queen of the village, as to why he has settled in

Flintlock, Byron gives an answer in which the contingent and the fated are equally mixed:

> **Johnny** I travelled the four corners of the globe, from Clacton-on-Sea to Shanghai and back up to Timbuktu, then I was passing by here on a day, and I thought, 'I know this place. Feels like I've been here before.' And I parked up in this wood for the night, but getting it down that slope from the road, I hit a tree, and when I tried to leave in the morning, my axle was broke. I thought, 'I'll fix that. I'll fix that tomorrow morning and be on my way'. (102)

This leaves the question of Byron's relation to the land interestingly poised. He claims elsewhere that he is as firmly rooted in this location as any tree; but his connection with the place is, possibly, as much an accident as anything else. Both options are held open. Either the land speaks to Byron, reaffirming a connection that exists from some unfixed point in the past, or it is entirely a matter of chance – a broken axle that wasn't fixed. Conceivably, too, neither story is true; Byron, after all, is a fabulist, and there is at this point no reason to assume that anything he says is objective fact. At the play's end, as noted above, Byron invokes all the folklore gods he knows to come and protect him from the developers who have come to take his land away:

> **Johnny** Rise up, Cormoran. Woden. Jack-of-Green. Jack-in-Irons. Thunderbell. Buri. Blunderbore. Gog and Magog. Galligantus. Vili and Ye. Yggdrasil. Brutus of Albion. Come you drunken spirits. Come, you battalions. You fields of ghosts who walk these green plains still. Come, you giants! (109)

In the original production, his calls were seemingly answered; but it is worth asking, given the jumble of names and stories in the invocation, precisely who it is that is coming to Byron's aid (if, indeed, the sound is not that of the developers, beginning to clear the land). As we have just noted, the links between Byron and this deracinated part of Deep England cannot be taken for granted. They are as likely to be a conscious invention as they are part of a deeply ingrained history. Moreover, the very fecundity of Byron's speech is itself something that should signal caution. This collection of mythical landspirits is drawn from a wide number of divergent traditions and cultures; a hodge-podge of Nordic, Cornish, and English gods and giants, all inhabiting the same terrain. So much myth, so much history, suggests not the presence of the gods but their absence. They are either the spirits of England, or they are merely an arrangement of names, as unconnected with each other and with this precise location as Byron is himself; there is no way to tell. The signs and symbols of Englishness within the play do not reflect a stable underlying sense of the nation; rather, beneath them, is an emptiness – a national narrative that stubbornly refuses to form. Boyle's final speech is an echo of the end of *The Night Heron*; like the birdwatcher's speech in Butterworth's earlier play, it is an attempt to will presence out of absence – to fill the eerie gaps in the landscape with living myths and stories. However, as in *The Winterling*, the precise provenance and history of the landscape in which he lives remains hidden – an absence, unfilled by any number of giants or gods.

A time for England

In Fisher's formation, one of the ways in which the eerie manifests itself is in the way that apparently stable, fixed objects and relations are displaced in time: 'The examples of Stonehenge and Easter Island make us realise that there is an irreducibly eerie dimension to certain archaeological and historical practices. Particularly when dealing with the remote past, archaeologists and historians form hypotheses, but the culture to which they refer and which would vindicate their speculations can never (again) be present' (2016: 63). Time obscures, rather than illuminating, the true nature of things. It does so, by masking the intention behind the creation and maintenance of cultural artefacts; in other words, it coverts presence into absence (in the way described in Gilpin's account of first seeing Stonehenge). However, the idea of time as absence exists in a paradoxical relation to another culturally sanctioned idea – that of time as a cycle, as an eternal, shifting present, a fixed and endless progression from planting to flowering, from seed-time to harvest. Two recent plays use this paradoxical idea of time (as eternal loss and eternal recurrence) to create narratives about rural England; they do so, however, by staging narratives that show the operation of time in sharply opposed ways.

Mike Bartlett's *Albion* stages an attempt to recreate an English country garden (the Albion of the play's title) and, with it, to recreate a way of life that seemed unchanging. In act one we encounter Audrey, who has recently bought the country house and garden where the play is set, with the intention of restoring it to the condition it was in when her uncle lived there. She rhapsodizes over the visits she made as a child to the house and garden:

> **Audrey**   As a child there were a number of big houses in the area. When we'd visit the adults would dress up in the evenings – us children would listen at the top of the stairs. It was the seventies but it felt timeless –

the music playing, the clatter of cutlery, and then they would retreat to their private conversations, in halls, in drawing rooms, or out on summer nights, down through the private rooms of the garden to the bathing pond, or the infinity walk. And I thought when I grew up that would be the world that I'd inherit, but then it was the eighties, and it was all... destroyed. (Bartlett 2017: 37)

This is England imagined as one immutable *Downton Abbey*; the grand house, with its fixed social rituals, standing foursquare against the tides of change. As Audrey herself makes clear, renovating the garden is in itself an exercise in time travel – a way of conjuring up not only the garden's past but her own:

Audrey   ... and down there was the long walk, which you can see in the photographs was framed with a magnificent structure they called Heaven's Gate. I just about remember it – the metal's frozen up now, but I remember the touch of them, along with my grandfather's pipe smoke, crumpets on the terrace, the lily pond. It's overgrown, but still there. (13)

If the garden can be brought back to what it was, then, by extension, not only the history of the location, but Audrey's own history can be reclaimed. At the moment, the Proustian sense impressions described here – the metal, the pipe smoke, the crumpets – exist on the edge of her memory; recreating the garden will make the memories, and the past that shaped them, concrete once more. The idea that fixing the garden means travelling backward in time lies behind one of the play's *coups de théâtre*; at the beginning of the second act, the characters come on stage in 1920s costume; the sound of 1920s jazz is heard, emanating from a gramophone on set. It is as though, for an instant, the work of renovation has achieved what Audrey wishes it to achieve; the past has been revived.

But what seems immutable is easily worn away; the great house disappears, and resists attempts at its recreation; and the unchanging seasons themselves change. The characters are uneasily aware that there is something wrong, something eerie, about the very climate. A moment before Audrey's speech (quoted above), another character notes that the world has changed – and that you never used to get 'Sun like this in early February' (36). At the end of the play, when the house is crumbling and the garden falling into ruin, the fixed progression of months also comes undone:

Matthew   There should be roses. Here. And snowdrops.

Cheryl   Not at this time of year.

Matthew   March.

Cheryl   It's November.

Matthew   Smells like March. (115)

The play's narrative traces the failure of Audrey's attempts to recreate a piece of Deep England; the play's staging does something more radical, and more uncanny – something which moves the performance squarely from naturalism to the eerie. At the end of the second act, we witness an odd, unplaceable action. A year before the play begins, Audrey's son James, a soldier, is killed. His partner, Anna, is a part of the group Audrey has gathered around herself at Albion. At the end of the act she begins a dance that grows increasingly frenzied. The dance seems to conjure up the memory of James; he appears on stage and dances with her. In the revival of the play in 2019, the link between Anna, James and the garden is made even more explicit; in the text, he walks on stage, and in the revival, she digs him out of the soil. Rain is falling; as the dance builds, the rain becomes a storm that breaks, abruptly, just before the end of the act. The image the audience is left with is of the natural world spinning out of control, as though the time of a normal storm has been compressed into a few short seconds of stage time. Something like the same effect happens at the end of the third act: '*the plants turn brown. The leaves die and fall to the ground*' (105) – and the fourth: '*The last pieces of the garden rot even more. The ground is returned to soil. The house is destroyed*' (123). Time, in other words, becomes an active, corrosive element in the world of the play; we see it doing what Fisher describes – effacing the visible marks of a culture, converting the present into the unknowable past. A play that begins with the desire to recapture lost time, and in doing so to collapse the past and the present, ends with the effacing of both past and present; the house and the garden move from presence to absence – from containing all of the timeframes the play invokes, to containing none.

Simon Longman's *Gundog*, according to the author, '*is set in the countryside. It is very quiet. The kind of silence that you can't hear anything over. The kind of silence that makes the world feel like it's turning too fast under your feet*' (2018: 2). In *Albion*, time speeds up at specific points in the narrative; in *Gundog*, time speeds up even as it seems to stop, and the narrative spools forward and backward between and in the middle of the play's four scenes. But for all the slipperiness of the play's temporal structure, actual change in the lives of the protagonists seems to take for ever. Near the beginning of the performance, an itinerant newcomer to farming, Guy, apologizes for his incompetence. One of the farm owners, Becky, tells him

'Then next year you'll be doing this with your eyes closed' (16). The next line is a stage direction – '*a year passes*' – and the dialogue scene continues, with Guy now able to perform the tasks he found difficult the year before. This is one of a large number of temporal slips; the action jumps forward, either by an unspecified amount, or by a year; and occasionally it leaps backward before moving forward again. However, even though the play dilates our experience of narrative time, it does not do anything similar to our sense of narrative action, or to the space in which the performance takes place. Characters stay in the same place, doing the same things, year after year after year; significant events do happen (parents and grandparents die; the farm's flock of sheep get infected and have to be shot; a brother leaves and returns) but the world they occupy stays fixed:

Becky   Can I tell you something?

Anna   What?

Becky   I'm really scared of him.

Anna   What? Of who?

Becky   Dad.
   Not like scared that he'll do anything to me like. Just scared that. I'm just scared of him.
   Like when I look at him. He doesn't look real anymore. Doesn't look like time is even going through him or around him or anything. That's not right is it? That shouldn't be happening should it? (49)

In *Albion*, time turns presence into absence, both by speeding up natural processes and by (seemingly) reworking the natural cycle of events on which the countryside depends. In *Gundog*, time is all too present; its inexorable progression cannot be halted or reversed – even though the play uses flashbacks, the events dramatized in them are all integrated into the forward motion of the narrative. In *Albion*, time eventually destroys everything that seems fixed; in *Gundog* time does not destroy – rather, the peculiar horror of it is that it leaves things as they are. At the end of the play, Anna asks her sister and brother:

Anna   Can you feel the world turning under our feet now? ... Me too. It doesn't stop, does it?
   It never does.

And I know that in one year's time we'll all still be here. I bet you anything. One year's time and we'll still all be here.
A year passes
Told you. And another one.
A year passes
And another.
A year passes
And another.
A year passes
And they won't ever stop.
A year passes (99)

Time is, in *Gundog*, all too present; rather than the calm, eternal present of Deep England, the play stages characters who are trapped in immemorial time – which both speeds past them and, in terms of the effect it has on their lives, barely seems to move. Or, at least, it barely seems to move until the very last minutes of the play. The final stage instructions read:

There is a thunderstorm. It is heavy… It keeps raining. It doesn't ever stop. **Anna**, **Becky**, *and* **Ben** *are still. The rain falls on them and years keep passing. They pass and pass and pass and pass and pass. They don't stop. Everything is still. Everything is silent.*
And everything turns to ruin. (100)

As decisively as in *Albion*, the idea of a sure, reliable, natural cycle is disrupted. But whereas in *Albion* time moves unpredictably and its effects are telescoped, in *Gundog* time is inexorable. The natural cycle of the year traps the characters, holding them in place; until everything collapses at once.

England's dreaming

At the end of *A Field in England*, the characters have been beaten, drugged, killed, revived and killed again; and yet the field has not yielded up its treasure. The lure that drew them there in the first place remains as hidden (if it is there at all) at the end as it is at the beginning; and yet they find they can't leave – the land itself, an ostensibly idyllic image of Deep England, won't let them escape. The film suggests that what they seek is something eerie; something that will remain absent, that will stubbornly refuse to show itself. The vision of England in Wheatley's film is one that is strongly echoed in Butterworth's, Bartlett's and Longman's plays. In each, the English landscape (a landscape which, as I have argued, occupies a hallowed place in the national imagination) reveals itself as structured around an absence. In Butterworth's plays, that absence resides in the landscape, in the unfathomable history of the places in which the characters find themselves; they try to establish a settled narrative that explains their locations; they tell themselves and each other stories in an effort to fix meaning to the landscape, but each attempt only reveals that the quest itself is doomed to failure. In Bartlett's and Longman's texts, the absence is created by the way that time operates on the ostensibly fixed cycles of the year. Both plays are structured around an annual progression that should remain essentially the same; and yet, in *Albion*, that cycle is rendered meaningless by the unpredictable way time operates on the house and the garden, and in *Gundog*, the forward temporal movement of the play seemingly has no effect on the lives of the characters. As Becky says, when talking about her father, time makes the characters unreal; it drains presence from them, turning them into ghosts. In these plays, the immutable landscapes of Deep England provide no respite from, or answers to, the troubling question of English identity in a shifting world. In each case, the landscape – an immemorial representation of Deep England – is treated as something fundamentally unknowable; something eerie, to use Fisher's term, something that, rather than providing a stable, secure image of England, suggests something troublingly absent at the heart of the image of the English nation.

References

Bartlett, M. (2017), *Albion*, London: Nick Hern Books.
Butterworth, J. (2009), *Jerusalem*, London: Nick Hern.
Butterworth, J. (2011a), *The Night Heron*, in *Plays: One*, 101–80, London: Nick Hern.
Butterworth, J. (2011b), *The Winterling*, in *Plays: One*, 181–244, London: Nick Hern.
Edgerton, D. (2018), *The Rise and Fall of the British Nation: A Twentieth Century History*, London: Penguin.
Edwards, G. (2020), 'Small Stories, Local Places: A Place-Oriented Approach to Rural Crises', *Journal of Contemporary Drama in English*, 8 (1): 65–82.
A Field in England (2013), [Film] Dir. Ben Wheatley, UK: Film4 Productions.
Fisher, M. (2016), *The Weird and the Eerie*, London: Repeater.
Harpin, A. (2011), 'Land of Hope and Glory: Jez Butterworth's Tragic Landscapes', *Studies in Theatre and Performance*, 31 (1): 61–73.
Longman, S. (2018), *Gundog*, London: Bloomsbury.
Matless, D. ([1998] 2016), *Landscape and Englishness*, London: Reaktion.

Ousby I. (1990), *The Englishman's England: Taste, Travel and the Rise of Tourism*, Cambridge: Cambridge University Press.
Priestley, J. B. ([1934] 1984), *English Journey*, London: Heinemann.
Readman, P. (2018), *Storied Ground*, Cambridge: Cambridge University Press.
Williams, R. (1973), *The Country and the City*, London: Chatto and Windus.
Wright, P. ([1985] 2009), *On Living in an Old Country*, London: Verso.

8

'Sinking giggling into the sea': Postdemocracy and the state of British politics in James Graham's *This House* and *Labour of Love*

José Ramón Prado-Pérez

The 2008 financial crisis has brought to the fore the ideological shortcomings of the dominant neoliberal doctrine concerning the social perception of vulnerability and the loss of personal and collective agency. The progressive erosion of the citizen's role as a participant and/or actor in the political arena, alongside the exclusion of any type of debate about alternative forms of political organization in the post-communist age, have resulted in the degradation of the liberal democratic systems and the subsequent disenfranchisement of the population. A fine example of such a sociopolitical crossroads can be found at the end of James Graham's *Labour of Love*, when Jean Whittaker, Labour's constituency agent for North Nottinghamshire, vividly outlines the context of her candidate's electoral defeat: 'You couldn't fix the problems. And I've never known such problems as now; health crisis, jobs crisis, Brexit crisis, crisis of confidence, crisis of trust, the country divided – ' (Graham 2017: 119). Her words chime with the playwright's own reflections about the current postdemocratic moment, which he has characterized as 'an increasingly polarized, angry and polemical political climate defined by its disunity and factionalism, both here and across the world' (2016a: xii), adding, in relation to another of his works, *The Vote* (2015), that 'The prevalent mood amongst communities and people in this country seems to be an increasingly very simple, ancient one – anger' (xiv). He also manifested his rejection of the ubiquitously negative mood in a *Guardian* conversation

---

José Ramón Prado-Pérez's work was supported by the Spanish Ministry of Economy and Competitiveness (MINECO) and the European Regional Development Fund (ERDF) project 'British Theatre in the Twenty-First Century: Crisis, Affect, Community' (FFI2016-75443).

with David Hare: 'I perhaps overemphasise the desire to return to politeness and courtesy, but what I really feel is the fear of a retreat into simplicity and fake fundamentalism in political debate' (Kellaway 2018), which reflected his concern about the perverse dynamics derived from the postdemocratic practice of anti-politics and utter confrontation.

The phenomenon of rapidly growing, social polarization alluded to by Graham has, of late, been tackled by Chantal Mouffe, suggesting that the present '"populist moment" points to a "return of the political" after years of post-politics' (2018: 6). The ideological boundaries traditionally dominated by class divisions associated with the right/left political divide and its celebrated them/us cultural equivalent have been re-formulated in terms of an affective rhetoric reliant on erecting insurmountable barriers: right-wing's populist alignment with negative affects of fear, terror, insecurity and precarity, firmly rooted in discourses of social and cultural crisis; versus its left-wing counterpart's re-signification of positive affects (Deleuze 1978–81), often times discredited as utopian, yet capable of mobilizing affective relations of empathy, cooperation, solidarity and human dignity. In line with the latter stance, Graham champions a mode of comedy that may engage the audience in critical laughter. In so doing, he discards other forms of humour, such as satire, since it can be potentially co-opted by the aforementioned strategies of anger and polarization at work in the present postdemocratic moment. Significantly, as early as 1962, Peter Cook, in his distinctive, provocative style, had derided the proliferation of political satire, warning that Britain would end up 'sinking giggling into the sea' as a consequence of the complacency associated with this comic form. Notwithstanding his own decisive contribution to the genre with the ground-breaking show *Beyond the Fringe* (1960) and London comedy club, The Establishment, Cook dismissed satire's sniggering, moral superiority and ironically questioned its suitability to effectively intervene in public affairs.

Jacques Rancière (1999), at the peak of neoliberal expansion, coined the term 'postdemocracy', later popularized by sociologist Colin Crouch (2004), to highlight the neoliberal oblique attacks on democratic values, intended to neutralize traditional sites of protest and contestation through ideological assimilation. Postdemocratic strategies, according to Rancière, rely on the eradication of difference as the mechanism of political subjectification, thus, suppressing politics *de facto*: 'The uncounted could make themselves count by showing up the process of division and breaking in on others' equality and appropriating it for themselves. The "exclusion" referred today is, on the contrary, the very absence of a representable barrier' (116). Such naturalization of discourses, of which discourses about crisis are a component part, may be effectively problematized by resorting to Stuart

Hall's definition of 'conjuncture', since it is at conjunctural periods of crisis that 'the contradictions that are always at play in any historical moment are condensed... Crises are moments of potential change, but the nature of their resolution is not given' (Hall and Massey 2010: 57). As a matter of fact, conjunctures manifest themselves as highly dramatic moments of uncertainty and disorientation, when previously effaced discourses resurface in contradictory fashion to dispute the existing, unstable ideological ground, thus creating the conditions of possibility to challenge the hegemonic, neoliberal regime of the real.

In recent years James Graham has established himself as an acute commentator of the political zeitgeist in Britain with such plays as *This House* (2012) and *Labour of Love* (2017). Centring on these two works, this chapter will examine how the playwright responds to the progressive dehumanization in the practice of politics so characteristic of postdemocracy. At conjunctures, the playwright seems to suggest, the terms of political engagement must be negotiated in ever-changing contexts. This implies discarding ideological or narrative closure in favour of the pivotal role conferred by disagreement and difference in the configuration of the democratic process, which, in Mouffe's notion of democratic 'agonism' (2000), construes the political other as adversary rather than as enemy. Accordingly, Graham seeks to reclaim the human element inherent in the political realm by resorting to popular comedy and the healing nature of laughter in an attempt to reinstate regenerative politics as part of the social debate.

This House and the boundaries of postdemocracy

This House premiered at the Cottesloe Theatre on September 2012, transferred to the Olivier in 2013 and had a West End run at the Garrick Theatre in 2016, followed by a national tour in 2018. The play originated as a response to the events leading up to the Conservative/Liberal Democrat coalition government of 2010, by taking a retrospective look at the 1974/9 span in British politics, dominated by a series of hung parliaments. Back in 1974, conservative PM Edward Heath's resignation precipitated two successive Labour minority governments under Prime Ministers Harold Wilson and James Callaghan, which had to survive in the face of growing social unrest against the backdrop of a global oil crisis. From a contemporary perspective, the close resemblance between the political issues at stake then, such as Scottish devolution or the recent accession to the EEC, and those faced by the 2010 Coalition government, reveals the inbred social operations by which unresolved or ignored faultlines tend to recurrently surface at moments of crisis.[1] So much so that, in a curious case of history repeating itself, on Wednesday 4 September 2019 British parliament witnessed a scene that could have been extracted from *This House* and its dramatization of the straining events during the 1974/9 Labour terms in office. An unidentified Labour source told *Guardian* correspondent Kate Proctor (2019): 'Our side are really ready for this though. For some it's taking them back to the all-night sittings of the 1970s in the Commons.' Eventually, the 'war of attrition' over a No Deal Brexit motion was avoided by the whips' negotiations, conducted by Lord Ashton of Hyde and Mark Spencer, Chief Whips for the Conservative and Labour parties respectively (Dyer and Ellcott 2019). Such nostalgic allusions to the turmoil that presided over the 1970s legislative period resonate with Graham's theatrical recreation, which offers an inside look into the whips' political manoeuvring and mutual concessions at a time when every single voting session posed a threat to the government's continuity.

The parallel circumstances regarding the two historical moments, as well as their divergent resolutions, may have prompted Graham to revise the exciting political events that would condition the generations to come. In so doing, *This House* calculatedly concentrates on the human component found in the private sphere of politics, rather than on the major historical movements or ground-breaking political achievements. Accordingly, the play fictionalizes the struggles and negotiations that took place behind the scenes so as to outline the inner affective history of power relations, which do not normally feature as part of the public, social space: 'I knew I wanted it [*This House*] to be set in the offices of the whips. I had no desire to portray the view of the leaders at the top, I wanted the dirty, mucky, grubby world of those turning the wheels in the engine room' (Graham 2016a: x–xi). The sense of chaos, instability and lack of direction implicit in that historical conjuncture was faithfully reproduced in Jeremy Herrin's production, underlining the striking similarities of the 1974/9 period with the political circumstances regarding the 2010 election, though in this occasion with the Labour and Conservative positions reversed. Audiences were thus presented

---

[1] In the TV play *Coalition* (2015), Graham dramatized the actual negotiations that resulted in the Coalition government between David Cameron's Conservative party and Nick Clegg's Liberal Democrats after the 2010 General Election, in what stands as the contemporary counterpart of *This House*. In interview, Graham stated that the political question that he was interested in was 'the processes and the procedures and the methods people used to get power, and the characters at the heart of it', rather than 'the policies of the campaign, or the rights of which parties to claim power' (Channel 4 2015). I would like to thank Jacqueline Wallace of Cuba Pictures for kindly granting me access to *Coalition*.

with a slice of political reality which dissected the circles of decision-making, but, simultaneously, foregrounded the necessary coexistence of friendship, decency and loyalty with the rivalry of ideological contention. In what could be considered a dramatic representation of Mouffe's agonism, Graham re-imagines the 1970s political struggles in comic fashion so as to recover their human element, reminding audiences that, eventually, the whole fabric of politics depends on the ability of politicians to bargain and compromise: such an exercise in giving visibility to the political process runs counter to an abstract, postdemocratic version of politics, where power operates autonomously and covertly, detached from the citizens that it is supposed to represent.

Among the humorous instances veering on the ridiculous that support the playwright's strategy to reinstate the human side of politics in the public debate, the inclusion of the infamous, actual fracas in the House of Commons, when the Conservative MP for Henley, an unidentified Michael Heseltine, grabbed the Parliamentary mace and brandished it against his Labour counterparts, highlights, through parody, the much-too-human passionate response of the MPs regarding the breach of unwritten agreements about parliamentary behaviour. In the episode, as well as similar others regarding battles over governance and bills, the Labour MPs appear as the stereotypical, sympathetic rascals who outplay the self-confident Conservative bullies to get political advantage, in accordance with the transgressive social image expected of them. Their mischief is met by the feigned indignation of their rivals, who believe that they own the playground. Thus, the ideological struggles are reduced to a mild caricature of childish behaviour that, nevertheless, stresses the humanity of these political actors. Accordingly, the whips from both sides resort to the recognizable political stereotypes of their times to refer to each other throughout, which accounts for a considerable amount of the play's broad humour and its reflexive, distancing effect on the audience. The Conservatives become, thus, the soft, upper-class villains, opposed to the romantic, comic-relief-cum-working-class heroes belonging to the Labour ranks.

Arguably, Graham's ability to extract the comedy out of such intense dramatic moments as the fight for political preservation underlines the healing effect of humour, via the recognition of fictional empathy, which stands as an alternative means to overcome the distrust and dissatisfaction with the current political climate. The playwright explains his stylistic departure from the mordant and biting satire featuring in 1980s and 1990s TV programmes like *Spitting Image* or *The New Statesman* thus: 'many people do cynicism and outrage and satire far better than I do ... I almost feel my job is to do a little bit of the opposite – I think I have a little bit of hope and optimism left in me still' (Fielding 2011: 345).² In the current climate of crisis in which liberal democratic regimes are immersed, satire's intrinsic aloofness may collude with self-reflexive political cynicism disguised as reformist possibilism (Castells 2017: 120). Moreover, the combination of self-reflexivity and satire's appeal to negative affective responses may compromise the genre's efficacy to articulate successful social criticism.³ Graham dismisses satire's common object of derision, namely, political personalities or specific ideological principles, and focuses on the political proceedings instead, understood as part of the rituals upon which all the parties involved in the game agree. Such a move allows him to avoid projecting any feelings of nostalgia on stage, which would turn the show into a costume-drama pastiche devoid of any critical edge. Graham explains it as follows: 'stars are normal men and women. It's about people who are struggling so that the play could be set in anyone's workplace. Essentially, the rules are the same' (National Theatre Live 2013). Similarly, the choice of a traverse staging, devised by designer Rae Smith, with the spectators symbolically occupying the parliamentary seats, reduces the physical distance between the characters/politicians and the audience, which, combined with laughter, contributes to establishing an atmosphere of complicity that brings the world of politics closer to that of the average citizen.

In his on-going exploitation of alternative interpretive frameworks that may supersede the use of satire, Graham invokes a female perspective, which had that far been absent from public affairs. Rendering women visible in the male-dominated world of Westminster underscores the productive possibilities offered by the recuperation of neglected sensibilities to both enhance and unsettle the political arena. In a subtle self-reflexive moment, Ann Taylor exposes her companions' patronizing attitude in the running gag that portrays them as a gang of working-class lads who must constantly apologize when they realize that they are swearing in front of the only woman in the team: 'Would you mind not apologising for swearing around me. I know it's a running joke, but I'm trying to fit in as one of the lads' (77). Yet, Michael Cocks, Labour's substitute Chief Whip, acknowledges her key role

---

² The issue of satire is revisited in *Monster Raving Looney* (2016), a fictional account of the extravagant, independent, political figure David Sutch. Each episode in the life of this fringe individual adopts the style of an emblematic satirical show, ranging from *Wise and Morecambe*, Monty Python, *The Blackadder*, etc., to offer a counter-cultural periodization of post-war British politics.
³ For example, UK Prime Minister Boris Johnson gained notoriety with his regular appearances in the classic, satirical TV programme *Have I Got News for You* (1998), cultivating a self-reflexive public persona reliant on self-parody, which the public recognized as a construct, but which, nonetheless, triggered uncritical affective identification.

in the group, 'I don't want you to be like the lads, I want the lads to be more like *you*' (77; original emphasis), with a self-explanatory reply that erodes the sexist humour and stresses the relevance of male/female equal interaction over assimilation of one sensibility by the other. In another disruptive comic moment reliant on the then incipient appearance of women on the political scene, the MP for Welwyn and Hatfield, Helene, is discovered breastfeeding on parliamentary premises after the Tories have suspended 'pairing' as retaliation for what they consider Labour's stratagems to artificially retain the majority in the Chamber. The Conservatives' refusal to withdraw one of their MPs from a voting session to cover for an absence in the other party forces all Labour MPs, without exception, to be summoned for the late-night parliamentary sittings. Helene's open behaviour in such an unprecedented situation provokes a comic commotion that reveals the anachronistic essence of the institution and embarrasses her male fellow politicians, who are not accustomed to such blurring of the divisions between the public and the private spheres of decency, let alone the antics of nurturing or bringing up children.

However, such unsettling, humorous moments are pitted against the hazards that may arise from straining the boundaries of ideological division when faced with the practical problems of local governance. One of those instances of dogmatic confusion shows the Labour MP for Coventry South West, Audrey, play along with the Conservatives, in her specific case, to punish her own government with a protest vote for what she considers a betrayal of working-class interests. Ironically, her decision will pave the way for the Tories to undermine the government and bring about its downfall. She justifies her stance thus: 'My understanding of this democracy is that people were sent to look after the interests of their neighbours, not just do as they were told by you lot', to which Ann Taylor replies:

> **Taylor** So you pay no heed of the benefits of working together as a party, with shared ideals... still able to come together? In order to get stuff done. It's not perfect, Audrey, but it's all we've got.
>
> **Coventry South West** It's only not perfect because no one is strong enough to challenge it. (95)

Even though, in abstract terms, the MP for Coventry South West's demands for radical change and the implementation of more progressive political measures are by themselves legitimate, what the depiction of the dilemma between compromising and the preservation of core values reveals is the undesirable consequences of treating such issues as incontrovertible truths, rather than as on-going, open debates. The democratic paradox emerging from Graham's dramatization of such internal factionalism demonstrates that attempts to disentangle its complexity, however well intentioned, may end up rendering ideological divisions indistinguishable, thus contributing to the propagation of postdemocratic disaffection. Audrey's appeals to perfection, which lead her to the logical conclusion of momentarily shifting sides to assert her political independence, somewhat resemble the sort of neoliberal homogenization that may follow from the cancellation of meaningful difference, as advocated by Rancière and Mouffe.

The overall comic tone changes into soberness when the play approaches its ending to reveal the Deputy Whips' unparalleled act of political acquiescence. Due to the absence of Labour MP Alfred Batley, who might not survive the journey from his northern constituency to London because of a major illness, Labour Deputy Whip, Walter Harrison, asks for a voting pair that will permit his party to save the government. The demand is met by his Tory counterpart, Bernard Weatherill who, in turn, compromises his own political career to honour a non-written code of conduct. For the action to be endowed with the potential to resignify the exercise of politics, the two politicians require a reciprocal gesture, which once granted, unlocks the stalemate situation and sets in motion historical forces beyond their control. Such mutual gesture, manifested as concession, displaces the ground of contention from the struggle over power for its own sake, to power as the means for the construction of communal affective spaces. The whips' acknowledgement of one another constitutes, on Graham's part, a fine dramatization of empathy which restores the agonistic nature of political confrontation and reconciles the citizen/spectator with politics beyond bi-partisan polarization. Earlier in the play, empathy had been presented visually in a succession of parallel scenes, where each party was immersed in the outsmarting of the other by anticipating their next move. The hilarious, frantic development of such alternate mirror scenes construed empathy as the ability to imagine oneself in the place of the other in order to neutralize or obliterate them. However, when the focus moves away from the comic political contention and falls on the deputy whips' relationship, its meaning evolves to denote sharing of one another's space by fostering mutual understanding.[4]

---

[4] The exploration of empathy features prominently in *The Angry Brigade* (2014). In the play, the police inspector assigned to the case requires his squad to put themselves in the place of the homonymous terrorist group in order to anticipate their next move and detain them. This unexpectedly causes the police members to develop more tolerant attitudes to criminality and their sociocultural milieu.

Graham's recovery of such a concealed, private piece of negotiation suggests that small, common attitudes might carry the potential to determine the course of events. The authenticity of the deputy whips' gesture defies any potential dismissive claim of utopianism, transforming the play into a 'bromance' with a happy resolution on the affective domain of friendship, but paradoxically leading straightforwardly into Labour's defeat and the rise of Thatcherite neoliberalism at the political level. Ironically, in the second act, the figure of Margaret Thatcher looms threateningly offstage, and it is her own party companions who seem to sense the menace that 'the lady' poses to the imperfect liberal democracy built around the post-war consensus, while Labour appears to sleepwalk into its own destruction.

The final reflection that the play demands from the audience is that they ponder where the ethical line should be drawn and whether such noble gestures as the one enacted by the two deputy whips may obtain any practical recompense, especially if they are not made visible, relegating them to the realm of the private. The answer to such questions about the boundaries of power is deferred so as to avoid narrative closure in the form of nostalgic mystification. With hindsight, however, the triumph of the ethical stance in the play, embodied in the characters of deputy whips Hamilton and Weatherill, is born out of defeat, giving way to an age that will exclude ethics from the previously shared understanding of the common good in the public and private spheres alike. Ultimately, Graham considers the present-day conjuncture as an adequate moment to render visibility to such suppressed gesture, considered inappropriate in its own time, but potentially regenerative nowadays, suggesting that the exploration of the formerly dismissed path could become an alternative departing point to the well-known turn of events that led to the politics of confrontation inaugurated in 1979.

The formulation of affective politics in *Labour of Love*

Produced by Headlong and the Michael Grandage companies and directed by Jeremy Herrin, *Labour of Love* opened on September 2017 at the Nöel Coward Theatre, winning the Olivier award for Best New Comedy in 2018. The play embarks on the periodization of New Labour by presenting the fictional trajectory of the MP for North Nottinghamshire, David Lyons, from 1990 to 2017. This exercise in 'soul-searching introspection' (Graham 2017: 13), as David himself calls it, traces the progressive depoliticization of society, resulting in the crisis of democratic legitimacy that makes him lose his constituency seat. He expresses his amazement over the electoral outcome, as well as the contradictory nature of the political landscape, in the following terms:

> Too radical for the old, too safe for the young. Too soft-Brexit for Leavers, too hard for Remain. Too left, too right, too old, too new; do you know what they can celebrate all they fucking like, I have no actual clue where we bloody well go from here.
>
> (12)

His perplexity reveals a politician who is unable to recognize that the political divisions running along hard/soft forms of neoliberalism, exemplified in the Blairite Third Way, have been superseded by the emerging configuration of political antagonism revolving around strong patterns of affective polarization. Jean Whittaker, David's constituency agent, replies to his bewilderment and confusion by stating the obvious: 'Well, it's a movement, int'it, movements don't stop, they "move"' (13), which brings echoes of the Big Ben image that presides over the stage in *This House*, to remind the audience about the inexorability of time and its ambivalent nature as the driving force behind progress, as well as destruction. Ironically, such words are uttered by the only character in the play who remains true to her socialist values throughout, while still understanding the importance of change, in contrast with his political boss, David, whose ideological convictions are malleable to the requirements of political ambition. Such a state of postdemocratic confusion is cleverly dramatized by Graham in Act One, scene two, when a prospective Chinese investor, Shen, more interested in attending the Nottingham Forest football match, teaches them a lesson in cynicism about the values of capitalism from a socialist perspective. In their attempt to explain to Shen where the Labour Party stands ideologically at the present moment, they come up with a number of labels that range from 'Democratic Socialist' to David's more moderate 'Social Democrat', which Jean privately re-brands as 'Social Corporatist', bringing the joke to a paroxysm when the Scottish Nationalists are drawn into the picture and Margot, the scene's comic relief, declares herself a 'National Socialist' to her party colleagues' dismay (29–30).

The reversal of roles between Old and New Labour political advocates, Jean and David respectively, articulates the contradiction around which the play revolves, by associating the notion of old with progress and that of novelty with stalemate: the desirable preservation of ideological positions must adapt to the demands of continuous historical transformation. In order to recreate such an atmosphere of paradoxical tension, the audience is allowed to get a vantage point on Labour's political evolution through a fictional, affective story, conveniently interrupted by transitional scenes that present the country's major political developments as high-speed, documentary news footage. These interspersed scenes prevent the audience from total identification with what otherwise could be considered a situational comedy. Furthermore, the overall dramatic structure encourages critical distance by presenting the audience with a non-linear time structure that upsets any expectation of cause/effect relation in the concatenation of plot events. The action in the first act moves backwards in anachronistic fashion, while the second act revisits the same scenes in chronological order, thus revealing their actual significance in the unravelling of the story. In such a way, Graham proposes a pendulum swing, starting and ending on the same scene, which defies political stasis. David strives to imbue such paradoxical issues related to change and certainty with a certain coherence in his campaign speech, which, as it had already been disclosed, led him to electoral disaster:

> 'Time' can be good, time can mean stability, but it shouldn't mean old. It shouldn't mean stuck. So I promise – in these times that can feel scarier, and more uncertain than ever – I want to look forward, not back. I don't want to repeat, I want to renew.
>
> (19)

However, his muddled statement becomes an empty exercise in duplicity when confronted with his earlier confession on the night of his defeat. As was the case with *This House*, the personal stories of anonymous characters will take centre stage over political positions, suggesting that private emotional spaces may bear the potential to condition larger historical events. No process of renewal is configured as a straightforward, congruous line of action, but as the contradictory ground of betrayal and disillusion, mixed up with progress and victory, not so different from a tempestuous love relationship, like the one that the play explores between David and his constituency agent Jean.

Act Two establishes the ideological conflict between reformist David and Old Labour Jean in the aftermath of Margaret Thatcher's resignation in 1990, marking it as the starting point of Labour's evolution towards postdemocratic disenfranchisement, a fact with which, later in the play, Jean reproaches David in mocking, right-wing overtones, after Labour's electoral victory of 2001:

> What a glorious peace it must be, to be on the Right. To wake up every morning and look around and think – yeah, this is pretty much as it should be. This is fine. As opposed to knowing you'll never be finished. We'll never be done.
>
> (95)

David, however, misinterprets Jean's point about Labour's betrayal for a complaint about her unsuccessful love life. His personal detachment comes as no surprise, since David's consecutive, uncontested victories have made him internalize the neoliberal strategy of fudging ideological differences until they cannot be distinguished from one another, as his original definition of democracy indicates: 'a platform that pleases the most amount of people, for the most amount of time. Down the middle.' (76) to which Jean retorts by calling him 'just a salesman, with nothing to sell' (77).

Understood in such terms, the play is not an indictment of Labour's policies, nor the chronicle of a betrayal of core principles, even though the themes feature prominently at both the political and the personal levels throughout. More likely, it suggests that the time has come to explore the path of an inclusive new pragmatism derived from the synthesis of Old Labour's resilience and the governing experience of New Labour's years in office, or as David had advanced in a fine moment of dramatic irony when he had been outwardly reproved by Jean: 'People just needed there to be a way to say – "love"' (77). This political and comic battle of the sexes, unlike most mainstream comedy, sides with women and progressive female experience, as suggested by David's revelation in the last scene, in which love triumphs through cooperation and empathy: 'I was wrong, Old Labour didn't hijack the party from me, New Labour didn't hijack it from them. We've *all* hijacked it – from *you*. The future ... the *answer* ... is you, Jean' (118; original emphasis). Such a representation of empathy, in which both characters agree on switching their respective positions, presupposes a configuration of power relations based on sharing and equality. David's initial affective shortcomings, derived from his concentration on naive ambition, explain his electoral defeat as a consequence of his inability to develop affective ties with his inner circle and, by extension, with his overall community. By contrast, Jean is the only character who addresses the demands of the fluctuating political scene while retaining her principles, which makes her a survivor in such a frantic, ever-changing context. As opposed to the one-dimensional quality of the male characters, who remain somewhat parodic and could be reduced to just about their ideological and human stereotypes, she is endowed with a more protean personality. As such, she can boast about having a personal life outside politics, while her learning process, built up as a succession of enduring moments, causes her to be firmly anchored in reality. The triumph of love in the play, of positive affect, and the subsequent renewal of politics, may constitute a bland political comment on reality. Nevertheless, what is at stake at the end of the piece is the articulation of an affective politics that will prefigure a future capable of drawing in a number of the malcontents and disenfranchised around Jean's inspiring life experience. David puts it thus:

> We've come full circle, we're at war again, this party, the Left. Here. Everywhere. The different tribes. But for once, just once, instead of it being one side or the other, if we can forge an – I don't know, an alliance. Finally. Of all the vulnerable, the angry, all the hopefuls and all the left behinds, not *sides* –
>
> (118; original emphasis)

Eventually, Jean's vital quest, as imagined by Graham, offers an alternative route to that of the dominant, divisive rhetoric that results in the citizens' disaffection and the disintegration of community.

As has already been pointed out about *This House*, the mildness in the presentation of the political message matches the playwright's aim of mapping the affective grounds on which to establish a different approach to politics. The historical review of the Labour Party should not be mistaken for a nostalgic longing for better times long gone, but rather as an assumption of the lessons learnt in a rapidly evolving sociopolitical scenario. The play's general acclaim, excepting some qualified criticism, such as Aleks Sierz's (2017; see also Bano 2017), who dismissed it for its sentimentality and predictability, indicates how much left-leaning audiences and, for that matter, society, demand optimistic proposals that may reach the public affectively: laughter, thus summoned on the stage, would prevent the portrayal of political defeatism disguised as critique which has predated a certain type of subsidized political theatre. Consequently, the play spells out the dramatic conflict between Old and New Labour with the broad ideological strokes of sit-com style, adopting the representational tactics of strategic penetration, which addresses dominant cultural assumptions by targeting wide sections of the population through received, popular, artistic forms associated with mainstream culture (Patterson 2003). Additionally, self-reflexive laughter undermines well-established left-wing stereotypes and simultaneously erodes the supposedly transcendental nature of potential epiphanic moments, such as the characters' final sentimental union:

Jean   Who's Eugene?

David   YOU! – JEAN!

Jean   Oh for – ! You need to fucking enunciate! No wonder we're always missing each other! (118)

Thus, the array of distancing devices employed throughout the play short-circuits any melodramatic sentimentality associated with the conservative nature of mainstream comedy. Moreover, audiences are encouraged to adopt the position of witnesses in the play's reconstruction of the period's affective history, being reminded of outside reality by the documentary video projections that strategically thwart dramatic illusionism.

Graham's gentle, debate-play approach to the issue of Labour politics rests on the combination of romantic comedy and sitcom, which very rarely upset the audience's status quo and prejudices, gravitating instead towards the communitarian and social dimensions of laughter.[5] Following Henri Bergson, the comic would bring to the fore the short-comings of neoliberal discourses of crisis, evincing laughter as a 'social gesture' that departs from extremes and recovers society's 'common centre' (2005: 10). The political sensibilities that appear to be sanctioned are those of progressive, middle-class theatregoers, whose ideological allegiances are never completely questioned. Nevertheless, commonplace assumptions about Labour are critically unsettled by portraying the private, human side of the party: the union of Old and New Labour, dramatized as the lived experience of the two protagonists' infatuation, implicitly dismisses the pose of fatalism and scepticism, disguised as pragmatism, held by a certain type of left-wing, high-brow intellectualism. Graham recurs here to the opposite image of that offered in *This House*, where conscious, working-class Mellish had enrolled Ann to infuse the party with the modernizing impetus and vigour of the female, educated youth. Jean's newly acquired leadership, while lacking any radical, transgressive import, beyond the superficial exploration of stereotypical male/female role-models, seeks to redress symbolically the historical imbalance to which women's claims concerning their access to the public domain have been subjected, either by being systematically postponed, as in the aftermath of *This House*, or ignored, as in *Labour of Love*.

Conclusion: The paradoxical reinscription of the human into politics

By concentrating on the evolution of post-war British politics up to the present, Graham's plays offer a telling account of the postdemocratic crisis that the country is immersed in. The staging of democratic decline by resorting to a fresh, comic perspective that recovers the private domain contributes to the representation of 'a legible world, the symbolization of collective

---

[5] See Redling (2014) for a discussion of the revival of the play of ideas in British political theatre of the 2000s.

power, and the testing of social differences' performatively in the playhouse (Rosanvallon 2008: 307). In such a multifaceted political landscape, historical and emotional spaces interact in complex and paradoxical ways, achieving a fine balance between realism and utopia so as to cater for the possibility of imagining alternative futures, albeit their provisional nature in the face of changing social contexts and uncertain political conditions.

Graham's depiction of British politics at various moments of conjuncture suggests that it is at such thriving, unstable times when politics and democracy may retain their original impetus and intended functionality. Paradoxically, at conjunctural turning points in the evolution of crises, a certain restoration of the balance of power is effected through the recovery of debate, argument and transactional tactics, even though the pervasive social perception might be one of turmoil, confusion and stalemate. This is reflected at the level of agonistic political contention in *This House*, or at the internal level of party organization, translated as renewal and change, in the case of *Labour of Love*. Ultimately, the playwright's attempt to restore the citizens' agency in the age of neoliberal hegemony becomes an act of resistance, resting on the promotion of positive, affective bonds through comic, popular genres, the configuration of the audience's critical viewpoint and the re-inscription of neglected social spaces back into the realm of politics.

References

Bano, T. (2017), '*Labour of Love* Review at the Noel Coward Theatre, London – "Light, Political and Nostalgic"', *Stage*, 4 October. Available online: https://www.thestage.co.uk/reviews/2017/labour-love-review-noel-coward-theatre-london/ (accessed 10 May 2020).

Bergson, H. (2005), *Laughter: An Essay on the Meaning of the Comic*, trans. Cloudesley Brereton and Fred Rothwell, Mineola: Dover Publications.

Castells, M. (2017), *Ruptura: La crisis de la democracia liberal*, Madrid: Alianza Editorial.

Channel 4 (2015), 'An Interview with James Graham, Writer of *Coalition*', *Channel 4*, 18 March. Available online: https://www.channel4.com/press/news/interview-james-graham-writer-coalition (accessed 19 October 2020).

Coalition (2015), [TV Film] Dir. Alex Holmes, screenwriter James Graham, Channel 4, 28 March, UK: Cuba Pictures/Channel 4.

Crouch, C. (2004), *Post-Democracy*, Cambridge: Polity Press.

Deleuze, G. (1978–81), 'Lecture Transcripts on Spinoza's Concept of Affect'. Available online: https://www.gold.ac.uk/media/images-by-section/departments/research-centres-and-units/research-centres/centre-for-invention-and-social-process/deleuze_spinoza_affect.pdf (accessed 30 April 2020).

Dyer, C. and C. Ellcott (2019), 'Boris Johnson "Set to Try Again with New General Election Bid on Monday": Government Pledges to Allow No Deal Bill to Pass through Lords by Tomorrow Night Removing Key Barrier to Labour Support', *Daily Mail*, 5 September. Available online: https://www.dailymail.co.uk/news/article-7429419/Peers-prepare-guerrilla-war-No-Deal-law-taking-sleeping-bags-House-Lords.html (accessed 17 May 2020).

Fielding, S., chair (2011), 'Roundtable: Why Do Dramatists Write about Politics?', *Parliamentary Affairs*, 64 (2): 341–53. Available online: https://academic.oup.com/pa/article-abstract/64/2/341/1424114 (accessed 18 September 2018).

Graham, J. (2016a), 'Introduction', in *Plays: 2*, ix–xvi, London: Bloomsbury Methuen.

Graham, J. (2016b), *This House*, in *Plays: 2*, 1–118, London: Bloomsbury Methuen.

Graham, J. (2016c), *The Angry Brigade*, in *Plays: 2*, 119–221, London: Bloomsbury Methuen.

Graham, J. (2016d), *Monster Raving Looney*, in *Plays: 2*, 315–86, London: Bloomsbury Methuen.

Graham, J. (2017), *Labour of Love*, London: Bloomsbury Methuen.

Hall, S. and D. Massey (2010), 'Interpreting the Crisis', *Soundings*, 44: 57–71.

Kellaway, K. (2018), 'State of Play: David Hare and James Graham Talk Drama and Politics', *Guardian*, 6 May. Available online: https://www.theguardian.com/stage/2018/may/06/david-here-james-graham-drama-politics-labour-party (accessed 25 October 2020).

Mouffe, C. (2000), *The Democratic Paradox*, London: Verso.

Mouffe, C. (2018), *For a Left Populism*, London: Verso.

National Theatre Live (2013), 'James Graham on *This House*', *National Theatre Live*. Available online: http://ntlive.nationaltheatre.org.uk/media/video/39207-this-house/OJYDZTKxdvI (accessed 4 June 2020).

Patterson, M. (2003), *Strategies of Political Theatre: Post-War British Playwrights*, Cambridge: Cambridge University Press.

Proctor, K. (2019), 'Tory Peers Accused of Wrecking Tactics over Bill to Delay Brexit', *Guardian*, 4 September. Available online: https://www.theguardian.com/politics/2019/sep/04/tory-peers-accused-wrecking-tactics-bill-delay-brexit (accessed 10 June 2020).

Rancière, J. (1999), *Dis-Agreement: Politics and Philosophy*, trans. Julie Rose, Minneapolis: University of Minnesota Press.

Redling, E. (2014), 'New Plays of Ideas and an Aesthetics of Reflection and Debate in Contemporary British Political Drama', *Journal of Contemporary Drama in English*, 2 (1): 159–69.

Rosanvallon, P. (2008), *Counter-Democracy: Politics in an Age of Distrust*, Cambridge: Cambridge University Press.

Sierz, A. (2017), 'Review of *Labour of Love*, Noël Coward Theatre', *Aleks Sierz. New Writing for the British Stage*, 3 October. Available online: https://www.sierz.co.uk/reviews/labour-of-love-noel-coward-theatre/ (accessed 15 May 2020).

Part Four

Contact zones

9

Theatre of migration: Uncontainment as migratory aesthetic

Verónica Rodríguez

Using Clare Bayley's *The Container* (2007) and Phosphoros Theatre's *Dear Home Office* (2016), this chapter considers how the selected examples of theatre of migration 'uncontain' both the concept of crisis and the representation of the migrant. The chapter argues that in form and content the uncontainment gestures present in these works open up the current limited understanding of crisis and humanize the vilified figure of the migrant. By the humanized representation, I do not mean the representation of 'an idealised human figure – the migrant/displaced Other' but a depiction of 'a multiply differentiated performing human' (Musca and Corrêa 2020: 379), through the portrayal and/or engagement with the migrant's lived experience and perception of his/her life events. For the purposes of this chapter, I have borrowed the image of the container and the related phenomenon of 'container plays', to which I will refer later in relation to Bayley's piece, since it aptly visualizes migrant theatres' attempts to free the conceptualization of migration and migrants from the constraints to which it is subjected by certain sectors of society and the media. I proceed with some terminological notes, in particular the definitions of asylum seeker, refugee, economic migrant, immigrant and migrant, which will frame my use of Emma Cox's concept 'theatre of migration' (2014).

The array of taxonomic categories attests to the complexity of the migratory phenomenon and challenges any bounded approach to it. According to Amnesty International Australia, 'An asylum seeker is an individual who is seeking international protection. In countries with individualized procedures, an asylum seeker is someone whose claim

---

Verónica Rodríguez's work was supported by the Spanish Ministry of Economy and Competitiveness (MINECO) and the European Regional Development Fund (ERDF) project 'British Theatre in the Twenty-First Century: Crisis, Affect, Community' (FFI2016-75443).

has not yet been finally decided on by the country in which he or she has submitted it. Not every asylum seeker will ultimately be recognized as a refugee, but every refugee is initially an asylum seeker' (2019). This is a temporary status, but for an overwhelming majority, if not all people, this process is tediously complicated, taxing and long (see, for instance, the title of Phosphoros Theatre's second show, *Dear Home Office: Still Pending*) often resulting in rejected applications. The United Nations' definition indicates that 'A refugee is a person who has fled their country of origin and is unable or unwilling to return because of a well-founded fear of being persecuted because of their race, religion, nationality, membership of a particular social group or political opinion' (Amnesty International Australia 2019). This definition does not mention displaced, pushed out persons or persons fleeing as a result of environmental disaster, for instance. It is also important to highlight that some migrants see themselves symbolically and materially as refugees. Thirdly, 'An economic migrant is someone who leaves his or her country of origin purely for financial and/or economic reasons. Economic migrants choose to move in order to find a better life and they do not flee because of persecution. Therefore, they do not fall within the criteria for refugee status and are not entitled to receive international protection' (Amnesty International Australia 2019). Needless to say, this is the preferred term of right-wing media outlets and commentators. A much wider term, 'An immigrant is someone who permanently relocates to a country for reasons that can be personal, economic or political' (Hatton 2005 qtd. in Cooper, Blumell and Bunce 2021: 198) – or a mixture of those. Finally, 'a migrant is a broader term that can refer to movement both within and between countries, temporary or permanent for different reasons' (UNHCR 2016 qtd. in Cooper, Blumell and Bunce 2021: 198). While with an immigrant, there is a specific relocation, a 'migrant' – an uncontained term – may refer to location-seeking people, relocated or relocating individuals as well as persons undergoing a series of dislocation and dislocating processes.

In *Refugee Imaginaries: Research across the Humanities* (2020), Emma Cox et al., quoting Nixon, have usefully complicated the differentiated boundaries between the concepts of the refugee and the economic migrant, to the point of almost subsuming the latter into the former by acknowledging the former's experiences of persecution and precarity: 'the idea of the refugee as someone who has experienced persecution struggles to comprehend the "persecuting" force of global capitalism and the forms of "slow violence" that routinely render certain places uninhabitable' (2020: 9). The chapter uses the notion of the migrant to denote a person moving (or having moved) within the same or to another country. The term migrant encompasses the concepts of asylum seeker and refugee while the opposite may not be the case.

A theatre of migration is a theatre concerned with telling and registering the experiences of the migrant. It may incorporate the migrant's viewpoint; include migrants in its staging; go beyond engaging exclusively with migration-related topics and/or tropes such as the journey to the receiving country or the numerous experiences of deprivation, suffering and hostility; expose and transgress pernicious migrant metaphors which include 'terrorist', 'benefits claimant' and 'job usurper' – 'victim' being an ambivalent one; defy victimhood narratives or other dominant narratives; tell its stories through emphasizing relation and co-transformation; leave aside the traditional migrant theatre model of testimony; mingle aspects pertaining to the real and the fictional; be interested in exploring politico-ethical concerns alongside aesthetic experimentation; and aspire to expand the understanding of the terms migrant and migration. A key feature of a theatre of migration, then, is uncontainment – even though, simultaneously, forms of containment are desirable in some respects, including the legal protection that comes with being granted an official status. Notably, the figures in both works straddle these identities: in *The Container* Bayley's characters, inspired by real people she interviewed, are not defined as asylum seekers or refugees; in *Dear Home Office* at the time it premiered, some of the members of the cast – and the character they perform collectively, Tariq – were themselves Unaccompanied Asylum Seeker Children (UASC), whose claims were being processed by the Home Office. Specifically, *The Container* decentres the idea of often-rehearsed migration tropes by focusing on the relations and dynamics that emerge between the migrant characters. *Dear Home Office* does the same by affording space and weight to the depiction of Tariq as a young male living in the UK.

Interestingly, Balfour, following Dennis, indicates that 'one of the main problems with refugee performance begins with the linking of "refugee" with "performance". It immediately sets up a fixed orientation between subject (the presence of the refugee voice) and the non-refugee audience (witness)' (Balfour 2009: 356). Refugee performance also generates expectations about the kind of theatre and the topics that are to be explored. For example, Christopher Hibma claims: 'I've heard exiles say they are whoring themselves, dramatizing stories they don't want to tell, in order to get funding and be seen onstage at all' (qtd. in Horwitz 2018). Some of these ambivalences also pertain to theatre of migration; nevertheless, I argue that its openness allows for a more nuanced understanding of the concept and the development of potential new relations.

Crisis discourse, the refugee crisis and migratory aesthetics

Crisis discourse as the amalgamation of mechanisms and narratives that activate and perpetuate a disconnected or confined understanding of crises in order to occlude the systemic nature of the crisis of capitalism applies to the way the refugee crisis has been conceptualized (Žižek 2015; Khiabany 2016; Musca and Corrêa 2020: 380). The way (the refugee) crisis is rendered as separate from other phenomena affects how individuals think, live and act in relation to it. With regard to the UK, Alison Jeffers, drawing on Simon Faulkner, highlights the recurrence of 'military metaphors reflecting Britain's island geography and underlining connections between refugees and being under siege, defending frontiers and fending off attacks' (qtd. in Jeffers 2012: 28). Jeffers describes how such 'metaphors figure national borders as frontiers that are vulnerable to attack and suggest images of the nation as what has been called a "spatial containment schema"' (Charteris-Black qtd. in Jeffers 2012: 28). Recently, the use of containment metaphors was especially notable in the context of Brexit campaigns and debates, where sealing borders and lowering immigration numbers were among the most important motivations for many leave voters longing to 'take back control' and 'secure our borders' (Hall 2016). As Marilena Zaroulia has argued: 'migration is conceived as excess in the logic of the system that we live in, a system of sovereignty and bordered spaces' (2018: 182), which justifies the subsequent need for migrants to be managed, controlled, quantified and therefore contained.

By calling attention to limits, by exploring outsidedness and by suggesting interrelatedness at many overlapping levels, *The Container* and *Dear Home Office* critique ideological, ahistorical and compartmentalized senses of crisis, the refugee crisis, the migrant and migration. In doing so, these plays are responding aesthetically, ethically and politically to those topics and perhaps – through their creative grammars – demanding an epistemological reconsideration of the meaning of such concepts. These works reflect migration not only thematically but also formally, both as plays and through strategies present in the plays. Indeed, this is a theatre 'that also engages with migration as a topic or trope' (Cox 2014: 7).

Cultural theorist and critic Mieke Bal coined the phrase 'migratory aesthetics' in the context of contemporary arts criticism. Migratory aesthetics 'is an aesthetic, but takes the latter concept literally, as a condition of sentient engagement. Thus, it is part and parcel of those concepts that attempt to establish an active interface between viewer and artwork' (2007: 23). As part of a genealogy of concepts that includes '"relational aesthetics" (Bourriaud), "empathic aesthetics," (Bennett) or simply "political art"' (Bal

2007: 23), migratory aesthetics is defined by 'movement and transition' (Bennett 2011: 115). It 'draws attention to those who are caught, even frozen, in transition, between lives and countries' (Durrant and Lord 2007: 12). Yet crucially, migratory aesthetics also applies to 'the degree to which the art work itself becomes migratory, the degree to which it mimics – at the level of form rather than content – that which it sets out to represent' (13). Vitally, migratory aesthetics has an affinity with uncontainment and the notion's relational ethos. As Bal states, 'Migratory, in this sense, ... foreground[s] the fact that migrants (as subjects) and migration (as an act to perform as well as a state to be or live in) are part of any society today, and that their presence is an incontestable source of cultural transformation' (2007: 23).

Migratory aesthetics thus favours an understanding of the migrant as a transformational figure in societies to which migrants relocate. As Thomas Nail suggests in *The Figure of the Migrant* (2015), there are 'two kinds of movement that define the migrant. The first kind, made up of units of space-time, is extensive and quantitative: movement as change of place, or translation. The second kind of movement is intensive and qualitative: a change in the whole, a transformation' (13). Indeed, 'The movement of the migrant is not simply from A to B but is the constitutive condition for the qualitative transformation of society as a whole' (2015: 13).

Both *The Container* and *Dear Home Office* uncontain the migrant as a bounded notion and decentre its distribution uniquely to subjects that move from one point to another. The migratory aesthetics strategies present in the works may urge the spectator to experience crisis and the migrant as uncontained, which allows a weaving of the spectator into crisis/es and of her body into the body politic, into the sets of relations occluded by a contained understanding of crisis. *The Container* potentially achieves this by issuing a bodily and visceral invitation to experience the body of the migrant as lived, whereas *Dear Home Office*'s bodily interplay situates knowledge about migration as knowledge lived and experienced by the migrant.

The Container by Clare Bayley

Originally commissioned by Nicolas Kent at the Kiln Theatre, Clare Bayley's *The Container* tells the story of a group of migrants who are smuggled across Europe inside a shipping container lorry in order to reach the UK. It was first directed by Tom Wright at the Edinburgh Fringe Festival and it was the winner of the 2007 Edinburgh Festival Fringe First and the 2007 Amnesty International Freedom of Expression Award. This chapter comments on the Young Vic's production (2009), also directed by Wright. *The Container* was staged inside a container parked outside the Young Vic Theatre and it allowed twenty-eight spectators per performance who sat in close proximity to the performers. In light of the idea of uncontainment as migratory aesthetic, this section will suggest ways in which 'the container [is] a box which cannot be boxed' (Parker 2013: 369).

One of the reasons why I have chosen a play that speaks to the experience of the migrant beyond the most recent peak in migration into Europe (2015–16) is precisely because it is important to see the movement of people into Europe and elsewhere historically and beyond the events and processes the media chooses to highlight – 'The frame... seeks to contain, convey, and determine what is seen', says Judith Butler (2009: 10). Bayley wrote *The Container* in 2002, and given the presence of two Afghani characters in the play, one may assume that the historical backdrop is the Afghan refugee crisis as conceptualized by the media. However, Bailey interestingly goes beyond a specific country as she includes a Turkish Kurd, a Turkish and two Somali characters. In so doing, *The Container* also tackles migratory flux globally and across continents as well as part of regional conflict. Adding to this more holistic picture of migration, the play also visualizes the figure of the trafficker.

The Container can be classified as a 'container play' (Helff 2016), which has as predecessors Christoph Schlingensief's *Bitte liebt Österreich! (Please Love Austria!* 2000) and, less famously, Maxim Biller's *Kühltransport: Ein Drama (Refrigerated Transport: A Drama* 2001). Regarding the first, a shipping container was placed outside the Vienna State Opera and covered with blue FPÖ flags, a sign reading 'Ausländer raus' ('Foreigners out') and the logo of Austria's most famous tabloid, the *Kronenzeitung*. Inside, there were twelve allegedly real asylum seekers. As Florian Malzacher suggests, 'the status of the participants remained dubious, since it was never officially resolved whether they were real asylum seekers or actors and if they fully understood the game being played' (2015: 22). The performance worked like a one-week-long Big Brother reality show, broadcast live on Austrian TV, where viewers could vote to deport one of the asylum seekers each night. Maxim Biller's piece 'turned a concrete memento of refugee reality in Europe into dramatic art when the dramatist traced and re-imagined the tragic deaths of 58 illegal migrants from China whose bodies were discovered in a freight container at the French–British border in June 2000' (Helff 2016: 104).[1] Schlingensief's and Biller's pieces were followed by a plethora of

---

[1] These extremely tragic events continue to happen (for instance, thirty-nine Vietnamese nationals were found dead in the back of a refrigerated truck near London after being smuggled into Britain on 23 October 2019).

container plays including Andreea Vălean's *Where the Smoke's Going* (2002), Tess Berry-Hart's *Cargo* (2016) and *The Container*.

In this one-act play in six scenes, the characters include Fatima, a Somali woman in her forties; Asha, her fifteen-year-old niece; Jemal, a Turkish Kurd in his twenties; Ahmad, an Afghan man in his fifties; Miriam, an Afghan woman in her twenties; and the Agent, a Turkish trafficker (there is also the unseen driver of the container lorry). At the beginning, the truck stops and the migrants are joined by Miriam. In the fourth scene, the Agent asks the migrants for an extra 50 dollars a head (after having paid the sum of 10,000 dollars previous to their journey). When Miriam reveals that she cannot pay the sum, the Agent suggests that there is an alternative way she can pay. Miriam leaves the truck and, although the play does not specify what happens to her, it is suggested that she is forced to choose between being sexually-assaulted in order to return to the container or abandoning her opportunity to reach her destination, pointing out the idea of migrating as gendered. Moreover, at the beginning of the play Jemal calls Fatima a 'stupid woman' so the play's attention to the disproportionate abuse regarding the female migrant experience is brought home in the last line of the play when Asha, a young woman, asks: 'Do you think we have arrived?' (*The Container* 2009).

While Michael Shane Boyle argues that 'the story that propels *The Container* gives audiences little choice but to interpret the infrastructural aesthetic as a narrative device' (2016: 67), I argue that the container in *The Container* is much more resonant. To begin with, the idea of the container connects with the migrant's experience, usually related to confinement in various ways: within bordered spaces, means of transport, other locked structures such as refugee camps and internment/detention centres, in liminal spaces/ states, unsupportive institutional structures, stifling movement limitations and restricted social mobilities.

The container also works as a powerful contradictory symbol of globalization: pivotal to the logistics of transporting consumer goods around the globe, it also evokes pollution, dehumanization and objectification. Using a device that represents Western societies' obsession with goods and consumerism and the transportation of objects under globalization can only have the metonymic effect of objectifying the people depicted inside. Furthermore, the suggestion made by this play's staging and proxemic relations (the cast and spectators share a very close and compact space, which makes it hard to argue for any form of disentanglement) is that the theatre itself and the spectators are also embedded in that circuit of objectification (and objectifying). This points out not only the spectators' imbalanced positioning, but also that the spectators could be in the migrants' position (as they are all physically inside the container) and that the depicted characters and the spectators are part of the same cosmos – all interdependent and interconnected.

The proxemic relation of audience and performers also reveals a sense of migratory aesthetics: the space is only illuminated by torches held by the actors in the dark; heat, smell and claustrophobic conditions that are part of the migrants' travelling experience become the spectator's experience as they all sweat, feel, see and smell in the same condensed space in close proximity (perhaps uncoincidentally, the play ran in the summer). This form of symbiosis, which transforms even the idea of immersivity, is pushed even further by having the container parked in a public space, in a specific borough (with a high refugee population) and in a specific country (the UK, where the migrants hope to arrive). This offers wider reflection about space and the interrelations between the story's migrants, the audience, the public sphere and lived geography.

Playfully and pragmatically, and suggesting a further step in this sense of uncontained selves and interwoven geography, the container in Bayley's *The Container* had holes because the actors and the spectators needed to breathe. This destabilizes the idea of setting and highlights the connection between the space of the story and the space of the real. Furthermore, the blurring of theatrical and public space means that life is made possible only by connecting with the outside, which, in turn, begs some reflection around the logic of insider/outsider. Usually, the citizens in the country of arrival are thought of as insiders and the migrant as the outsider, or 'out of place' (Ahmed 2000: 78). *The Container*'s staging reverses these roles, placing the migrants (outsiders) inside (a container and the UK, which simultaneously signifies their desire and uncertainty), while placing the spectators (insiders) outside (in the world of the outsiders, outside a comfortable position, outside the theatre building and the usual migrant image and narrative depicted on the media).

Other contradictions are revealed by the show's appeal to the idea of movement. This enclosed space, the container, is stationed, but in movement in the story as the story may 'move' spectators into an uncontained understanding of crisis and of the migrant. Moreover, a pre-recorded soundscape replicates road travel (truck noise, vehicles driving past, et cetera), which clearly suggests the idea of movement while making it difficult for the spectator to listen to the story. This perhaps mirrors the idea that migrants are indeed speaking but crisis discourse and a contained understanding of the migrant make it difficult for these voices to truly be heard.

The spectator has the certainty that she can leave the performing space at any time, being aware that the people whose lives are evoked through the characters do not. In this sense, even though this may not reflect *The Container*'s creative team's intentions, the spectator's investment may turn into a mere voyeuristic experience (see Musca and Corrêa 2020: 376). At the very least, with a visceral approach that crucially engages spectators' bodies, I would argue that the experiential impetus of *The Container* attempts to bodily turn spectators into the characters it depicts. Rather than witnesses of migrants construed as depersonalized numbers and figures, as portrayed in the media, or as people removed from their experience, *The Container* casts spectators not only as witnesses but also alongside the performers (all now migrant) as fragile bodies in one space.

Dear Home Office by Phosphoros Theatre

Phosphoros Theatre (hereafter PT) is a London-based UK theatre company whose productions star refugees and asylum-seeking actors, all of whom arrived in the UK as Unaccompanied Asylum Seeking Children (UASC). The group's first show, *Dear Home Office*, is about fourteen-year-old Tariq Ali, an unaccompanied asylum-seeking minor in the UK who has escaped persecution in his birth country. Although Tariq is a fictional construct, the character was devised by the company by resorting to fragments from each of the refugee and asylum-seeking actors' stories, which then surface in Tariq's story. These include not only scenes of his migratory journey across continents, suffering imprisonment, danger and hunger, but also and, crucially, experiences pertaining to his life in the UK as a young male. *Dear Home Office* premiered in 2016 at the Underbelly Med Squad during the Edinburgh Fringe and was then performed in several venues across the country, mainly in London, due to the proximity to most of the cast's home in North London. *Dear Home Office* was nominated for Amnesty International Freedom of Expression Award 2016.

The refugee and asylum-seeker members of *Dear Home Office*'s cast did not have previous theatrical experience. Their expertise has grown over the past few years, which highlights Phosphoros Theatre's work around the training and professionalization of their members. This is evident in the work the company has produced to date beyond *Dear Home Office*, including *Dear Home Office: Still Pending* (2017), *Pizza Shop Heroes* (2018), *All the Beds I Have Slept in* (2020) and *But Everything Has an Ending* (2020) – an anthology of digital performances in response to Covid-19 – and in the company's effort to train people with experience of forced migration as workshop assistants. Phosphoros Theatre states in their website, unveiling the rationale for the company's name, that their 'mission is to bring the unseen to light, making bold, informed, resistant theatre that speaks to our lived realities' ('About Phosphoros Theatre' n.d.).

PT, officially recognized as a Theatre Company of Sanctuary by the umbrella organization, City of Sanctuary, and now a registered charity with solid links with other charities and numerous organizations and with notable advocacy work experience to date, grew out of applied theatre practitioner Kate Duffy's (now Kate Duffy-Syedi) job as key worker in a Supporting Housing project run by Afghan Association Paiwand. There, she helped a number of unaccompanied minors in Harrow, North London, to deal with daily tasks such as going to the GP, opening a bank account, buying clothes and food or enrolling in an English course. Interestingly, 'The idea for Dear Home Office came to Kate at the suggestion of one of the residents' who one day approached her and said 'I think I'm quite funny and I have an interesting story to tell' (Rodgers Johns 2016). Duffy-Syedi's mother, Dawn Harrison (an experienced script writer) and Harrison's collaborator and Duffy-Syedi's friend Rosanna Jahangard (intercultural theatre practitioner and secondary school drama teacher) soon joined the project and they started working on *Dear Home Office*, also becoming the company's co-artistic directors (Jahangard has lately been replaced as co-artistic director by Juliet Styles).

While 'traditional forms of migrant theatre' include 'mainstream testimony-focused models (e.g. documentary, verbatim, testimonial, and forum theatre)' (Musca and Corrêa 2020: 378), *Dear Home Office* seems to be non-prescriptively located somewhere at the crossroads of testimonial and documentary theatre. It conforms to Michael Balfour's description of testimonial theatre as 'refugees "performing" their experiences on stage' (2009: 356–7), where the stories of real UASC find a voice, in this particular instance via the specific character of Tariq. This permits the migrant's narrative and the migrant subject to be productively uncontained. The artistic co-directors repeatedly state that the construct of Tariq does not imply a unified refugee narrative, which is clearly laid against the 'singular refugee narrative told by the UK press' (Jahangard and Duffy 2016).

In *Performing Statelessness in Europe*, Stephen Wilmer states that documentary theatre 'include[s] productions devised and performed by refugees who recount their past experiences and ambitions, using their own bodies as evidence, such as in *Letters Home* by the Refugee Club Impulse in Berlin and *Dear Home Office* by Phosphorus [*sic*] Theatre in London' (2018: 4). Of all the functions of documentary theatre Wilmer reminds us about by using Carol Martin's taxonomy in her article 'Bodies of Evidence', the one which aligns best with PT is: '*To intermingle autobiography with history*' (qtd. in Wilmer 2018: 74; emphasis added). In fact, in the 'Home' section of

PT's website, they describe their work as autobiographical. And for instance, history has been given a prominent role in their show *Pizza Shop Heroes*, as a play that engages with the UK's colonial history. 'Lived experience' is another key term for Phosphoros Theatre, which they highlight, for instance, in the description of their show *All the Beds I Have Slept in*.

In contraposition to *The Container*, which was written by a playwright after a series of interviews with migrants, *Dear Home Office* was devised and performed by refugees and asylum-seeking actors. The process started with a series of collective workshops, followed by the artistic directors' work on ideas for the scenes, story line and characters. Next, they developed the script (mainly Harrison), which underwent a series of edits in response to the company's collaborative and creative readings and rehearsals. This was later turned into a creatively rich show with the use of different media, techniques and forms of artistic expression on stage, which, non-exhaustively, included physical theatre, comedy, storytelling, live traditional music, singing, video projection, mime, dance and spoken word.

PT states the rationale behind their exploration in *Dear Home Office* and the background against which the piece was created and performed, a background of raising UASC figures and unfair treatment: 'The majority of unaccompanied minors (around 72%) receive Discretionary Leave, which means they are granted leave in the UK until the age of 18, at which point around 70% of applications to extend their leave are refused' (Refugee Council qtd. in Jahangard and Duffy 2016). The play traces Tariq's journey to the UK, his experiences of finding accommodation, new friends, learning English, as well as his asylum claim experiences with the Home Office (court appearances, appointments with solicitors, et cetera). Tariq faces a series of difficulties: he has to prove his age, constantly face disbelief and cope with the fragility of memory. However, by resorting to some uncontaining techniques which challenge the media's insistence on highlighting unidimensional identities, *Dear Home Office* shows that Tariq's life also shares some aspects with any other young male in the UK including having fun with friends, feeling lonely and having dreams and hopes. Importantly, a tactic 'in applied theatre with refugees' that 'necessarily involves a... staging of suffering and victimhood' (Jeffers 2008: 218) is no longer adopted in the case of *Dear Home Office*.

Abdul, Awet, Emirjon, Faheem, Goitom, Mohamed, Sied and Syed, who come from Somalia, Afghanistan, Eritrea and Albania (I am stating their names as they appear in *Dear Home Office*'s free sheets) take turns performing character Tariq, who is a synthesis of fragments from their own voices and stories. However, expanding the definition of *Dear Home Office* as testimonial and documentary, the company emphasizes that the resulting account is fictional, and the fragments delivered by particular cast members may or may not coincide with their own story. '[E]xperimenting with naming and identity positions offered by the fictional space of the theatre' (Jeffers 2012: 40) in this case was not only an artistic choice but also a pragmatic one – expressing their views while their asylum claim was ongoing could endanger the potential success of the applicant. Not assigning story was instrumental in protecting the unaccompanied minors and providing them with a sense of safety. To make clear that they all are Tariq, each actor placed one piece of their own clothing on a mannequin that read 'Tariq'. That is, while all the actors' bodies represented Tariq, the mannequin was also a representation of Tariq and the actors' bodies, suggesting that the real and fictional accounts, as well as real bodies of asylum seekers and the symbolic mannequin representation of the asylum seekers, become confounded.

The fragmented and fragmentary technique utilized via storytelling as well as stage design offers a series of disconnected narratives and moments which evoke the vulnerability, fragility, dislocation from home and language, and mental suffering and disturbance, among other forms of deprivation migrants go through. It is, in other words, a migratory aesthetic, an aesthetic that reflects the experience of the migrant. The narrative of one's self may no longer be a coherent one so perhaps seeing oneself in others' voices (and from a different standpoint) and seeing other stories maybe reflecting back at one's own story and self may bring some form of solidarity and commonality to a solitary and highly traumatizing experience. Besides, the narrativization of one's story, no matter how fragmented, may raise some possibilities around proximity/distance, which may afford some new forms of understanding. This chapter is not the first to use the idiom of 'aesthetics' regarding *Dear Home Office*. Amanda Stuart Fisher, for instance, argues that 'caring within this play emerges not only as part of its material content but also as an aesthetic practice' (2020: 3).

In the piece, Duffy-Syedi plays herself as Kate, the boys' 'Key Worker and, occasionally, a mother and a teacher, acting not as a narrator to the story, but as a character in her own right and as a depiction of an integral part of the boys' experience since they arrived in the UK and have forged surrogate relationships in absence of their family' (Jahangard and Duffy 2016). At a crucial moment, Kate reads the letter that is to be handed at the Home Office in order to have Tariq's asylum claim assessed, emphasizing the right of her character to be a character and the fact that this aesthetic experience of migration has to be thought alongside the company's everyday life. As Harrison puts it, 'We're not just a theatre company, we offer support so they can actually be in the play, which includes going to court with them, being witnesses in court, and going to the Home Office with them to report' (qtd. in Fotheringham 2017) – conferring the phrase 'Phosphoros family' its full meaning.

It is not only that theatre reflects life and that theatre becomes part of life but also that the cast goes from the theatre and other spaces of practice to the world, a world that very often is profoundly hostile towards them.[2] Theatre making, the stage and working spaces become a vital rehearsal environment for real life's institutional and extra-institutional encounters including interviews, exams or making friends. Space for rehearsing and rehearsal spaces become a staple as, according to Jeffers, '[a] weak "performance", in the context of claiming asylum, can lead to failure no matter how strong the story/script and failure in these circumstances can be deadly' (2012: 30).

At present, PT's core group of actors have some form of leave to remain in the UK. As the company has evolved, the cast has taken more and more ownership of the shows 'as individuals or artists' (Sharifi and Wilmer 2016). Increasingly, for PT, 'performance provides a space in which migrants and refugees can author and perform their stories of exile' (Cummings qtd. in Fragkou 2018: 303) and indeed, beyond exile. The spaces of contact PT crafts have always had an ally in their audiences, which are at the heart of their work. For instance, at the Bunker in London, they offered the audience to stay after the show to continue the conversation, uncontaining the theatrical event as such. The composition of their audience clearly uncontains the usual white middle class audience majority. They visibly and notably engage educational institutions, community groups, charity groups, legal professionals, social workers, et cetera. With their unique blend of the personal and the political, day-to-day issues and historical engagement, humour and urgency, authenticity and fictionality, autobiography and the universal, lived experience and the impact of macropolitical decision-making, PT is a theatrical powerhouse with minimal theatrics and serious thinking about (and action around) migration.

Theatre of human experience

In *Theatre & Migration*, Cox asks 'who does the imagining?' (2014: 5). In both *The Container* and *Dear Home Office*, the imagining does not come from one person and does not come from the person in the arrival society

---

[2] According to The Joint Council for the Welfare of Immigrants, 'hostile environment' alludes to 'a set of policies introduced in 2012 by then-Home Secretary Theresa May, with the aim of making life unbearably difficult in the UK for those who cannot show the right paperwork' (JCWI 2021).

uniquely. The imagining is uncontained, shared and co-created, which hopefully allows for its journey to be expanded to the spectator and beyond. *The Container* and *Dear Home Office* have been suggested as examples of uncontainment because they challenge a confined understanding of (the refugee) crisis, the migrant and migration. Indeed, theatre of migration's insistent ontological pressure may result in an eventual epistemological shift to other ways of understanding and living those concepts. By exhibiting a migratory aesthetics across many overlapping levels, i.e. an architecture of uncontainment, and inviting a new set of unbounded relationships with the world, these plays' subtle and refined engagement with the trope of migration urges connections (and opens up migrancy distribution) rather than reinforcing subject positions. The logic of uncontainment allows both performers and spectators to question fixed roles regarding migrant theatre (i.e. witness and victim, spectator and migrant). A theatre of migration is a theatre that is simultaneously in and out, where participants collapse into being bodies, humans with lived experience – a lived experience that may migrate at any time – in one space.

References

Phosphoros Theatre (n.d.), 'About Phosphoros Theatre'. Available online: https://www.phosphorostheatre.com/about (accessed 4 October 2020).
Ahmed, S. (2000), *Strange Encounters: Embodied Others in Post-Coloniality*, London: Routledge.
Amnesty International Australia (2019), 'What's the Difference between a Refugee and an Asylum Seeker?', *Amnesty International Australia*, 24 January. Available online: https://www.amnesty.org.au/refugee-and-an-asylum-seeker-difference/#:~:text=An%20asylum%20seeker%20is%20an%20individual%20who%20is%20seeking%20international%20protection (accessed 3 October 2020).
Bal, M. (2007), 'Lost in Space, Lost in the Library', in S. Durrant and C. M. Lord (eds), *Essays in Migratory Aesthetics: Cultural Practices between Migration and Art-making*, 23–35, Amsterdam: Rodopi.
Balfour, M. (2009), 'The Politics of Intention: Looking for a Theatre of Little Changes', *RiDE: The Journal of Applied Theatre and Performance*, 14 (3): 347–59.
Bayley, C. (2007), *The Container*, London: Nick Hern.
Bennett, J. (2011), 'Migratory Aesthetics: Art and Politics beyond Identity', in M. Bal and M. Á. Hernández-Navarro (eds), *Art and Visibility in Migratory Culture: Conflict, Resistance, and Agency*, 109–26, Amsterdam: Rodopi.
Boyle, M. S. (2016), 'Container Aesthetics: The Infrastructural Politics of Shunt's *The Boy Who Climbed Out of His Face*', *Theatre Journal*, 68 (1): 57–77.

Butler, J. (2009), *Frames of War: When Is Life Grievable?* London: Verso.
The Container (2009), [Streamed production] Young Vic Theatre/Digital Theatre +, London 22 July. Available online: https://www.digitaltheatre.com/consumer/production/the-container.
Cooper, G., L. Blumell and M. Bunce (2021), 'Beyond the "Refugee Crisis": How the UK News Media Represent Asylum Seekers across National Boundaries', The International Communication Gazette, 83 (3): 195–216.
Cox, E. (2014), *Theatre & Migration*, Basingstoke: Palgrave Macmillan.
Cox, E., S. Durrant, D. Farrier, L. Stonebridge and A. Woolley (2020), *Refugee Imaginaries: Research across the Humanitie*s, Edinburgh: Edinburgh University Press.
Durrant, S. and C. M. Lord (2007), 'Introduction: Essays in Migratory Aesthetics', in S. Durrant and C. M. Lord (eds), *Essays in Migratory Aesthetics: Cultural Practices between Migration and Art-making*, 11–19, Amsterdam: Rodopi.
Fisher, A. S. (2020), 'Introduction: Caring Performance, Performing Care', in J. Thompson and A. S. Fisher (eds), *Performing Care: New Perspectives on Socially Engaged Performance*, 1–17, Manchester: Manchester University Press.
Fotheringham, A. (2017), 'Fringe Drama Returns with Update on Refugees in the UK', *Herald Scotland*, 21 August. Available online: https://www.heraldscotland.com/arts_ents/edinburgh_fringe/15484118.Fringe_drama_returns_with_update_on_refugees_in_the_UK/ (accessed 5 November 2017).
Fragkou, M. (2018), 'Strange Homelands: Encountering the Migrant on the Contemporary Greek Stage', *Modern Drama*, 61 (3): 301–27.
Hall, C. (2016), 'The Racist Ideas of Slave Owners Are Still with Us Today', *Guardian*, 26 September. Available online: https://www.theguardian.com/commentisfree/2016/sep/26/racist-ideas-slavery-slave-owners-hate-crime-brexit-vote (accessed 4 October 2018).
Helff, S. (2016), 'In the Name of the Other? Refugee Theatre and the Value of "Illegal" Life in Britain', *Journal of Postcolonial Writing*, 52 (1): 102–13.
Horwitz, S. (2018), 'The Refuge of the Stage: What Roles Can Theatre Play in the Global Refugee Crisis? Healing, Representation – and Diversion', *American Theatre*, May/June. Available online: https://www.americantheatre.org/2018/04/24/the-refuge-of-the-stage/ (accessed 25 May 2019).
Jahangard, R. and K. Duffy (2016), 'Unheard Voices, Unseen Faces: Staging Stories of Male Refugee Youth', *Critical Stages/Scènes Critiques*, 14. Available online: http://www.critical-stages.org/14/unseen-faces-and-unheard-voices-how-a-group-of-refugee-teenage-boys-living-in-the-uk-brought-their-hidden-stories-to-the-stage-in-dear-home-office/ (accessed 5 May 2018).
Jeffers, A. (2008), 'Dirty Truth: Personal Narrative, Victimhood and Participatory Theatre Work with People Seeking Asylum', *Research in Drama Education: The Journal of Applied Theatre and Performance*, 13 (2): 217–21.

Jeffers, A. (2012), *Refugees, Theatre and Crisis: Performing Global Identities*, Basingstoke: Palgrave Macmillan.

Johns, T. R. (2016), '"I Guess We're Trying to Go Against the Expectation of What Refugee Stories Are", An Interview with Kate Scarlett Duffy – *Dear Home Office*', *The Unapologists*, 25 November. Available online: http://theunapologists.com/kate-scarlett-duffy%E2%80%8A-%E2%80%8Adear-home-office (accessed 4 February 2018).

The Joint Council for the Welfare of Immigrants (2021), 'The Hostile Environment Explained', *The Joint Council for the Welfare of Immigrants*. Available online: https://www.jcwi.org.uk/the-hostile-environment-explained (accessed 5 January 2021).

Khiabany, G. (2016), 'Refugee Crisis, Imperialism and Pitiless Wars on the Poor', *Media, Culture & Society*, 38 (5): 755–62.

Malzacher, F. (2015), *Not Just a Mirror: Looking for the Political Theater of Today*, Berlin: Alexander Verlag.

Martin, C. (2006), 'Bodies of Evidence', *TDR*, 50 (3): 8–15.

Musca, S. and G. P. Corrêa (2020), '"White People All Over": Refugee Performance, Fictional Aesthetics, and Dramaturgies of Alterity-Empathy', *Contemporary Theatre Review*, 30 (3): 375–89.

Nail, T. (2015), *The Figure of the Migrant*, Stanford: Stanford University Press.

Parker, M. (2013), 'Containerisation: Moving Things and Boxing Ideas', *Mobilities*, 8 (3): 368–87.

Sharifi, A. and S. E. Wilmer (2016), 'Reflections on Theatre and Statelessness', *Critical Stages/Scènes critiques*, 14. Available online: http://www.critical-stages.org/14/reflections-on-theatre-and-statelessness/ (accessed 6 November 2017).

Wilmer, S. E. (2018), *Performing Statelessness in Europe*, London: Palgrave Macmillan.

Zaroulia, M. (2018), 'Performing That Which Exceeds Us: Aesthetics of Sincerity and Obscenity during "the Refugee Crisis"', *Research in Drama Education: The Journal of Applied Theatre and Performance*, 23 (2): 179–92.

Žižek, S. (2015), 'We Can't Address the EU Refugee Crisis without Confronting Global Capitalism', *These Times*, 9 September. Available online: http://inthesetimes.com/article/18385/slavoj-zizek-europeanrefugee-crisis-and-global-capitalism (accessed 1 October 2018).

10

The crisis of multiculturalism in Charlene James's *Cuttin' It* and Gloria Williams's *Bullet Hole*

María Isabel Seguro and Marta Tirado

Despite the fact that Female Genital Mutilation (FGM) was criminalized in the UK with the 1985 Prohibition of Female Circumcision Act, it did not become a widely discussed public issue until the 2010s. The 2013 Channel 4 documentary *The Cruel Cut* sparked widespread debate in the mass media, raising awareness of the extent and impact of this practice on immigrant and British women and girls (Williams 2013). British Home Office reports 'estimate [that] 170,000 women and girls are living with FGM in the UK, and since September 2014 more than 2,603 women and girls who went through FGM have been treated by the NHS' (qtd. in Collier 2016). Yet, first prosecutions only occurred in 2014, and first convictions as late as 2019. FGM is an extreme example of what is often perceived as a crisis of multiculturalism, unmasking a confrontation between values: women's rights recognized by liberal Western democracies and respect for cultural differences.

This chapter examines some of the ways recent British theatre has responded to the controversy around what is considered by some as a cultural practice and an identity marker of African immigrant communities, by others as an abusive act and, by law, a crime. Often produced by local/regional theatres with strong community links, a diverse body of theatre work on the intimate politics of this phenomenon has emerged since 2014. For instance, Baretruth Theatre Company's *Little Stitches* (2014) collected four short plays performed at Theatre 503 in Battersea, Areola Trent in Hackney and the Gate Theatre in Notting Hill; Cora Bissett and Yusra Warsama collaborated to create *Rites* (2015), first presented at Glasgow's Tron Theatre; Charlene

María Isabel Seguro and Marta Tirado's work was supported by the Spanish Ministry of Economy and Competitiveness (MINECO) and the European Regional Development Fund (ERDF) project 'British Theatre in the Twenty-First Century: Crisis, Affect, Community' (FFI2016-75443).

James's *Cuttin' It* premiered at the Young Vic in May 2016, then transferred to the Royal Court before touring to schools in London and Birmingham, with a new production opening at Manchester's Royal Exchange Theatre in 2020; Gloria Williams's *Bullet Hole* was first performed at the 2017 Camden Fringe Festival and later at Park Theatre; and in 2019 Bedminster's acta community theatre presented *Judging Without Knowing Us*, a play written and performed by women from Bristol's Somali community. While these examples display a variety of views on FGM, the plays all share a strong sense of community commitment, seeking to engage audiences with the public debate about, and consequences of, FGM.

Focusing on James's *Cuttin' It* and Williams's *Bullet Hole*, we will explore the crisis of the prevailing liberal view of multiculturalism as it intersects with feminism. As Black British women assimilated in mainstream culture and familiar with issues concerning minority groups, the playwrights in question give voice to the silenced victims, while simultaneously questioning the official discourse of multiculturalism, according to which cultural practices should be tolerated. As James argues, 'We must stop saying FGM is a cultural thing: it's child abuse' (qtd. in Urwin 2016). Both playwrights nevertheless present the complexities of the issue through characters who, having experienced FGM, continue to perpetuate the practice. By exposing the physical pain undergone by female bodies and its psychological consequences, James and Williams undermine the justification for FGM, providing arguments for eradicating the practice from within the communities. Moreover, we argue that a global feminist view is offered as a tool against FGM, understood as one which incorporates a non-Western perspective, prioritizing women's rights as a counterbalance to dominant positions held by certain forms of Western feminism that embrace multiculturalist views.

The crisis of multiculturalism

The view that issues around FGM are evidence of the crisis of multiculturalism can be traced back to the cultural racism after 9/11 and, in the British context, the 7/7 London bomb attacks. Once idealized as a means of creating harmonious societies in diversity, it has become apparent that multiculturalism was not the solution, but the problem. Championing respect for cultural difference over social cohesion and shared values (based on those of the host country, mostly understood as a Western liberal democracy) has led, so the argument follows, to the creation of marginalized spaces in which hostile attitudes develop, undermining thus the possibility of social integration (Lentin and Titley 2011). As political thinker Bhikhu

Parekh underlined in *Rethinking Multiculturalism: Cultural Diversity and Political Theory* (2000), multiculturalism is an impossibility:

> Multicultural societies throw up problems that have no parallel in history. They need to find ways of reconciling the legitimate demands of unity and diversity, achieving political unity without cultural uniformity, being inclusive without being assimilationist, cultivating among their citizens a common sense of belonging while respecting their cultural differences, and cherishing plural cultural identities without weakening the shared and precious identity of shared citizenship. This is a formidable political task and no multicultural society so far has succeeded in taking it.
> (2000: 343)

Liberal multiculturalism, according to Will Kymlicka (1989, 1995), considers that group rights should be conceded to immigrant communities so that their individual members may have the choice to pursue their cultural heritage as a means of guaranteeing equality within liberal democracies. Traditionally, liberal multiculturalism assumes the 'civic integration' of minorities, according to which they will accept the social, economic and political parameters of the liberal democratic host countries, while preserving their cultural difference. As Tariq Modood states, 'migrants should be able to retain their distinct cultures while they adapt to working and living in their new countries. No doubt, some assimilation would take place, but it should not be required' (2007: 3).

However, feminism has questioned the viability of protecting minority groups and simultaneously guaranteeing the individual rights of its members – particularly concerning gender equality and sexuality, as Susan Möller Okin has suggested. Individual rights are perceived as not political enough for state protection. Consequently, practices such as forced and/or arranged marriages, deemed as cultural, are ignored by public authorities, increasing gender inequality via the control of female sexuality. Thus, granting group rights fails to 'recognize that minority cultural groups are, in this respect like the societies in which they exist, though to a greater or lesser extent, *gendered*' (1998: 664; original emphasis).

While acknowledging Okin's claim about gender discrimination within Western majority cultures, a number of critics (such as Azizahy Al-Ahibri, Homi K. Babha and Sander Gilman) included in the volume *Is Multiculturalism Bad for Women?* (1999) – in response to Okin's much-debated article of the same title originally published in 1997 in the *Boston Review* – question her ethnocentric stance in relation to non-Western cultures. Even though Okin does not explicitly proclaim the superiority of Western cultures, such a position has been deduced from her aforementioned article (Zerilli 2009: 295): if, according to Okin, 'women in more liberal cultures [understood as Western/Westernized] are ... legally guaranteed many of the same freedoms and opportunities as men' (in Cohen, Howard and Nussbaum 1999: 16–17), then the argument would follow that immigrant women could be liberated from their more oppressive cultural origins through adherence to Western liberal ideals related to the individual's freedom and rights. Their civic integration would thus secure their recognition as equal citizens in diversity.

Such a view of multiculturalism offers the 'social promise by extending freedom to migrants on the condition that they embrace its game. Multiculturalism becomes in other words a happy object' (Ahmed 2017: 549). Therefore, a dichotomy is established whereby the happy migrant – and in particular the happy female migrant – is the one who integrates successfully within the majority culture at the expense of sacrificing certain aspects of her family's cultural tradition. Although, as Sara Ahmed highlights, the official discourse does not clearly state that integration means complete assimilation, the unhappy migrant (or 'melancholic migrant' (549) in her words) would be the one who resists such a process.

The attempts to reconcile feminism and multiculturalism along the lines discussed above obviate such issues as the hierarchization of coexisting cultures in Western liberal contexts and the resulting racial discrimination, as the presence of FGM among immigrant women who are considered integrated would stubbornly attest. In fact, the persistence of FGM in the UK reveals that immigrant women who are considered integrated are also subjected to clitoridectomy. The focus on the assimilation/non-assimilation binary conceals the unbalanced relationship between majority and minority cultures, obscuring its biased foundation that immigrant women's assimilation implies their liberation from their oppressive patriarchal cultures. As Carolyn Pedwell argues, this opposition between the 'liberated' and 'oppressed' (immigrant) women 'represents a framework for thinking through apparently divergent gendered identities in contemporary multicultural and transnational contexts' (2011: 189).

Addressing FGM in Black British theatre

Both *Cuttin' It* and *Bullet Hole* can be contextualized within post-millennium Black British theatre, which reflects British cultural diversity, and Black feminist theatre insofar as they deal with Black women's experiences, such as inter-generational cultural conflicts, notions of sisterhood, beauty, sexuality and sexual abuse (both within and without immigrant communities)

(Goddard 2007: 47). James and Williams are performers and playwrights who were brought up and educated in Britain; both participated in The Royal Court Theatre Young Writers' Group. As Lynette Goddard points out, the Royal Court is a venue that 'has by far been the most consistent in staging black British women's theatre' (2007: 22) as part of a policy of representing cultural diversity from the mainstream. Neither of the playwrights is an FGM victim, but their decision to tackle the issue reflects their commitment with their communities and their feminism by resorting to theatre as an adequate platform from which to condemn oppression against women and, in Williams's words, 'to raise awareness, using drama as a tool to educate audiences' (qtd. in Masso 2018).

Cuttin' It: A binary perspective and the fallacy of assimilation

Cuttin' It, directed by Gbolahan Obsesan, takes place in a prototypical English urban setting. Joanna Scotcher's set design with its grey stairs topped with a red and twisted metal fence gestures towards an impoverished environment of social housing. The main characters, Muna and Iqra, are Somali-born teenagers who have undergone FGM. Having been raised in England since the age of three, Muna believes herself to be more assimilated and speaks English with the accent of the city she was brought up in. Iqra, by contrast, arrived when she was ten after the traumatic experience of the Somali civil war and speaks with a 'strong Somali accent' (James 2016: 9), signifying her otherness. Although both characters share the same origins, their experiences make them radically different to the point that each incarnates the opposite side of the binary 'liberated and Westernized' and 'oppressed and non-Westernized', according to Pedwell's terms (2011: 188–9). Additionally, both have to face, not only racism, but also the painful rite of passage of FGM from their two divergent perspectives, which foregrounds the two major reasons behind the crisis of liberal multiculturalism as revealed by FGM practices: racial discrimination that affects British immigrant girls and the impossibility of complete assimilation in Western societies.

Whereas Muna's resistance to her own FGM is based on her conception of civil rights, Iqra's participation in FGM ceremonies becomes an act of resistance against the loss of her family memories and a homeland destroyed by war. For Iqra the cutting is necessary because, as women, it is not only important 'to be clean', but it also makes them good, decent, Muslim women '[i]n the eyes of our community' (41). Notwithstanding its obvious link to patriarchal structures that control women's bodies, through such a construction, FGM is brandished as a means of opposing European cultural imperialism implicit in assimilationist policies. The practice was considered to be a protection against rape, in particular type 3, which consists of 'the narrowing of the vaginal opening through the creation of a covering seal. The seal is formed by cutting and repositioning the inner, or outer, labia, with or without removal of the clitoris' (Eltahawy 2015: 117). In this sense, FGM could be reconceptualized as an act of symbolic resistance against the appropriation and possession of the land, and by extension, of the female body – whose penetration by colonial powers entailed the expansion of Western domination and, ironically, the miscegenation of the colonized.

The teenagers' characterization enhances the binary assimilated/non-assimilated immigrant construct. Iqra's costume, comprising a black hijab and a long skirt that covers her legs, suggests that she has not completed her process of cultural assimilation. By contrast, Muna is dressed in tight and stylish black trousers, being indistinguishable from any British teenager. The linguistic expression of the girls also adds to the idea that each narrative is the result of their two different histories and levels of assimilation. The slow pace of Iqra's speech, punctuated with silences and hesitations, denotes her insecurity with English and highlights her traumatic war experience as well as her discomfort with Western culture, whereas Muna's fluid, expressive and ironic tone highlights her confidence and reflects her acceptance of the majority culture.

Despite the fact that Muna identifies herself as a Western teenager, she still experiences racial discrimination that reminds her of her position as an immigrant. At the opening of the play, when she is about to miss the bus to school and the driver pretends not to see her, she reacts as follows:

> **Muna** My man's got too many shades of brown on his ride. Probably thinks the ones with the hoods are gonna stab him up an' the ones with the scarves are gonna blow him up.... I bet ya if I was some white girl standin here in this uniform, some blue-eyed, blonde-haired white girl, Mr Bus Man would be stoppin then, wouldn't he, stoppin to have a nice little look? I should report him. Watch me report him. (16)

Muna recognizes that she has rights and seems ready to exercise them. However, she is powerless when she needs to address the conflicts between her family's values and those of British society. When she suspects that her younger sister, who is about to turn seven, is going to be cut, she feels she cannot tell her closest friends, even less her school counsellor. Muna's position reveals how society at large, which apparently provides legal, political and social protection of human rights to all its population, seems to neglect the most vulnerable and invisible sector: immigrant girls and young women.

Dramaturgically, the play alternates the characters' monologues addressed to the audience. The predominant use of the monologue, only breaking into direct conversation twice, allows them to expose not only their inner thoughts, but also the impossibility of communication with the Western external world, thus creating a sense of helplessness on the audience. In the same vein, this dramatic form bears witness to the silence – individual and collective – by both immigrant cultural groups and Western societies on issues that evince multiculturalism's crisis:

> **Muna** It's hard not bein able to tell your best mates everythin about you, but jus' cause they're your mates, don't mean they're gonna understand. Not even I understand. What if they find out an' don't wanna roll with me no more? They think I'm a freak or summat? I'd miss them too much to tell them. (47)

To let anyone from outside her family and community know about her cutting, and that of her sister, would alienate her even further from the social background that connects her to the majority culture she willingly wants to be a part of, and would provoke the legal indictment of her family. Muna's situation reflects the impossibility of achieving Ahmed's 'promise of happiness' offered by multiculturalism. Her assimilation does not guarantee the protection of her individual rights, since she lacks any control over her body and suffers from racial discrimination. This would apparently uphold Okin's view that the private sphere of minority groups should be the object of protection by the state. FGM discloses the fallacy of assimilation for Muna and her sister by highlighting the division among women in minority communities. James states that her play was written in order to make British audiences, and specifically teenagers, aware that FGM is not a foreign, distant phenomenon that does not affect them, but which takes place around us: 'When people think of FGM they picture a girl in Africa or faraway countries with flies around their eyes and it's not: it's happening here. It's that eye-opening moment that it's happening to girls in this country.' Being conscious that FGM is still an active practice in some communities in the UK, James's aim with *Cuttin' It* is to make society take responsibility on this pressing concern: 'If you think someone is at risk of FGM don't say "it's not my business, it's not my problem, it's not my community". It's your duty to report it and it's up to the authorities to investigate' (qtd. in Brooks 2016).

As mentioned, Iqra is presented as the least assimilated – the invisible one. The hijab and the long skirt she wears literally conceal her face and body, emphasizing her otherness. This orphaned refugee of the Somali civil war clings to memories of home and conveys her British life experience in the form of an inner monologue that highlights her cultural marginalization and disconnection from the new environment:

> **Iqra**   I am the girl who has no parents any more, no brothers left. The girl living with a woman she calls her aunt, but isn't her aunt. I am the girl who has been through a real-life war, like the war they see on their televisions – the films, the news. I want to forget all that but they will not let me. (21)

Being the new girl who eats alone in the canteen, she is nevertheless thrilled to establish contact with Muna, regardless of their differences. In exchange for Iqra's kindness in offering her help when she feels dizzy on the bus, Muna offers Iqra an empathetic ear. She also lends Iqra her old iPod with pop tunes, one of them being Rihanna's 'Diamonds'. Significantly, this is the first time both monologues break into direct conversation in the play – with the corresponding eye-contact between the girls. The moment when both teenagers share the earphones and listen to the song symbolizes their union and feeling of agency in their desire to achieve recognition by the majority culture. Together they are able to express the pain which the host culture is unwilling to listen to. At another point in the retelling of her story, Iqra, who is provided psychological help by a school counsellor, realizes that this apparently integrative measure 'is not for me… it is for them. They do not want me breaking down in the halls screaming for my dead family when this Ofsted come' (22). Iqra's perspective seems to problematize the possibility of a complete assimilation through one of the main state's integrating institutions, the school, even in those countries where multiculturalism is an emblem.

The play's ending clearly manifests the split between both teenagers due to their opposite attitudes towards FGM via their exchange of words, each facing the audience on different sides of the stage. First of all, through staging two direct monologues addressed to the audience claiming '[t]his is real. They're cuttin little girls in tower blocks on a Saturday mornin… Like it's nothin' (52), the play reveals its purpose to raise awareness that FGM affects the whole society, including the white, middle-class population in mainstream audiences. Secondly, the girls' estrangement is staged through a powerful piece of stagecraft. There is a huge incision right through the set of stairs that progressively separates them into two blocks, opening a gap in the middle, which, like a neat cut, suggests the physical wound that British society refuses to heal or assume as its own. Even the red fence at the top of the staircase now evokes the bloody rite of passage narrated by the girls, who circle the gap but cannot look down directly at it, in a clear example of their difficulty to think about and express their pain. Nonetheless, there seems to be a point of contact when both compare the female body subjected to FGM to the embodiment of war:

> **Muna** An' that sickness stays with me in my pit as I make my way past the waitin' women, get to the back of the room an' see two of them lyin there, tiny bandaged bodies like casualties of war. ...
>
> **Iqra** She is next to her. Kneeling. Crying. It reminds me of when my mother found Hdafur and wouldn't leave his side. She stayed there with him like that until they came to take the body away.
>
> **Muna** Feels like a battle's jus happened. Feels like war jus took place on her body. (53)

What this exchange of words reveals is the common experience of bodily pain which, in turn, can open a space of encounter despite the girls' initial opposing views on FGM. The dramatic form consisting in intertwining monologues addressed to the audience, that results in a kind of common narrative of painful memory, elucidates the play's claim to give voice to immigrant women's silenced suffering in multicultural societies apparently welcoming and protective of all citizens' rights. Bodily pain, thus, leads to the recognition of what Judith Butler terms as the 'intertwinement' of one's life with other lives, since our pain displays the shared precariousness of human beings (2012: 140–1). The body in pain as represented by FGM opens the door to the possibility of female bonding, which eventually may lead to the eradication of female infibulation. However, the ending of *Cuttin' It* appears to deny such promise of encounter between the girls when Iqra is discovered as a voluntary assistant in Muna's sister's cutting. As a result, both teenagers become definitively separated, thus representing the two sides of the argument around FGM.

Bullet Hole: A multiple perspective from within the community

In *Bullet Hole*, directed by Lara Genovese, Williams explores the possibility of female bonding by presenting three female characters who initially stand for different perspectives on FGM. However, their pained bodies become the common ground from which to construct a shared female consciousness of their vulnerability within their communities, as well as the majority British culture. This, in turn, establishes the foundation for the development of a global feminism which gives voice to women from minority groups about their own concerns beyond the dichotomies assimilation/non-assimilation, liberated/oppressed, happy migrant/unhappy migrant, imposed by liberal multicultural and feminist views. As journalist and activist Mona Eltahawy contends, Western liberals who denounce imperialism but, simultaneously, ignore their own cultural imperialism when discarding criticism towards misogyny in the Middle East and North Africa,

> behave as if they want to save my culture and faith from me, and forget that they are immune to the violations about which I speak. Blind to the privilege and the paternalism that drive them, they give themselves the right to determine what is 'authentic' to my culture and faith. If the right wing is driven by a covert racism, the left sometimes suffers from an implicit racism through which it usurps my right to determine what I can and cannot say.... Cultures evolve through dissent and robust criticism from *their* members.
>
> (2015: 27–8; emphasis added)

In *Bullet Hole*, characters Cleo, Eve and Winnie portray three perspectives on FGM as previously mentioned. Unlike *Cuttin' It*, the characters are adults originally from Sierra Leone from different generations, who have been infibulated (FGM type 3). Cleo and Eve are referred to as 'African British', while Winnie, the matriarch, is just described as an 'African Female' (Williams 2018: xiii). Cleo suffers the dire consequences of FGM after being raped by her husband and is subsequently taken under the supervision of the other two women. Although Eve and Winnie do not recognize the act as rape, for Cleo, there is no other way of defining sexual intercourse, since her husband forces her despite the pain she experiences. Eve's situation is the reverse: her husband is unable to penetrate her due to the pain it causes him too. Feeling his virility to be diminished, he leaves her. Winnie, on the other hand, lost her son at birth due to 'complications' resulting from her stitched 'bullet hole' (41). Cleo wants to reverse the procedure, but in order to prevent her from doing so, she is sent to Aunt Winnie to reconsider her position, and thus accept the 'gift' of femininity (9). Eve, who undertakes to look after her, also suffers the consequences of infibulation as she is unable to become pregnant. This lack is compensated by adopting a motherly attitude towards Cleo as well as a devotion to beauty.

The play follows the tradition of British social realism, set in a London household interior with much emphasis placed by Eve and Winnie on feeding Cleo so that she can recover her strength and go back to her husband. The set, thus, highlights not only issues of domesticity traditionally associated with femininity – but also the fact that the domestic space is neither one of safety or belonging. Cleo is held against her will – in fact, towards the end of the play she is literally tied up by Aunt Winnie – highlighting how the home is a space of danger and oppression. The play's realism is reinforced by the use of Black British accents, references to African myth, storytelling and down-to-earth activities, such as African cooking.

Via the interaction of the three characters within a limited space, the play offers a multi-layered perspective on assimilation and loyalty to one's culture through the discussion of FGM. Eve functions as a bridge between two worlds. On the one hand, she does not judge Cleo negatively for her wish to reverse FGM, but, on the other, she views FGM as a rite of passage that sublimates femininity. This is particularly reflected in her memories of the Bondo ceremony, which she conceives as a moment of female bonding and empowerment:

> **Eve** I never blackout when I think 'bout my Bondo ceremony. People be tweetin' sayin' 'it's trauma', 'it's a crime', 'we need help'. But naw – how can it be when I just love to remember the sound of them drums – you remember your drums? Dem, dem drum beats dat let the whole bush know dat you are a woman. That's why I think I love to dance... them drums beatin' in my heart, got every woman in the forest dancing and cheering for me. (12)

Cleo, however, sees the ceremony as a tradition that cuts their bodies as well as their voices. For most of the play's first scenes, Cleo is silent and does not reply to Eve's entreaties – at times she screams as the only way to express the unspeakable. Physical pain, as Elaine Scarry highlights, 'does not simply resist language but actively destroys it, bringing about an immediate reversion to a state anterior to language, to the sounds and cries a human being makes before language is learned' (1985: 4). Notably, Cleo sleeps with and carries the doll she was given at the ceremony, signalling her desire to return to her childhood before being cut.

When Cleo directly challenges the community by threatening to report on them to the authorities, she is literally tied up at Winnie's command. Winnie embodies African cultural resistance to what she perceives as colonization, dismissing healthcare workers as people who see themselves as their 'saviours' for wanting to 'fix' their bodies (8), while being also aware that for a sector of British society they are 'like sum research project' (11). Winnie regards FGM as a means of protecting women's bodies from sexual abuse. The reversal surgery, so she tells Cleo, 'makes you an open target' (8).

Ironically, Cleo was submitted to FGM at seven precisely to protect her after confessing to her father, uncle played footsie with da 'dirty' 'tween my legs' (13). Nonetheless, for Cleo the reversal process implies recovering the voice of her mind and body, the uncutting of her lips to express herself verbally and sexually, an imagery that is explicitly represented in the play's poster, where the characters appear with sewed lips. Hers will be the final process which Eve's body had initiated of its own accord at the beginning of the play, when she explained how her stitches were beginning to stretch: 'Now one side of the stitch peeks through like it don't wanna be no secret no more – like it ain't forbidden...' (1). For Cleo, female bonding consists in protecting other girls from undergoing the cutting by voicing her Bondo experience and its painful consequences, in the same way that Muna wants to prevent her sister's infibulation ('I wanted to protect other girlz. That's da power that a dream and a needle should make' (13)). In this case, the binary opposition is built upon the antagonistic attitudes towards FGM from within the minority community, and not so much based on the level of assimilation into the majority culture. Williams does not offer a straightforward perspective whereby assimilation is equated to condemning FGM and non-assimilation to its acceptance, as in *Cuttin' It*, whose binary approach is highlighted due to the play's didactic purpose. *Bullet Hole* focuses on the opposing perspectives of women who suffer from FGM within a minority community so as to give them a voice and thus deconstruct such a hierarchical cultural dichotomy. As Pedwell highlights, 'In a historical context in which African women's bodies have been routinely fetishized, pathologized and violated by westerners, interventions in discourses relating to FGC by feminists speaking from western locations, have been perceived by many indigenous African women as ethnocentric and imperialist' (2007: 61).

In *Bullet Hole*, by giving voice to these women, Williams disrupts the cultural hegemony of the Western feminist empathetic gaze thus disassociating notions of cultural difference from assumptions of progress or regression. Cleo's aim is to make the other two women acknowledge their pain in order to make the problematic of FGM visible, which would ultimately create a common consciousness for African British women. In fact, as a reflection of her commitment with this cause, in *Bullet Hole*'s production at the Park Theatre, Cleo was played by the author, who declared in an interview that her aim was to 'get people thinking about female genital mutilation' in order for it to be considered a 'national issue' (qtd. in Masso 2018).

As a result, pain is clearly the central motif of the play. As Christina Carè in her review for *LondonTheatre1* states, the characters expose on stage 'all the pain and conflict of a community tradition in direct contradiction of both their bodies and a modern, Western lifestyle'. The suffering of each woman is not merely an individual, physical experience, but one that represents how the female body has been used as the 'battleground of cultural, religious and gendered expectations' (2018), in this case, those of a Sierra Leone community in the UK. In *Bullet Hole*, the voicing of their experience is based on real testimonies from women subjected to FGM, as offered by diverse NGOs, NHS midwives and various institutions supporting survivors. In giving voice to FGM victims, the play can be aligned with what Eltahawy describes as her right as a Muslim woman 'to critique both my culture and my faith in ways that I would reject from an outsider. I expose misogyny in my part of the world to connect the feminist struggle in the Middle East and North Africa to the global one' (2015: 29). This use of pain to effect a critique from within is shown by Cleo when she confronts Aunt Winnie with the physical and psychological suffering of having lost her baby boy in childbirth due to infibulation. This is potentially the first step to bond with Winnie, who embodies FGM practices as a form of cultural conservation. It might also enable Winnie to achieve consciousness of patriarchal control over the female body:

Winnie   Why? Why do you want to do this?

Cleo   For my peace of mind. They can fix the problem with the construction of the narrowing. Can you believe that! They say it's a reversal Aunt Winnie. A reversal! You can pee naturally and *give birth naturally*! You can really really live!

Winnie *(pause)*   That's what you believe is it?
Pause.
   I see... *(Beat)* Nobody hears me. Our type have healthy babies all the time. It's misleading. What?! A 'reversal', *please*. It is not gold dust and it is not going to undo anything. These fake rumours about horror births. There's a separate God for children.

Cleo   You went into labour with Gabriel your son? Right Aunt Winnie? Your third pregnancy?

Winnie   So?

Cleo   Wasn't he meant to be a year younger than me?
Pause.
   You carried him for the full nine months and then what happened?

Winnie   There were complications. (39–40)

However, even though Cleo and Eve bond at the end of the play, Winnie's position remains unchanged. The painful consequences of FGM for the three characters ignite in a British audience, not only the awareness that the practice exists within its modern and supposedly integrated society, but also that the experience of suffering is common to all bodies.

Conclusions

By giving voice to FGM survivors, James and Williams highlight the need for Western women to listen to their non-Western counterparts in their common struggle against omnipresent patriarchy. As Eltahawy underlines, the way to eradicate misogyny 'is for each of us to expose and to fight against local versions of it, in the understanding that by doing so we advance the global against the hatred of women' (2015: 29). Eltahawy's global feminist perspective, which can be identified in *Bullet Hole*, contrasts with the dichotomy present in *Cuttin' It*. The point of connection between the pieces lies on how the characters in both plays offer the audience their personal experiences about the consequences of FGM from within their specific cultural context and away from the majority culture's point of view, in an attempt to overcome the possible appropriation of their narratives on pain by the 'privileged western subject' (Pedwell 2007: 60).

The crisis of multiculturalism as a discourse is particularly enhanced in its interaction with feminism, since the latter insists on female agency based on the control of one's body. The body, thus, becomes a discursive battlefield over women's empowerment, based on binary oppositions such as assimilation/non-assimilation, Western empathetic gaze/minority cultural resistance. In James's and Williams's plays, the contradictions and inequalities inherent in multiculturalism are exposed via the pain of the culturally, and physically, scarred female bodies.

The range of characters in both plays provides a picture of heterogeneity within minority cultures that subverts reductionist received notions that construe them as impermeable blocks. The ultimate aim of such a problematization of minority groups would be to raise awareness on the audience as to the complexity of FGM affecting young immigrant and British women and girls in a liberal, democratic society, underlining that it is not an issue relegated to distant countries. In their own specific ways, the plays suggest that the dichotomies often resorted to by liberal multiculturalism and feminism provide a limiting framework to represent the diverse perspectives on FGM within the affected communities. Both James and Williams offer an inside-outside look through characters who display their inside and outside position within mainstream culture, while retaining strong bonds with their minority communities. Such a take on the issue, as Catherine Riley proclaims (in Riley and Pearce 2018: 101–2), would stand as a kind of corrective to hierarchical attitudes in relation to race and cultural difference, reflecting the necessity to advocate a more global feminism whereby the history, culture and politics of the immigrants' communities are not merely included, but prioritized as a means of linking their experiences to those of Western women.

References

Ahmed, S. (2017), 'Multiculturalism and the Promise of Happiness', in C. R. McCann and S.-K. Kim (eds), *Feminist Theory Reader: Local and Global Perspectives*, 539–54, New York and London: Routledge.

Brooks, L. (2016), 'Interview: Playwright Charlene James', *Culture Whisper*, 11 May. Available online: https://www.culturewhisper.com/r/things_to_do/interview_charlene_james_cuttin_it_play/6972 (accessed 3 October 2020).

Butler, J. (2012), 'Precarious Life, Vulnerability, and the Ethics of Cohabitation', *Journal of Speculative Philosophy*, 26 (2): 134–51.

Carè, C. (2018), '*Bullet Hole* by Gloria Williams at Park Theatre: Review', *LondonTheatre1*, 7 October. Available online: https://www.londontheatre1.com/reviews/bullet-hole-by-gloria-williams-at-park-theatre-review/ (accessed 3 October 2020).

Cohen, J., M. Howard and M. C. Nussbaum (eds) (1999), *Is Multiculturalism Bad for Women? Susan Moller Okin with Respondents*, Princeton: Princeton University Press.

Collier, R. (2016), 'How Charlene James' Play *Cuttin' It* Is Introducing Audiences to the Reality of FGM in Britain', *New Statesman*, 12 July. Available online: https://www.newstatesman.com/culture/music-theatre/2016/07/how-charlene-james-play-cuttin-it-introducing-audiences-reality-fgm (accessed 3 October 2020).

The Cruel Cut (2013), [Documentary] Dir. Vicki Cooper, UK: Love Productions.

Eltahawy, M. (2015), *Headscarves and Hymens: Why the Middle East Needs a Sexual Revolution*, London: Weidenfeld & Nicolson.

Goddard, L. (2007), *Staging Black Feminisms: Identity, Politics, Performance*, Basingstoke and New York: Palgrave Macmillan.

James, C. (2016), *Cuttin' It*, London: Faber & Faber.

Kymlicka, W. (1989), *Liberalism, Community and Culture*, Oxford: Oxford University Press.

Kymlicka, W. (1995), *Multicultural Citizenship: A Liberal Theory of Minority Rights*, Oxford: Oxford University Press.

Lentin, A. and G. Titley (2011), *The Crises of Multiculturalism: Racism in a Neoliberal Age*, London and New York: Zed Books.

Masso, G. (2018), 'Playwright Gloria Williams: "I Want to Get People Thinking about Female Genital Mutilation"', *The Stage*, 1 October. Available online: https://www.thestage.co.uk/features/interviews/2018/playwright-gloria-williams-i-want-to-get-people-thinking-about-female-genital-mutilation/ (accessed 3 October 2020).

Modood, T. (2007), *Multiculturalism: A Civic Idea*, Cambridge: Polity Press.

Okin, S. M. (1998), 'Feminism and Multiculturalism: Some Tensions', *Ethics*, 108 (4): 661–84.

Okin, S. M. (1999), 'Is Multiculturalism Bad for Women?', in J. Cohen, M. Howard and M. C. Nussbaum (eds), *Is Multiculturalism Bad for Women? Susan Moller Okin with Respondents*, 7–26, Princeton: Princeton University Press.

Parekh, B. (2000), *Rethinking Multiculturalism: Cultural Diversity and Political Theory*, Cambridge: Harvard University Press.

Pedwell, C. (2007), 'Theorizing "African" Female Genital Cutting and "Western" Body Modifications: A Critique of the Continuum and Analogue Approaches', *Feminist Review*, 86: 45–66.

Pedwell, C. (2011), 'The Limits of Cross-Cultural Analogy: Muslim Veiling and "Western" Fashion and Beauty Practices', in R. Gill and C. Scharff (eds), *New Femininities: Postfeminism, Neoliberalism, Subjectivity*, 188–99, Basingstoke and London: Palgrave Macmillan.

Riley, C. (2018), 'Ethnicity', in C. Riley and L. Pearce (eds), *Feminism and Women's Writing: An Introduction*, 94–109, Edinburgh: Edinburgh University Press.

Scarry, E. (1985), *The Body in Pain: The Making and Unmaking of the World*, New York and Oxford: Oxford University Press.

Urwin, R. (2016), 'Playwright Charlene James: We Must Stop Saying FGM Is a Cultural Thing: It's Child Abuse', *Evening Standard*, 18 May. Available online: https://www.standard.co.uk/culture/theatre/playwright-charlene-james-we-must-stop-saying-fgm-is-a-cultural-thing-it-s-child-abuse-a3251196.html (accessed 12 February 2021).

Williams, G. (2018), *Bullet Hole*, London and New York: Samuel French.

Williams, Z. (2013), '*The Cruel Cut*; One Born: What Happened Next?', *Guardian*, 7 November. Available online: https://www.theguardian.com/tv-and-radio/2013/nov/07/the-cruel-cut-tv-review (accessed 7 December 2020).

Zerilli, L. M. G. (2009), 'Toward a Feminist Theory of Judgement', *Signs*, 34 (2): 295–317.

Part Five

New directions

11

'Imaging' crisis: Photodramas in focus

Elisabeth Angel-Perez

The recent development of 'risk studies' and of 'hazards research' (Burgess, Alemanno and Zinn 2016; The UCL Hazard Center 2021) corroborates the fact that crisis is no longer a situation of exception but a *régime de croisière*, a *modus vivendi* in our post-millennial world. Crisis has become structural. The proclamation of a Covid-related state of emergency, protracted for months on end in many countries has allowed governments to restrict the citizens' liberties, thus turning crisis into normality. Emergencies are neither fewer nor punctual but have become a recurrent, not to say constant, catalyst in the advent of personal or collective transformations or even of the status quo. Yet inside this life-long situation of crisis, some particular moments single themselves out as cases of emergencies, cases of crisis-within-the-crisis, meta-crises so to speak.

If crisis is theatrical by nature and has precisely always been the subject of drama – it constitutes the kernel of traditional and well-made theatre and functions as the point of convergence towards which all action is heading – today it keeps challenging playwrights and urging them to experiment with new forms to capture the unrest of our times (Angelaki 2017). While in the 1990s British theatre was marked by an overaggressive frontality and graphic representation exemplified by the early work of Sarah Kane and Mark Ravenhill, then it has also developed an In-Yer-Ear aesthetics based on narrativization or epicization, as evidenced in plays by Martin Crimp or Alice Birch. A myriad of other strategies, from participative theatre which addresses issues of terrorism or political crisis (such as David Greig's 2010 *The Events* or his 2013–14 Twitter-based project, *The Yes/No Plays*, on the Scottish independence referendum) to verbatim theatre which foregrounds the experience of the crisis of the Middle East (Jonathan Holmes's 2007 *Fallujah*, Gregory Burke's 2007 *Black Watch*), have offered fascinating redefinitions of the genre of political theatre. Poetically, crises may spur unstoppable logorrheas contrasting with infra-verbality or aphonia (as in debbie tucker green's 2018 *ear for eye*), or paradoxically trigger a catastrophic laughter as is the case with Caryl Churchill's 2016 *Escaped Alone* or with Nick Gill's witty yet sordid plays about pre-Brexit grotesque little-Englandism (*Mirror Teeth* 2011) or about Abu Ghraib (*Fiji Land* 2014). Crisis, it seems, acts as a dramaturgic impulsion. Among all these inventive new modalities, a new theatrical aesthetics seems to emerge which, as I intend to show, allows for an unusual take on what the concept of crisis covers, taking its cue from photography.

Crises (from Greek verb *krinein* meaning 'to judge' and 'to decide') always capture the decisive moment, the pith, a temporality that may come close to what the Greeks called *kairos*. They occur at the crucial moment when a choice has to be made, precisely when the tipping point is reached, thereby interrogating what Anne Dufourmantelle calls 'our intimate relation to time' (2011: 12).[1] Moments of crisis foreground the present and require making urgent decisions and taking risks. Risk-taking, which is constitutive of crises, opens an unknown space which places the protagonist in an unprecedented, even pristine, state of ontological suspension. This state of ontological suspension, characterized by an in-between liminality, a state of undecidability – hovering between life and death, resilience and doom, 'teetering at the edge, between improvement or decline' (Angelaki 2017: 2) – is also the 'noeme' of photography. In its capacity to open a temporality of its own, a 'heterochrony' (Foucault 1984: 46–9) often verging on spectrality – photography is always concerned with the negative of the event – but also on immortality. Roland Barthes in *Camera Lucida* defines photography as a 'micro-experience of death', declaring that photography dwells in the 'future perfect' (2010: 150).

It is therefore not surprising that among the various dramatic forms prompted by situations of crisis, photo-based dramas stand out as particularly innovative not only in expressing the referentiality of historical traumatic events (as Barthes puts it, 'this has been' or 'it was there' (120)), but also in rendering palpable the sense of ontological suspension attached to the notion of crisis. They open up both a possibility for risk and newness and a sense of bereavement, since making a choice implies the possibility of mourning that which has not been chosen. Focusing on Simon Stephens's *Rage* (2018), inspired by Joel Goodman's 2016 Manchester New Year celebrations photographs, Lucy Kirkwood's *Chimerica* (2013) and Chris Thorpe's *There Has Possibly Been an Incident* (2013), (partly) based on Jeff Widener's famous photograph 'Tank Man' (or 'The Tiananmen Protester'), I will here contend that in these plays, photography, insofar as it is essentially linked to the temporality of crisis, functions both as a thematic inspiration and as a dramaturgic and poietic method. The plays, just as photography already 'engraves' the subject it represents, build an altogether different kind of visuality based on a sense of loss while concomitantly opening a space for transition.

---

[1] All translations by the author unless otherwise specified.

Photography, theatre and 'dramatic pressure points of history'

Crisis – a moment when meaning collapses – is brilliantly captured by photographs that hit on the emblematic gesture or posture and succeed in metonymically conjuring up the whole situation at once. Recently a corpus has emerged, politically engaged and even at times militant, which brings together plays federated by their being photo-based. These photodramas, as I will call them, have not only been inspired by the various critical historical events taking place in the world – crises, be they economic, ecological or political, when seen through the prism of photography allow us to conceive of 'the dramatic pressure points of history' (Starn 1971: 12) – but take their cue from an iconosource. Based on a series of photographs entitled 'New Years Night Revellers' by Joel Goodman, Simon Stephens' 2016 play *Rage* experiments with the photodrama form as a reaction to the state of contemporary Britain in the aftermath of the Brexit referendum. Goodman's photos captured the violent, chaotic atmosphere of the 2015 New Year's Eve celebrations in Manchester; they were first published in the *Manchester Evening News* before circulating widely in the media. Stephens had been asked by his long-term German collaborator Sebastian Nübling to write a play in response to Nobel Laureate Elfriede Jelinek's new drama, *Wut*, written after the Charlie Hebdo attack in Paris in January 2015. In his Preface to the play, Stephens explains that he decided to focus on the rage he experienced during the final months before the Brexit referendum:

> There was much about Britain that was making me furious and a sense of increasing anger throughout the country. But nevertheless I didn't have an anchor. I needed something to steady my anger if I was going to be able to make something for [Nübling] ... And then, in the first weeks of 2016 I saw Joel Goodman's photographs of the New Year's Eve around Well Street in Manchester.
>
> (2018: iii)

Stephens dedicated one hour every day of March to writing a scene inspired by almost each of the thirty-one photographs making up Goodman's series.[2] All of them, he wrote, were '[a] chaotic disordered exploration of rage for a culture of chaotic disorder ... Nights like the night on which Goodman saw humanity fracture. Through their booze and chaos and pure, distilled anger,

---

[2] These photos are accessible on Joel Goodman's site: https://joelgoodman.net/2016/12/31/press-photographer-2016-viral/new-years-night-revellers/.

they are events of dehumanization. I wanted to capture that' (2018: v). The play therefore is a montage, or even a collage, of these many extrapolations and variations inspired by the heart-felt rage experienced simultaneously by the community and by the playwright himself.

The play stages a range of protagonists as midnight is about to chime on New Year's Eve in 'a major British city' – among whom Sister and Brother going to a party, Ralph Lauren and the Girl Who Sparkles's impromptu love declaration, violent passengers in public transportation, a Man With Sideburns and a Woman With A Bag arguing, and of course police officers. Goodman's photos inspire the play its fragmented and chaotic structure: a rhapsodical juxtaposition of brief vignettes which read like a disorganized series of snapshots. These scenes read as images of a community whose crisis is emblematically epitomized and exacerbated on this particular night, as well as the objective correlative of Stephens's own furious frame of mind. The most well-known photo – one that went viral on the internet – represents police officers detaining a man whilst another lies in the middle of the road still reaching out towards a bottle of alcohol nearby, around them revellers are enjoying a New Year night out at the bars and clubs of Manchester City Centre.[3] This photo has been described by Stephens as capturing 'the sense of dislocation and disorder of a country that, as it voted to dismantle its own economic security by leaving the EU, seemed to be committing a kind of suicide. It captured completely what I felt when I considered rage or fury in my country at that time' (2018: iv).

Optical unconscious

The published version of the play is slightly different from the one that was staged in Germany, as Stephens wanted to give the collage a dramaturgy of his own that would grant the play its total autonomy (in regards to both Jelinek's play and Goodman's series). Consequently, Stephens reorganized the series of scenes in collaboration with the students of the Royal Welsh College of Music and Drama who were working on the play (Stephens 2018: v). In Nübling's production at the Thalia Theater, Hamburg in 2016, Goodman's photos were projected on a screen while Stephens's text constructed what I would call a sort of unconscious for them. The link between photography and the unconscious has been elaborated by Freud, who often took photography (and its negatives) as a metaphor to speak of the unconscious. Yet perhaps a more appropriate tool for thinking of crisis

---

[3] See Joel Goodman's site: https://joelgoodman.photoshelter.com/gallery/01-01-2016-New-Years-Day/G0000AoNW9V4e170.

as a possible moment of transition is Walter Benjamin's notion of 'optical unconscious' (Benjamin 1999; Kofman 1973).[4] Even though Benjamin was afraid that the proliferation of images and photographs might obstruct our perception of things, he thought of photography as retaining a capacity to capture phenomena that only the unconscious was able to perceive. In other words, photography reveals an optical unconscious. What Simon Stephens proposes with his series of fractured vignettes and loose characterization is precisely that: he allows for the scenes to render this optical unconscious conspicuous. Each scene – almost a response to Caryl Churchill's twenty-five repetitions of the phrase 'Terrible rage' in *Escaped Alone* (2016: 42) – evokes one fragment of a 'fractured psychosis':

> The psychosis of *Rage* is fractured, and sexually needy, incoherent, drunken, sometimes racist and terrified. I think it is so because that state is what Goodman captured in his photographs on that New Year's night, and it is what I recognized as being a defining tone of the country I lived in as it plunged its way towards economic self-destruction at the start of that year.
>
> (2018: vi)

Stephens brings our attention to the fact that only a few characters in his scenes have a name, therefore somehow preserving the anonymity of the photos, as he wanted them to be 'manifestations of feeling or tone rather than imagined human beings' (2018: v). The photographs – topical as they are – similarly provide us with the comprehensive idea of the situation in its dense complexity rather than with the mere situation itself. Stephens places words inside the photo's mute characters' mouths, turning them into the representatives of their social group performing their 'habitus' (Bourdieu 1980: 187) and speaking out the conclusions they were determined (as in urged by a determinism) to reach. Hence the infamous and outrageous passenger's speech in the eighth scene spits out the xenophobia and racism which, according to Stephens, explained the Brexit vote:

> **Passenger** He's not a gentleman. Don't call him a gentleman. He's not a gentleman. He's a fucking Paki. He's a fucking nigger. He's a fucking Al Qaeda he is. He's a raghead fucking ISIS cunt.
>
> (2018: 19)

---

[4] Sarah Kofman's seminal study of the links between photography and Freud's theory of the unconscious offers a highly stimulating elaboration of the Benjaminian concept of optical unconscious and helps bridge the gap between the collective and the individual subject's unconscious in crisis.

The photographs prompt a hyper realistic dialogue which connotes not only a psychological state but also an almost Brechtian *gestus* allowing for the individual crisis to be seen as the locus of the collective national crisis.

Photogenic theatre

This same correlation between the individual and the collective was already what prompted Stephens in his particular use of the sadly well-known Abu Ghraib photographs in *Motortown* (dir. Ramin Gray, Royal Court Theatre, 2006). In this play, 'manifestly a play *about* something – Abu Ghraib', as Billy Smart puts it in a polemical and much commented upon text (2016; emphasis original), Stephens tells us of Danny, who is returning from Iraq only to find that he no longer recognizes the country for which he has fought. The Iraq War veteran, inspired or haunted by the images of torture-as-power promoted by the barbaric photographs, takes one picture of each new act of torture he performs on his fourteen-year-old victim, who happens to be a young, Black woman. The Abu Ghraib photographs, epitomizing the acme of the Iraq War,[5] have been commented upon by Judith Butler in *Frames of War*. These photos, in particular those staging woman soldier Lynndie England, dressed as a dominatrix, with a naked Iraqi prisoner at the end of a leash, have become icons of American barbarity. Just as, for the perpetrators, the Abu Ghraib photos acted as an ontological proof of the American domination, Danny's photos not only perform his dominance but provide it with a reality of its own (Al-Azraqi 2017; Fragkou 2019: 196). Butler is concerned with the ethics of 'embedded reporting'. She points to the fact that the photo of the event creates the apex of the ethical crisis almost more so than the event itself:

> By regulating perspective in addition to content, the state authorities were clearly interested in regulating the visual modes of participation in the war. Seeing was tacitly understood as linked with the occupation of a position and, indeed, a certain disposition of the subject itself. A second place in which embedded reporting implicitly occurred was in the Abu Ghraib photographs. The camera angle, the frame, the posed subjects, all suggest that those who took the photographs were actively involved in the perspective of the war, elaborating that perspective, crafting, commending, and validating a point of view.
>
> (2009: 65)

---

[5] Susan Sontag coins this phrase in reference to Bergen-Belsen and Dachau (1977: 19).

As shown by Marion Coste (2021), in *Motortown*, the photographer becomes a stage director of sorts: he does 'not only organize visual experience but also generates specific ontologies of the subject' (Butler 2009: 3). The image provides a surplus of being to the event.

By his recourse to photography, Stephens makes it explicit that theatre is not only a seismograph of the crises, it is photogenic in that it augments the *ontos* of the referential reality. The photogenic covers 'any aspect of things, beings and souls which has its moral quality augmented by cinematographic reproduction. And any aspect that is not enhanced by cinematic reproduction is not photogenic, is not part of the art of cinema' (Epstein qtd. in Aumont et al. 1999: 115). Theatre and crisis share the same paroxysmic ethos.

Crisis and *kairos*: Anatomizing crisis

More specifically capturing the precise moment of the crisis, a number of plays concentrate not on the metonymic representation of the whole critical situation, but on the indeterminacy of the pending moment. Buttressed by Hannah Arendt's vision of what a crisis is, sociology has recently shown that the acme of the crisis may be an opportunity. In *Between Past and Future*, Arendt explains that what characterizes a crisis is the fact that it cuts us off from our culture and experience. She claims that tragedy began 'when it turned out that there was no mind to inherit and to question, to think about and to remember'. She insists that '[i]n every crisis a piece of the world, something common to us all, is destroyed. The failure of common sense, like a divining rod, points to the place where such a cave-in has occurred' (1961: 6, 178). A crisis conjures up a radically new situation, an unexpected element of novelty, what one calls an 'event' (Alain Badiou describes the event as 'the outlaw of the situations' (1988: 38)). One is yet to discover who they are in this unprecedented face to face between oneself and the situation that confronts one with one's yet unknown (in)capacity to adapt one's response so as to continue building the world for oneself and for the community. For Arendt, if one can address this event with an equally unprecedented type of answer, then this event can be turned into an almost 'new mundane beginning', allowing the world to be 'bound back once more' or else in terms of 'miracles' and 'infinite improbabilities' (1961: 126, 169). More recently, sociologist Michel Dobry has both acknowledged and interrogated this position. Although less adamant than Bourdieu on the subject of the inevitable regression towards the habitus even in times of unrest (Bourdieu 1972), Dobry claims that although a crisis can open broader choices and horizons for the subject in a critical situation (he even speaks of 'creative effervescence') than the ones they have at their disposal in more routine-based or steady contexts (2009: 257–74), it very often ends up in a restructuration of habits which does not allow stepping out of the crisis.

The becoming-hero

The plays I am concerned with in this section anatomize the momentum of the crisis by focusing on the specific temporality it opens. A decision has to be made urgently, a risk has to be taken one way or another, as to what to do or what not to do. It is this precise moment – the *kairos* of the crisis – which is captured, for example, in a photo as well known as the 'Tank Man' or the 'Unknown Protester'. Although several photographs captured the moment, perhaps the most famous is the one taken by Jeff Widener.[6] It features an unknown Chinese protester who stood in front of a column of tanks on Tiananmen Square on 5 June 1989, the day after the massacre repressing the workers and students' demonstrations for more democracy and less corruption. The photo, which became viral around the world, grasps the situation at its most unstable, ready to tilt over one way or the other: either the Republic of China's super powerful army – embodied by the soldier who appears in command of the first tank – is going to crush the man in the street (literally) in yet another display of state violence or the man in the street, standing all by himself, will succeed in stopping them. This image, tragically emblematic, is the matrix of Lucy Kirkwood's *Chimerica* (2013) – a term coined by economist Niall Ferguson that collapses China and America – as well as of part of Chris Thorpe's *There Has Possibly Been an Incident* (2013). Whereas Kirkwood elaborates from the enigmatic Unknown Protester's life and retraces the genesis of the situation, Thorpe addresses the question of heroism and of risk-taking which is central to the notions of crisis and of *kairos*.

Kirkwood's play, which was adapted by Kirkwood herself for a Channel 4 mini-series in 2019, premiered at the Almeida Theatre in London in May 2013 in a production directed by Lindsey Turner. Providing the photograph with a genesis and therefore helping reframe the frame, *Chimerica* tells the story of photojournalist Joe Schofield who tries to find out who the Tank Man was. He undertakes this mission with the help of his Chinese friend, Zhang Lin, who cannot get over the death of his fiancée murdered during the slaughter. This double quest sheds light on the political relationships between China and the United States, and the way China squanders its

---

[6] The 'Tank Man' photo is available on: http://www.jeffwidener.com/stories/2016/09/tankman/.

freedom of speech for economic prosperity. What Kirkwood's play reveals is that the Unknown Protester's act, an icon for dissent, may precisely not have been an act of dissent, but an act of despair. After the hospital nurse has announced the tragic news to Zhang Lin and packed up his dead fiancée's clothes in two white grocery bags, he is shown '*turn[ing] to us*': '*We are looking, for the first time, at a front view of the Tank Man*' (Kirkwood 2013: 135):

> *A lighting change. ZHANG LIN walks, into the gallery. He has reached the avenue. ZHANG LIN turns. His back, more familiar view. The tanks approach. ZHANG LIN walks into the tank's path. ZHANG LIN's movements are synchronised with the projected, real film of the Tank Man. JOE, and we, watch it with the knowledge of who this man is for the first time. Of how he came to be there and what is in his bags.* (135)

The whole situation enables the understanding that the rebel is probably not the Unknown Protester, but the soldier in command of the first tank who takes the risk not to run over the dissenter. Drawing on Howard Becker's conceptualization of deviance (1963), I suggest the play 'images' the crisis not only as depending on the decision of a protagonist but on the interaction between the dissenter and those around him who invent and implement the norms. The moment of decision making may be more excruciating for the soldier who embodies the norm than for the protester who is driven by a sense of doom, colliding his lethal grief with both his anger and his hubris. The officer's deviance, which opens an unprecedented chronotope of risk-taking, gives the play its tragic, yet investigative, structure while focusing on the 'becoming-hero' of the protagonists.

Similarly, the 'becoming-hero' of the ordinary person is the subject of Chris Thorpe's photodrama *There Has Possibly Been an Incident*. The play was part of the 2013 edition of the Edinburgh Fringe Festival (Northern Stage, St Stephens). Chris Thorpe always addresses sociopolitical issues – access to health care, hypercapitalism and cell phone dependence as in *I Wish I Was Lonely* (2013), co-written with poet Hannah Jane Walker. In his recent *Mysteries* (2018), Thorpe delivers six State-of-the-Nation plays in which he gives an account of the critical situations he has experienced in person by immersing himself in six different rural communities. For him, theatre is the place of a 'conversation' with the public, in the etymological sense of the word which means 'to be with', and above all a space dedicated to collective introspection (Gardner 2015). He holds theatre as the place for an ethical reflection on human action in and on the world. *There Has Possibly Been an Incident*, directed by Sam Pritchard at the Royal Exchange

Theatre (Manchester) with Gemma Brockis (G), Nigel Barrett (N) and Yusra Warsama (Y) interweaves three fragmented narratives, one of them developing from an identifiable photographic matrix, again the 'Tank Man', whereas the two others are only very likely to have developed from a photo as well, although none are immediately recognizable.[7] All of them, however, conjure up an identifiable episode of a recent political or human crisis in which the narrator experiences a feeling of doubt and emergency as to his role and commitment in the situation. In between these three narrative threads, are six dialogues in which one speaker interrogates the other. Though never named, it becomes clear that these dialogues are between the police and Norwegian terrorist Anders Breivik. The police's rational questions confront the implacably terrifying supremacist vision of Breivik who slaughtered 77 people in Oslo and Utøya and wounded 151 on 22 July 2011. The play ends with a moment of shared enunciation or chorus between the three actors on the stage voicing the police who heroically arrested Breivik. Thorpe is concerned with experiencing and having the audience experience the crises he is talking about and posits crises as specific moments when the ordinary person may qualify as what Haïm Burstin calls a 'protagonist'. The concept of 'Protagonism' that the sociology of crisis claims for itself, borrows from the terminology of theatre and refers to a network of behaviours by which a person, out of participation, self-celebration, spontaneity or even unintentionality, becomes a self-determined actor of their own freedom and destiny by their intervention in public life (Burstin et al. 2015).

The first narrative thread is unravelled by G, a revolutionary woman. Repeated references to a scene on a balcony are suggestive, among other possibilities,[8] of the overthrow of Ceausescu, a crisis also at the centre of Caryl Churchill's 1990 play, *Mad Forest*. A number of famous photographs were taken on 21 December 1989, when Ceausescu appeared on the balcony of the Communist Party Building in Bucharest. Instead of greeting him, the crowd started chanting 'Timisoara' to the point that the leader had to take refuge inside the building as riots broke out. Although soon after Ceausescu and his wife Elena escaped the building by helicopter, they were promptly captured and executed.

Because of the accidental gesture of one of her partners, who lifted his hand, G finds herself propelled to the forefront of the stage, turned into first

---

[7] The role played by Yusra (Y) was played by Chris Thorpe himself in the early stages of the productions so that C may replace Y in certain versions of the play. Sam Pritchard's production transferred to the Soho Theatre in London (2013).

[8] It could also beckon, for instance, towards the Jasmine Revolution in Tunisia which saw the exile of the Ben Alis.

a revolutionary leader and then into the leader of a repression. The third narrative thread is that of Y, possibly a passenger of the Turkish Airlines crash (also known as the 'Poldercrash') that took place on 25 February 2009 (Thorpe 2017). The crash landing of Turkish Airlines Flight 1951 resulted in nine fatalities (126 passengers out of the 135 survived). The small boy whom Y could perhaps have saved dies in the plane's explosion: the heroic act fails to happen. The second narrative thread, which will be my main focus, is that which explicitly has the Tank Man as its matrix. N is the ocular witness of what happened on Tiananmen Square on the second day of the repression. The crisis is pungent: N has to decide in the spur of the moment whether he will join the anonymous hero in front of the tanks.

Paradoxically, Thorpe does not show us the matricial photograph(s), nor does he decide to have the actors enact the actions. On the contrary, all there is to see is the line made up by the three speakers sitting on their chairs with their (fake and never read) scripts in hand. The audience is given an aural *ekphrasis* of the photograph.

Adding pathos to these situations of crisis, these voices anchor their enunciators in the event as would be protagonists grappling with the issue of heroism, responsibility and ethical action (resisting State oppression and then enforcing it, saving a child in a plane crash, solidarity with heroic actions). Thorpe anatomizes minds in a state of crisis; the characters must decide in the twinkling of an eye whether to act or not – 'Y. something has happened or something has failed to happen' (38) – and in this particular moment of decision what is at stake is their unicity, their serenity, their atonement. Thorpe's photo-based play precisely dramatizes the undecidability of the situation, the suspense or suspension of time that alters the linear temporality and opens a heterochrony. Faced with this unprecedented situation, the protagonist may find that a new definition of themselves is at hand (this is the Marxist point of view) or may find that old determinisms are being reassessed (habitus), what Pierre Bourdieu theorizes as the 'hysteresis', a word he uses to describe the discrepancy between changing field conditions and habitus (Bourdieu 1972: 178–9). Whereas Y tries but fails to rescue the little boy, N, speaking out the unknown protester's thoughts in front of the tanks, endorses both his own capitulation as well as the apprehensive becoming-hero of Tank Man. N, a witness to the scene, maybe the photographer himself, does not join the unknown protester in spite of his inviting look, conveying both his own demise and the protester's stream of consciousness:

N. Tanks are fucking big. And I wish I'd put my shopping down. But can't do that now. Because the weight of these cabbages is the only thing stopping me from running away. The only thing keeping me on the ground. (42)

The photograph emblematizing the political crisis gives the play this sense of temporal and ontological suspension:

> **N.** A crowd waiting for something to happen. Something big is happening, but the centre of that thing has deserted us, temporarily, and faded to just a low rumble in the air. A vibration in the ground and a few scraps of something, maybe paper, maybe what used to be paper but is now ash in the shape of paper, suspended in still spring air and a vibration and a low rumble and someone has to decide what happens next. (21)

This frozen stasis, an omen of both slaughter and resistance, is a 'becoming' which has already been. Thorpe senses the 'hermeneutic manna' enclosed in the image (Bailly 2005: 126). He somehow, here again, recreates an optical unconscious for this photograph. Benjamin's concept allows for a perception of photography as pointing backwards but also forward, towards a future: 'he seized upon this temporal disruption as key to photography's revolutionary optical unconscious' (Smith and Sliwinski 2017: 19).

Obliteration

Moreover, the suspension contained in the image justifies the photograph being abstracted from the play as if a sense of apnoea contaminated the very poietic devised by Thorpe. The 'centre' that 'has deserted us' digs a hole in the middle of the text so as to voice the wound, the trauma – and trauma and 'trou' (hole) share the same etymology – both past and to come. The matrix photograph is indeed paradoxically never shown on stage. It is obliterated, absented as soon as conjured up, thus capturing the 'micro-experience of death' contained in it.

As if to drill a vertiginous abyss, the *ekphrasis* of the obliterated photograph concentrates on the face of the Protester whereas the well-known photograph only shows us his back. Yet in this face, it is here again an absence and not a presence which is described: 'But he opens his mouth like a sudden crack in the bottom of his face. A hinge into blackness' (32). The mouth which is open but deserted by words, like Munch's or Bacon's silent cries, en-graves the anonymous heroes whose massacre has taken or will take place. The violence of Thorpe's vocabulary – the crack slashing the face – convokes an empty inner crypt (Abraham and Torok 1975) engulfing the thousands of victims of the day before and of the days after and points to the performative power of those who are in the position to condemn thousands with just one word as opposed to those deprived of the freedom to speak:

> In the seconds that the man in the white shirt stands there, he might have said. He might have said a lot of things. I know I don't speak the language he grew up speaking. But he could say. He might say. As if he's addressing me. Or the whole crowd. All of us. He might say.
> This is a photograph waiting to happen. A photograph in which no one will ever see my face. (39)

Crises act as a dramaturgic drive. They propel new dramatic strategies and innovative aesthetics onto the contemporary stage so as to voice the various epistemological collapses of our times of unrest. The photodramas studied here, which focus their lens on emblematic situations, underline the historical significations while restoring a humanist vision of crisis and, in the words of Angelaki, 'expos[ing] the hues in humanity that render individuals more than the sum of the neoliberalist context' (2017: 2–3). Crisis compels us to try to think of a way out and theatre helps us conceive of these new paths.

Photography, in its capacity to capture the moment of suspension that characterizes crisis, functions not only as a thematic inspiration for contemporary playwrights but as a methodology. Photography reveals crises yet paradoxically, photography is not concerned with writing or drawing with light: 'Photography is melanography' (Milner 2005: 406); it makes forms out of blackness. This is how traditional, gelatin silver, photography works. As such, it is an art that addresses contemporariness. By writing photodramas, playwrights, in the words of Agamben,

> firmly hold [their] gaze on [their] own time so as to perceive not its light, but rather its darkness. All eras, for those who experience contemporariness, are obscure. The contemporary is precisely the person who knows how to see this obscurity, who is able to write by dipping [their] pen in the obscurity of the present.
>
> (2009: 44)

Innovatively, Simon Stephens, Lucy Kirkwood and Chris Thorpe, by conjuring an optical unconscious to the photographs they have in mind, give credit not to what appears in the light but to the negative of the form so as to promote a present situation that will not be marred by illusion. Starting from the image of the crisis, they dig their way back to the dark room where the pith of the crisis is at hand, and doing so, they reconstruct this suspensive conversational space where the individual exists as part of a community in transition, teetering on the brink of revolution.

References

Abraham, N. and M. Torok (1975), *L'Ecorce et le noyau*, Paris: Flammarion.
Agamben, G. (2009), 'What Is the Contemporary?', in *What Is an Apparatus?* trans. D. Kishik and S. Pedatella, 39–54, Redwood: Stanford University Press. Available online: https://soundenvironments.files.wordpress.com/2011/11/agamben-what-is-and-apparatus.pdf (accessed 30 September 2020).
Al-Azraki, A. (2017), 'The Representation of Political Violence in the Plays about Iraq (2003–2011)', *Theatre Times*, 11 May. Available online: https://thetheatretimes.com/representation-political-violence-plays-iraq-2003-2011/ (accessed 30 September 2020).
Angelaki, V. (2017), *Social and Political Theatre in 21st-Century Britain: Staging Crisis*, London: Bloomsbury Methuen.
Arendt, H. (1961), *Between Past and Future*, New York: The Viking Press.
Aumont, J., A. Bergala, M. Marie and M. Vernet (eds), (1999), *L'Esthétique du film*, Paris: Nathan.
Badiou, A. (1988), *L'Etre et l'événement*, Paris: Seuil.
Bailly, J-Ch. (2005), *L'Instant et son ombre*, Paris: Seuil.
Barthes, R. ([1980] 2010), *Camera Lucida: Reflections on Photography*, trans. R. Howard, London: Hill and Wang.
Becker, H. S. (1963), *Outsiders: Studies in the Sociology of Deviance*, London: Free Press of Glencoe.
Benjamin, W. (1999), 'Little History of Photography', in M. W. Jennings, H. Eiland and G. Smith (eds), *Walter Benjamin: Selected Writings, Vol. 2, Part 2, 1931–1934*, trans. R. Livingstone et al., 507–30, Cambridge: Belknap.
Bourdieu, P. (1972), *Esquisse d'une théorie de la pratique*, Genève: Droz.
Bourdieu, P. (1980), *Le Sens pratique*, Paris: Minuit.
Burgess, A., A. Alemanno and J. Zinn (eds) (2016), *Routledge Handbook of Risk Studies*, London: Routledge.
Burke, G. (2007), *Black Watch*, London: Faber and Faber.
Burstin, H., I. Ermakoff, W. H. Sewell and T. Tackett (2015), 'Protagonisme et crises politiques: histoire et sciences sociales. Retours sur la Révolution française', *Politix*, 112 (4): 131–65. Available online: https://www.cairn.info/revue-politix-2015-4-page-131.htm (accessed 30 September 2020).
Butler, J. (2009), *Frames of War: When Is Life Grievable?* London: Verso.
Churchill, C. (2016), *Escaped Alone*, London: Nick Hern.
Cohen, S. (2014), 'Coq/Cock'. Available online: http://www.heure-exquise.org/video.php?id=8926 (accessed 30 September 2020).

Coste, M. (2021), 'Frames of Violence and Recent History in Simon Stephens' *Motortown* (2005)', *Sillages Critiques*, 31 (2021). Available online: https://journals.openedition.org/ (accessed 12 January 2021).
Crimp, M. (2005), '*Sophocle à l'aéroport*', trans. E. Angel-Perez, Dialogue avec les Classiques, *OutreScène*, 5: 11–15.
Dobry, M. (2009), *Sociologies des crises politiques*, 3rd ed., Paris: Presses de SciencesPo.
Dufourmantelle, A. (2011), *Eloge du risque*, Paris: Rivage.
Foucault, M. (1984), 'Des espaces autres', *Architecture, Mouvement, Continuité*, 5: 46–9.
Fragkou, M. (2019), *Ecologies of Precarity in 21st-Century Theatre: Politics, Affect, Responsibility*, London: Bloomsbury Methuen.
Gardner, L. (2015), 'Interview: Chris Thorpe: Theatre Is a "Laboratory for Thinking about How We Think"', *Guardian*, 7 May. Available online: https://www.theguardian.com/stage/2015/apr/07/chris-thorpe-theatre-confirmation-a-nations-theatre (accessed 30 September 2020).
Gill, N. (2011), *Mirror Teeth*, London: Oberon.
Gill, N. (2014), *Fiji Land*, London: Oberon.
Greig, D. (2010), *The Events*, London: Faber and Faber.
Greig, D. (2013–17), '*The Yes/No Plays*', [Twitter post], 14 December 2013–18 April 2017. Available online: https://twitter.com/yesnoplays.
Holmes, J. (2007), *Fallujah*, London: Constable.
Kirkwood, L. (2013), *Chimerica*, London: Nick Hern.
Kofman, S. (1973), *Camera Obscura: de l'idéologie*, Paris: Galilée.
Milner, M. (2005), *L'Envers du visible*, Paris: Seuil.
Smart, B. (2016), 'Things That Always Tend to Happen in Simon Stephens' Plays', Interventions, *Contemporary Theatre Review*, 26 (3). Available online: https://www.contemporarytheatrereview.org/2016/things-that-always-tend-to-happen-in-simon-stephens-plays/ (accessed 30 September 2020).
Smith S. M. and S. Sliwinski (eds) (2017), *Photography and the Optical Unconscious*, Durham: Duke University Press. Available online: https://www.dukeupress.edu/Assets/PubMaterials/978-0-8223-6901-1_601.pdf (accessed 30 September 2020).
Sontag, S. (1977), *On Photography*, New York: Farrar, Straus and Giroux.
Starn, R. (1971), 'Historians and "Crisis"', *Past and Present*, 52: 3–22.
Stephens, S. (2006), *Motortown*, London: Methuen.
Stephens, S. (2018), *Rage*, London: Methuen.
Thorpe, C. (2013), *There Has Possibly Been an Incident*, London: Oberon.
Thorpe, C. (2017), Interview with Elisabeth Angel-Perez, 23 February.
Thorpe, C. (2018), *Mysteries*, London: Oberon.
Thorpe, C. and H. J. Walker (2014), *I Wish I Was Lonely*, London: Oberon.
tucker green, d. (2018), *ear for eye*, London: Nick Hern.
The UCL Hazard Center (2021), *University College London*. Available online: https://www.ucl.ac.uk/hazard-centre/ (accessed 30 September 2020).

12

Playing in the dark: Tim Crouch's *Total Immediate Collective Imminent Terrestrial Salvation*

Stephen Scott-Bottoms

At the start of his author's note, the author makes a simple proposition: 'A play creates its own world where things can be done differently. Plays are not bound by our natural laws.' He then goes on to list some of the ways in which this is so: 'Time can travel backwards as well as forwards. People become other people; they can die and not die' (Crouch 2019a: xii). The list of imaginative propositions continues, and most readers will probably consent to the premise without much hesitation: yes, we might think, in a play we can do anything! All we need is an empty stage, an actor, some words and our imaginations. After that, the possibilities are endless. Or so we might imagine.

In reality, of course, possibilities are never endless, and the author – Tim Crouch – knows it. The play he is introducing here is a play about the end of the world. It's called *Total Immediate Collective Imminent Terrestrial Salvation*, and it ends in the (imagined) darkness of a solar eclipse. It is a play that first appeared at the Edinburgh International Festival in 2019, but the following year, the unimaginable happened, and the Edinburgh International Festival did not.[1] Eclipsed by coronavirus, theatres in the Scottish capital and around the world remained dark for most of 2020. As I write this, it remains uncertain when they will fully reopen, or what condition the industry will have been reduced to by the time they do. Covid-19 has reminded us forcibly that plays are indeed bound by natural laws, such as those that involve breathing. Yet we are also faintly conscious that this pandemic is just the starter portion. All around us there are other harbingers – the floods and droughts and cataclysmic wildfires – as we begin to understand that the end

---

[1] The play was produced by the National Theatre of Scotland in association with London's Royal Court Theatre, Lisbon's Teatro do Bairro Alto, and Brighton's Attenborough Centre for the Creative Arts (ACCA). Following the Edinburgh premiere, it appeared at each of these venues during an autumn tour, and also at Dublin Theatre Festival.

of the world really does need to be imagined. If that task remains difficult, it is because so much else still seems so familiar. So normal.

The term 'cognitive dissonance' was coined in the 1950s by the American social psychologist, Leon Festinger. It refers to any situation in which an individual is simultaneously aware of two or more contradictory cognitions. The mental discomfort arising from such dual awareness will, Festinger argued, drive most people to *reduce* such dissonance by *altering* one or other of the conflicting cognitions. Put simply, we will reimagine the situation into one that makes sense for us. Festinger's classic demonstration of this rationalization process is presented in *When Prophecy Fails* (1956), a book in which, together with his colleagues Henry Riecken and Stanley Schachter, he recounts the process of infiltrating a middle-American doomsday cult. This group, the Seekers, whose members were in all other respects just ordinary, middle-class Midwesterners, believed in the prophecies divined by one of their number through the séance-like process of automatic writing. The messages received from beyond, by Mrs Keech, told them that the world was going to end in an apocalyptic flood on 21 December 1953.[2] The faithful few, however, would be saved from the deluge by aliens in flying saucers.

Festinger wanted to see what this group would do when the world did not, in fact, end. He predicted, according to his emerging theory of cognitive dissonance, that the Seekers would not simply abandon their beliefs in the face of disconfirming evidence since to do so would bring on shame, embarrassment and confusion. 'Suppose an individual believes something with his whole heart', Festinger wrote by way of explanation; 'suppose further that he has a commitment to this belief, that he has taken irrevocable actions because of it'. Confronted with a crisis of faith, such an individual 'will frequently emerge, not only unshaken, but even more convinced of the truth of his beliefs' (Festinger, Riecken and Schachter 2008: 3). The Seekers, Festinger thus predicted, would double down on their convictions by amending the detail of the prophecy but not its substance. They would, moreover, start to proselytize for new members (they had not actively done this prior to 21 December), because the social support added by new believers would confirm them in the truth of their revised beliefs. And sure enough, Festinger's hypothesis was validated by events. When the world did not end, the Seekers concluded that their faithfulness had been rewarded with a temporary reprieve from the sky gods. It was now their responsibility to recruit more people to be saved, prior to the rescheduled end of the world.

---

[2] Mrs Keech was a pseudonym chosen by Festinger and colleagues to protect the identity of Chicago housewife Dorothy Martin (1900–92).

When Prophecy Fails is part scientific thesis and part social comedy. Festinger and his colleagues bring a bone-dry sense of humour to bear on their descriptions of this group's increasingly bizarre rationalization processes. They do so from the smugly comfortable position of sensible, mainstream humans who would not buy into such self-evident nonsense as sky gods in flying saucers. In 1953, if the world was going to end, it would be because the Russians dropped the bomb, and there would be nothing that ordinary folks could do about it besides 'duck and cover'.[3] Today, though, two decades into the twenty-first century, the situation is somewhat more complicated. Most of us are creepingly aware that the world as we know it is ending by incremental degrees, as the signs of environmental breakdown become ever more unavoidable. Most of us are probably also conscious of being somehow complicit in this crisis, because we have 'taken irrevocable actions' in our commitment to an energy-consuming way of life that is the very source of the problem. Yet we also know that little we do at an individual level will make the smallest bit of difference in the face of the oncoming crisis. And so, to medicate the resulting dissonance, most of us indulge daily in climate denial – numbing our discomforting cognitions by hastily thinking about whatever else just popped up on our phones.

These are, I think, the psychological realities that Tim Crouch has dramatized in *Total Immediate Collective Imminent Terrestrial Salvation*. Whether or not that is what Crouch himself intended is a moot point: 'There's an element of my thinking that thrives from not knowing too much', he explained to me of the largely intuitive creative process behind this piece, in particular (Crouch 2019b).[4] The play, it should be noted, makes no direct allusion to the climate crisis. Yet in terms of Crouch's creative process, it seems telling that *Terrestrial Salvation* was written in between two plays for young people – *Beginners* (2018) and *Superglue* (2022) – that are explicitly concerned with the implications of environmental breakdown. As the written-for-adults filling in this creative sandwich, *Salvation* seems rooted in a more immediately personal crisis – the death of a young child and his parents' conflicted responses. Yet given that the child's father defers his grief into doomsday prognostications, it seems clear that Crouch is concerned here – just as in *Beginners* – with the older generation's failure to take adequate responsibility for the fate of the young.

[3] 'Duck and cover' was a slogan promoted by the US government during the 1950s, aimed particularly at schoolchildren, which instructed citizens how to protect themselves in the event of a nuclear attack.
[4] All references in this essay to Crouch's views and opinions, including those where he is not directly quoted, are drawn from this personal interview.

In what follows, I will pursue this line of argument with reference to *Down to Earth: Politics in the New Climatic Regime* (2018), a recent, rhetorical essay by the French philosopher of science, Bruno Latour. According to Latour, the world's political polarities have now tilted decisively away from the old, familiar axis of progressive left versus reactionary right. The essential choice is now different. At one pole lies a 'terrestrial' orientation that asks us to work realistically within the laws of nature, and to fashion a future for our children that recognizes our shared inhabitation of Spaceship Earth. Yet since this orientation requires some difficult rethinking of almost everything we treat as 'normal', it may be psychologically easier to double down on those normalities instead. By insisting on defending what we already have, by closing borders and pulling up the drawbridge to repel migrants, we are drawn magnetically towards Latour's other pole, where an 'out of this world' fantasy politics takes refuge in strident ideological posturing and strawman enemies. 'We understand nothing about the vacuity of contemporary politics', Latour writes, 'if we do not appreciate the stunning extent to which the situation is unprecedented' (2018: 44).

In the expository prologue of Crouch's play, we see Miles and his young son Felix attempting to cross a frozen lake, hand in hand. They are heading towards the rest of their family – mother Anna and daughter Bonnie – on the far side of the lake. Yet the ice cracks under Felix's small footsteps, and he slides into the murky depths to drown. 'Each of us is beginning to feel the ground slip away beneath our feet', Latour writes: 'We are discovering, more or less obscurely, [that] there is no longer an assured "homeland", as it were, for anyone' (2018: 5). Miles survives the accident, but he is no longer at home in his city or his skin. While in a coma, he has had a cosmic vision of the earth's oncoming destruction. Yet through miraculous mathematical extrapolation, he calculates the exact spot from which the wise few will somehow be saved. On leaving hospital, he leads Anna and Bonnie far away from everything they knew to resettle in a remote spot in South America. There they found a settlement reminiscent of Jonestown (the remote spot in Guyana to which the Reverend Jim Jones led his cultish congregation in 1977, prior to their mass murder the following year). Miles sets himself up as a visionary prophet, publishing quasi-scientific papers and attracting devoted followers whose social support confirms his wisdom. It would be difficult to imagine a more extreme instance of dissonance reduction than the one depicted here. The death of a son becomes the end of the world, as sudden disaster and unbearable loss transmute into a salvation fantasy, in which Miles acquires godlike insight into the precise time and date of the inevitable apocalypse: 'This moment was fixed before the continents were formed' (Crouch 2019a: 69).

This entire back-story, it should be noted, is told through pictures in a book. As Crouch's play begins, audience members sit facing each other in a large circle – like the congregation at some evangelical church meeting. Each of us holds in our hands a slim, olive-green hardback. When instructed by an actor-celebrant, we open this hymnal-like volume, and then turn its pages together, whenever we hear the word 'Okay'. We examine hauntingly evocative pencil drawings by Crouch's collaborator, Rachana Jadhav. (Is it graphite or charcoal? Either way, it's carbon.) The wordless story told by Jadhav's pictures is given further depth and weight by Pippa Murphy's immersive sound design as we hear ice cracking, parents crying out, hospital equipment beeping, and a dissonant electronic drone. The sounds, images and carefully paced page-turning bring the audience together in hushed contemplation of imagined loss.

The graphic novel as theatre? It's unorthodox, but Tim Crouch's plays have always sought fresh ways in which to emphasize the spectator's role as a creative participant in the making of the live event. There is always something for us to do – some leap of imagination for us to make. In *An Oak Tree* (2005), for example, one of the two characters is played by Tim Crouch, but the other is played by a different actor every night, who has neither seen nor read the play prior to walking onstage. The spectator must thus negotiate the inevitable gaps in the representational illusion – the gaps between the story being told and the means of its telling – as the second actor sight-reads her lines from pieces of script handed to her on clipboards, or simply repeats whatever Crouch tells her to say. As a play, *An Oak Tree* works rather like that old optical illusion – the line drawing that simultaneously looks like both a rabbit and a duck. Just as one can never quite 'see' both animals at the same time, so with *An Oak Tree* one has to flip, perceptually, between watching the actors grapple with the play's theatrical challenges and engaging with the dramatic narrative in which a father meets a stage hypnotist. Each cognition seems to exclude the other. Yet as Crouch argues, his work simply highlights the perceptual processes inherent in decoding any form of representation: 'I would say that cognitive dissonance exists in every work of art – from Frank Bruno playing Widow Twankey on down' (Crouch 2019b). As I have argued elsewhere (Bottoms 2009), the theatrical miracle of *An Oak Tree* is that the spectator's intuitive attempts to reduce such dissonance function to deepen the emotional experience of the play. Somehow, the edge of disoriented hesitancy that inevitably colours the second actor's performance becomes a theatrical metaphor for her character's situation – that of a father grieving the sudden death of his teenage daughter.

Terrestrial Salvation returns to that same trope of parental mourning. Here, though, the cognitive contradictions refuse to be reduced or resolved, because the theatrical means of textual delivery (the book) is also an essential component *within* the dramatic fiction. As we read on in the hymnal, and the play 'proper' begins, two women appear in the circular stage space and enact a scene of meeting. Every word they speak is read aloud from copies of the same green book held by each spectator. The theatrical conceit here is that Miles's desperate need to control the uncontrollable has turned him into such a monomaniac that nobody in the settlement he has founded is permitted to speak a word that he has not scripted for them in advance. No independent speech or thought is sanctioned, and reading ahead in the book is not sanctioned either (no spoilers!). Thus, the younger woman, Sol, can only be the person Miles has scripted: 'This girl is me. Described as me here. Is me' (Crouch 2019a: 30). There is a darkly Pirandellian joke here about the godlike power of the playwright over characters-in-search-of-an-author. And yet the ostensible author here, Miles, is so monstrously controlling that he even denies reading glasses to his own daughter. Sol is Bonnie, the little girl who watched her brother drown fifteen years earlier. Miles has rechristened her after the blazing star around which the earth itself revolves; yet without glasses she is obliged to squint closely at the pages of her book, slavishly following the words with her finger.

The woman who now approaches Sol wishes to save her from the author's all-abusing power. This is her mother, Anna, who lost faith with Miles's dictates a decade ago – leading a faction that broke with his leadership and fled. Now though, on the very eve of the predicted apocalypse, Anna has plucked up the courage to return – hoping to redeem her daughter from the cognitive crisis that will engulf her when the world does not end. Sol, however, is understandably troubled by the fact that Anna's presence seems to be both illicit and somehow anticipated:

Sol Did you tell him you were coming?

Anna He'll know, won't he?

Sol He wrote all this.

Anna So he knows we're talking.

Sol He's seen everything. (45)

The woman who is ostensibly here in defiance of Miles reads lines ostensibly written by Miles. It makes no sense. Indeed, as Sol later observes, Anna cannot possibly have any lines: 'You don't exist here. You died. You got written out.

No one mentions you anymore. Not in the readings, not in the – ' (81). As she speaks these words, she is still reading them from the book.

The cognitive contradictions here are glaring. Yet even so, as audience members who begin to root for these characters, we want Sol to be saved from her monstrous father, and we want Anna, her mother, to do the saving. And so, in spite of all the evidence to the contrary, we try to imagine that this is what is happening. We attempt to reduce the inevitable cognitive dissonance by believing what we *want* to believe. (When I say 'we', here, I am extrapolating both from my own experience and from conversations with others.) The audience thus becomes paradoxically complicit, with Miles, in the process of reality-denial. We want to believe in something which is manifestly not the case.

Spectators are further encouraged in this contradictory enterprise by the subtle details of *Salvation*'s staging. In the original 2019 production – as co-directed by Crouch's longstanding collaborators, Karl James and Andy Smith – the actors would carefully read almost every line they uttered from their books, rather than letting them seem memorized, but they would also frequently look up from Miles's words at each other. As in any stage play, a great deal seemed to be communicated through eye contact and body language. Pauses would sometimes seem to be held for agonizingly long periods of time, as Sol (Shyvonne Ahmmad) and Anna (Susan Vidler) gazed searchingly at each other, as if for some contact beyond their assigned words. In a few isolated moments, they would speak stolen words that do not appear on the pages of the hymnal: 'This is not sanctioned', Sol protests, off book (51); 'I'd love to hold you if you'd let me', Anna tells her daughter (80). In the context of the play's established performance conventions, these moments feel thrillingly illicit – like sudden, puncturing holes in author-Miles's suffocating membrane of control. And yet these lines *do* appear in the published, paperback version of the play text (as my page references here indicate). As written and rehearsed, they represent another layer of authorial manipulation. 'This has been thought through', Sol reminds Anna, and us, as if Miles himself is speaking through her to mock all hope of freedom: 'We are his patterns, you understand. All of us' (52). Moments later, as the audience obediently turns the page with the next 'okay', we become immersed in the deafening sound of fuzzing white noise. The double-page spread in the book that now confronts us is a deluge of over-printed words, with only two clearly visible: 'DARK' and 'MATTER' (54–5). Crouch has plunged us into a theatrical black hole of unreconcilable contradictions. Humans cannot see or detect dark matter, physicists tell us, but we know that it exists because of its effect on objects that we *can* observe directly. Much the same might be said of playwrights.

But then, in the second of the play's two main scenes, the playwright himself appears, visibly, onstage. Tim Crouch walks onstage in the role of Miles, and in doing so he seems to collapse any imagined distance between the actual author and character-as-author. Simultaneously, he removes our own, notional invisibility as an audience: the circle of chairs in which we are sitting is now, explicitly, the circle of Miles's congregation. Previously, we could imagine ourselves as functionally invisible witnesses to the outdoor meeting of Anna and Sol, but now we are directly implicated. Indeed, don't some of those people peering at hymnal-like books – the people in Jadhav's establishing drawings of this scene – look a lot like some of these actual people sitting around me? (Conversely, Jadhav's drawings of a tousled, bearded Miles remain cognitively dissonant with Crouch's clean-shaven baldness.) In the scene that follows, Crouch-Miles invites a series of spectators to stand and recite passages from his book, as if from holy scripture. Those invited invariably comply, because nobody wants to spoil the play. And so, from having imagined ourselves to be on Anna's side, as resisters of Miles's monstrous autocracy, we find ourselves complying with his authority. We are a people divided amongst ourselves, obliged to take sides in an argument we didn't choose.

In the UK, in 2019, there were certain resonances in this scenario that were hard to avoid. The suggestion of a breach in the body politic – with Anna having been among a group of leavers from Miles's cult, while the majority remained – recalled the ongoing, acrimonious split in the UK population between Brexit-supporting Leavers and pro-EU Remainers. It is probably safe to assert that a comfortable majority of the nation's liberal-minded, middle-class theatregoers saw themselves as Remainers. Crouch's audience, however, find themselves 'remaining' with Miles – a man who is in many ways exactly the kind of Trumpian demagogue that liberals typically find repellent. (Indeed, Crouch readily admits that Miles's monomania was inspired in part by Donald Trump and his unquestioning base.) In this scene, rather than marvelling smugly at the self-evident stupidity of those gulled by demagogues, we find ourselves compliantly reading along with a leader who seems curiously reasonable. Where would we be, Miles asks, without his leadership and prophecies? '[W]e'd be going through our lives, drinking expensive coffees, staring at smartphones, rushing around like malfunctioning automatons. Lied to by the media. Manipulated and divided by the money-grabbers, the politicians... blithely going along with the old fantasies' (102).

In Miles's rhetorical construction, this alternative scenario seems laughably awful. Why would we want to live like that? (Oh wait, we already do.) Miles speaks quietly and persuasively, and rather than appealing to petty nationalism or racism to rally his adherents, he appeals to the authority of science and mathematics. 'There's no faith involved', Sol repeatedly explains to Anna, of her father's reliance on cosmological calculations (69); 'Belief is the end of intelligence' (77). Here, Crouch gently mocks our conventional faith in the wisdom of science, since most of us – as he remarked to me in interview – 'have absolutely no idea' how it works. Instead, we take the authority of experts (like Miles) on simple trust: 'The great thing about the extreme edge of astrological physics is that it reads like God. A black hole is a perfect metaphor for God' (Crouch 2019b).

Compared to the awesome power of such authority, ordinary human subjectivity seems vulnerable and awkward, with its sticky emotions and uncertainties. Empirical science, Latour contends, excludes such things from its realms of consideration, by dismissing them as being 'at worst, simple fairy tales; at best, ancient myths' (2018: 69). And certainly, grief at the loss of a son is the stuff of stories and myths, which may be why Miles the scientist has no use for it. Instead, he has calculated that the earth is about to be sucked into a black hole. The drawings in our hymnals that picture Miles's visions of destruction seem to give him an almost god-like omniscience, as if standing outside of the crisis itself. Yet for Latour, this is merely the default setting for scientific objectivity: a refusal of emotional engagement, which amounts to 'a sort of sadistic asceticism', goes hand in hand with the distanced gaze of the observer (2018: 69). Whether looking through microscopes at petri-dishes, or through telescopes into space, scientists habitually picture themselves as being somehow outside of that which they are studying, rather than surrounded by it, or embedded within it, or affected by it. As Latour argues, following James Lovelock's Gaia hypothesis (Lovelock 2016), these habits of thought can prevent us from seeing the cognitive wood until it's too late, because we are too busy peering in close-up at individual trees.

But wait. Now we really are lost in the dark matter. If we are to question the wisdom of experts, won't that lead us into irrational scepticism and conspiracy theories? Isn't that sort of thing driving our current state of crisis? Or should we doubt even what the scientists are telling us about climate change? Well, no. Because the evidence for that is now staring us in the face. A better question might be whether any of us is *behaving* as if we believed in climate science to begin with. As Latour notes of the flagrantly fictional political platforms offered by Trump, Bolsonaro and the Brexiteers, 'for the first time, a large-scale movement no longer claims to address geo-political realities seriously, but purports to put itself explicitly outside of all worldly constraints' (2018: 36). These fantastical politics are literally 'out of this world' – just like Miles's cosmological visions. Yet it does no good simply to point fingers and mock the stupidity of those who fall for such ludicrous posturing, because – just like Crouch's audience – we are all complicit in the problem. As divisions mount, all sides double down on the righteousness of our own convictions, and in so doing, we distract ourselves from the most urgent priorities facing us all.

What is the audience of *Terrestrial Salvation* supposed to do with the unresolvable tangle of dark matter and cosmic dissonance that the play throws up? Must we somehow resist the controlling authorship of playwrights and politicians, and learn to confront reality for ourselves? Crouch admits privately that he would love it if spectators simply stopped complying with Miles's lead. He cites the moment in the play when a spectator – selected to speak momentarily as a theatrical surrogate for Sol – is asked: 'Are you just saying what you've been told to say?' (60). Crouch fantasizes that someone – just once – would say 'Yes' instead of the 'No' scripted in the book. Yet, paradoxically, any such affirmative answer would indicate that the non-compliant speaker is still complying with Crouch's wider design (*yes*, I'm saying what I've been told to say). And while non-compliance of a less compliant sort is certainly possible in *Terrestrial Salvation*, true resisters would risk vacating the experience of the play itself – as is the case, for example, with those spectators who simply refuse to turn the pages of their books or follow along with the text and images (these have mostly been bored-looking men, Crouch notes, apparently brought to the play by more enthusiastic partners). In the end, it would seem, a more constructively resistant reading of the play would need to take place in the spectator's unscripted imagination, rather than through the limited options for audience participation.

Without trying to foreclose on the possibility of other such readings, let me try to outline some responses of my own. I will do so by focusing on the question that Crouch leaves deliberately unanswered at the end of the play: what happens next? The climax of the drama comes with the scheduled solar eclipse. We experience this cosmic phenomenon not by lighting blackout but by simply turning the pages of our books, on the word 'okay'. The closing pages, largely blank, become progressively darker as Jadhav's pencil shades them in with a heavier touch across three double-page spreads. Total blackout is reached on the fourth such spread, and continues through two more, carefully timed 'okays'. After that, the pencil-shading goes into reverse and the pages start to get lighter again. As they do so, the sound of birdsong becomes faintly audible in the theatre. The eclipse is receding and the earth is coming back to life. Yet the actors leave the stage without uttering another word, and the book comes to an end with blank, white pages. So what has just happened, and what will happen next?

In literal terms, of course, nothing comes next because the play has finished. Nothing will come of nothing. Without an author to grant it further life, this Pirandellian world really has come to an end. Indeed, as Crouch explains of his early thinking for this piece, 'I wanted to write about the moment when the suicide bomber blows themselves up and there is nothing' (Crouch 2019b). The playwright explodes himself and we are left with blank pages. Perhaps the sound of birdsong indicates that he has taken us all with him to *jihadi* paradise. 'We're going to the place where no world and every world exists', Miles tells his congregation during his last sermon; 'Where the dead died and never died' (110). That is, indeed, a pretty good description of what happens in theatres on a nightly basis. In theory, at least, dramatic characters have eternal life, because plays are endlessly reproducible. Each role can be endlessly surrogated by the next speaker's body. 'For an observer, we would always be here forever', Sol tells Anna, parroting her father's theory of relativity. Anna, however, points out that if the apocalypse comes, 'there will be no observers ... And it will be dark' (72). Theatre *is*, as we have already noted, subject to the laws of nature.

But what if the world has not ended? What if Miles's power as author-god is actually quite limited? What if the returning birdsong hints at the world now carrying on, without his controlling obsessiveness? If the end is not nigh, will Miles now just shut up and go away, having been proved wrong? Leon Festinger's theory of cognitive dissonance would suggest not. According to his analysis, any hypothetical future for these characters would involve Miles and his followers doubling down on their beliefs and evangelizing for new followers. Indeed, that is the future that Anna foresees, in the event of non-apocalypse: 'you'd all start again', she tells Sol. 'Yes. He'll rewrite. Of course he will. And off you go again. New hope, new expectation' (85). In this scenario, some fresh spin will be found on Miles's out-of-this-world fantasies, and nothing meaningful will change. Moreover, since Miles is – at least in theory – the author of Anna's scripted lines, we might reasonably ask whether *he* is the one who foresees himself rewriting, after the failure of his own prophecy? So did Miles ever really believe anything he foretold, or has the entire, insubstantial pageant of this play been the work of a nihilistically cynical con-artist? In the current political climate, this possibility feels all too plausible.

Yet there remains, I would suggest, a third potentiality in that returning birdsong. What if we could hear the birds and see the earth around us, for what they are – instead of clouding our heads with apocalyptic dissonance? Recall that Latour proposes 'Terrestrial' as the opposite political pole to 'Out-of-This-World' (2018: 109), and then look again at the title of Crouch's play: *Total Immediate Collective Imminent Terrestrial Salvation*. Might the terrestrial, indeed, be our salvation, if we can somehow tilt ourselves away from the magnetic pull of Miles's profound denialism? It seems to me that the potential for such an outcome lies seeded within the play itself – not so much in the words ostensibly scripted by Miles, as in the visual counterpoint offered by Jadhav's drawings (under Crouch's guidance).

To explain my thinking here, it may be useful to consider Latour's choice of that word 'terrestrial'. He deliberately avoids the more familiar alternative, 'natural', because the habituated thought patterns of human culture have already placed us on the *outside* of it. Nature is that which lies *beyond* the human, rather than being intrinsic to it. Nature is something to feel nice about, but not something to be fought for tooth and nail: 'the emotions involved are not the same when you're asked to defend nature – you yawn, you're bored – as when you're asked to defend your territory – now you're wide awake, suddenly mobilized' (Latour 2018: 8). Of course, territorial defensiveness can manifest simply as jingoistic nationalism, but what if it invited – instead – a renewed attention to our shared terrestriality?

Terrestrial Salvation, Crouch readily acknowledges, owes a significant debt to *The Tempest*. Miles is Prospero, not burning his books; Sol is Miranda, growing up in a fantasy world invented by her father. But could we, the audience, be like the earthy Caliban – finally resisting this colonizer of minds and laying claim to the territory that is our birthright? As Caliban famously asserts, 'This island's mine, by Sycorax my mother' (1. 2. 396). Motherhood haunts Crouch's play as an implied counterpoint to Miles's patriarchal mastery. Indeed, he is apparently so threatened by it that he administers supplements to all the women in the settlement, to arrest their menstrual cycles. In *The Tempest*, of course, Miranda has no mother, but in *Terrestrial Salvation*, Sol's comes back for her. And while every word that Anna speaks seems to have been preordained for her by author-magician Miles, she nevertheless represents something awkwardly unresolved within his male-centred creation: a maternal ghost in the machine. According to Latour, the kind of 'hard science' invoked by Miles has always entailed 'hatred of a large number of values traditionally associated with women' (2018: 72). The domestic, the maternal, the subjective, the earthy – these are the means by which humans survive and thrive (rather than divide and rule). And in Crouch's play, these things are apparent both in Anna's presence as mother and in the terrestrial landscape that is conjured so lovingly into being.

'Hello earth, ground, grass', says Sol at the beginning of the play's first scene, as she 'wakes' to 'the smell of earth and flattened grass' (28–9). She refers to the ground around her as 'Mum beneath all me' – evoking both Mother Earth and her birth mother, Anna (whom Sol has been told is dead, and buried in this spot). In the drawing that establishes this setting, Jadhav shows rings of solar heat emanating out across grassy scrubland, with mountains looming in the background. This is not a 'beautiful' landscape in terms of conventional spectacle, but Jadhav augments her drawing with a series of in-set, zoomed-in images that highlight the abundant life all around: insects in the grass, crawling; the structure of leaves, photosynthesizing; even microbial forms, clustering and reproducing. These things lie beyond the human, but Crouch's text nonetheless implies a strong connectivity between the terrestrial and the human. '*Nausea. Needle grass*' reads one stage direction, as Sol shelters her eyes from the sun (42). Such prompts are never acknowledged by the actors, but they may trigger the reader-spectator's imagination, as we read along. '*A large bird circles high above them*' (50). We might patch this image of flight into the imaginary landscape already conjured by Jadhav's drawings and by Murphy's wraparound soundtrack of chattering insect life. There is just a hint, here, that the circling bird might be tracking Sol as potential carrion. She has, at least according to the stage directions, just doubled over in pain. Nothing about Crouch's terrestrial texturing suggests any cosy or comforting view of 'nature', but this is, identifiably, the earth we live on.

The richly evoked patch of landscape on which Sol and Anna meet is also boundaried land – human *territory*. A high, mesh fence runs across several of Jadhav's pictures, policing the threshold between grassland and mountains. In one image we see this fence in close-up, and Anna – with bolt-cutters – breaking her way through it (a large dragonfly perches on the fence as she does so). 'How'd you get in, anyway?' Sol demands to know of Anna: 'How'd you even get this close? This land is circumscribed, protected' (35). The paradox for Anna is that, while in one sense she is encroaching on alien territory, in another sense she is returning home – to her daughter, and to the place she fled but could not leave behind. In another set of images, depicting Anna's back-story prior to this moment on stage, the storyboard both begins and ends with Anna in the air, on a plane (temporarily detached from the terrestrial). The captioning tells us that these first and last pictures bracket a period of ten years, in which she returned home to normality, but could not find normality. Thus, finally, she has flown back to the site of her unresolved trauma.

In a later image – a double-page spread – we see yet another plane, high above the clouds. It appears to be carrying mother and daughter home, away from Miles's controlling grasp. Sol, it seems, has consented to be saved. We have even seen her being taken out through the boundary fencing. Even so, as we turn the page and the plane vanishes, we are back with Miles – surrounded by his congregation (us). Miles calls out for Sol, and she reappears onstage with the book that never leaves her hand. She has left with her mother and she has stayed with her father. Like Anna, Sol is both grounded and mid-air, caught in a double bind of the imagination. What would it even mean for her to go back to that strange world of expensive coffees and mobile phones, which she does not remember and where even Anna is not at home? Today, Latour ventures, we are *all* suspended between destinations – distrustful of the future having left behind the past: 'People find themselves in the situation of passengers on a plane ... to whom the pilot has announced that he has had to turn around because he can no longer land at the airport' (2018: 32).

Perhaps the only future scenario that makes sense would be for Anna and Sol to stay grounded, on that patch of terrestriality that Crouch evokes so richly, in the very place where the author-god will need to be faced and outthought. 'Either we deny the existence of the problem', Latour writes, 'or else *we look for a place to land*' (2018: 5). What if, rather than leaving Miles to rewrite more out-of-this-world fantasies, mother and daughter could work to bring him back down to earth? The earth is, after all, the element in which his son lies buried. In one of Jadhav's most haunting drawings, Felix's small coffin is seen at the bottom of a deep, vertical shaft dug into dark, moist ground. Beneath it lies a mysterious tangle of snake-like roots, or subterranean monsters – the engulfing, subconscious horrors of grief that Miles has been evading all this time. Indeed, Miles himself is missing from the graveside image, even as Anna stands silhouetted, with the three-year-old Bonnie – almost literally astride the grave. What if Miles – what if *we* – could be brought to honest terms with the earth on which we stand, finally acknowledging our engulfing fears of the future, and the inescapable fact of death itself?

Total Immediate Collective Immanent Terrestrial Salvation is a play that seeks to inhabit the dissonance, the uncertainty and the sheer, unholy mess of the crisis situation in which we now find ourselves. It approaches the abyss and looks tentatively for ways to cross it. Or at least, that's how I see it. And on the other side of that abyss stands another play by Crouch's longstanding collaborator Andy Smith, titled *Summit* (2018). Premiering just a year earlier, this piece is not about dissonance but about harmony. It's a piece that begins 1,000 years in the future, at a time of utopian accomplishment for humankind. Three actors tell the same story in three different languages simultaneously (two spoken and one signed), and in performance these three registers blend together in joyous, rhythmic counterpoint. It is as if, 1,000 years from now, we have all discovered the secret of effortlessly pleasurable communication with other human beings. Facing up to the climate crisis, Latour argues, 'is not a matter of how to repair cognitive deficiencies, but rather of how to live in the same world, share the same culture, face up to the same stake' (2018: 25).

Smith's three actors tell the story of a global summit that took place in their distant past – at a time right around now – when harmony seemed hard to come by. 'It was like this', they explain, gesturing to the stage and audience arrangement of speakers and listeners, 'summit like this' (here Smith plays puckishly with the Yorkshire slang word *summat* – something):

> Summit all happen
> Because of a crisis
> There was a *crisis*...
> People at summit were talking and listening
> We don't know what was being said...
> There was talking and listening
> And then suddenly
> Suddenly
> *Suddenly*
> The lights just went out.
>
> (Smith 2018: 25–6)

In *Summit*, unlike *Terrestrial Salvation*, the stage lights actually do go out – on several occasions – as the contrapuntal text returns to recount this catchy, pop-song hook about that moment when (suddenly!) all the lights went out. What happened? We don't know, but summit definitely happened. And that moment of darkness, that temporary eclipse, is remembered by people 1,000 years in the future as the mythic moment in which people finally started to sort everything out. It was the moment when we stopped talking over each other and actually listened – the moment when dissonance ended and harmony began. Smith's optimism, like the looping, percussive rhythms of *Summit*'s text, is absurdly infectious. And as knowingly naïve as it is, its crystalline simplicity shines all the brighter when placed side by side with the tangled darkness of *Terrestrial Salvation*. Does the end of the world really have to happen at all, Smith asks? Might we fix our problems readily enough if we just stopped trying to control each other, or ridicule each other, or deny that our problems even exist? What if we could just talk to each other? Here on this earth. Because really, how hard can it be?

References

Bottoms, S. (2009), 'Authorising the Audience: The Conceptual Drama of Tim Crouch', *Performance Research*, 14 (1): 65–76.
Crouch, T. (2005), *An Oak Tree*, London: Oberon.
Crouch, T. (2018), *Beginners*, London: Oberon.
Crouch, T. (2019a), *Total Immediate Collective Imminent Terrestrial Salvation*, London: Oberon.

Crouch, T. (2019b), Interview with Stephen Scott-Bottoms, Brighton, 7 November.
Festinger, L., H. W. Riecken and S. Schachter ([1956] 2008), *When Prophecy Fails*, London: Pinter and Martin.
Latour, B. (2018), *Down to Earth: Politics in the New Climatic Regime*, trans. C. Porter, Cambridge: Polity Press.
Lovelock, J. (2016), *Gaia: A New Look at Life on Earth*, Oxford: Oxford University Press.
Smith, A. (2018), *Summit*, London: Oberon.

13

Re-membering assembly

Louise Owen and Marilena Zaroulia

On 22 October 2020, over half a year since the eruption of the most acute public health emergency in living memory, the authors of this essay gathered to attend a theatre work. Of course, we did not *actually* go to the theatre: most theatre venues in Britain, where we live, were then closed due to government measures preventing in-person, indoor congregations, in an attempt at controlling the spread of Covid-19. On that Thursday, we watched a piece of digital performance, simultaneously yet separately in our homes in London. The piece was Lost Dog's *In a Nutshell* (The Place, 2020) – a performance to camera speculatively presenting a time after theatre as we know it has ceased to exist, which had premiered free of charge on YouTube on 23 September 2020. Rather than indicating a 'new direction' as such, we found in Lost Dog's work an invitation to revisit the intersection of crisis and theatrical assembly, a theme which we first explored together in the aftermath of the financial crisis which emerged more than a decade ago. Like Covid-19, the financial crisis was cataclysmic and experienced across the world, with unequally distributed effects, and elicited a range of theatrical responses. Under the conditions of austerity imposed in Britain during the 2010s, and in tandem with uprisings taking place elsewhere, people demonstrated in the streets, in protest at attacks on public services. British theatre artists and institutions also reacted: works engaging with economic inequality, and practices, histories and ideas of people gathering gradually proliferated. As theatregoers and researchers, we saw the dynamics of public demonstrations begin to resonate in works staged in theatre buildings. Mike Bartlett's *13* (National Theatre, 2011) and Lucy Kirkwood's *NSFW* (Royal Court, 2012), for instance, thematized popular uprising and workplace gender politics. Productions including Alecky Blythe's *Little Revolution* (Almeida Theatre, 2014), Penelope Skinner's *Linda* (Royal Court, 2015), Gary Owen's *Iphigenia in Splott* (Sherman/NT, 2015/16) and Alexander Zeldin's trilogy of plays *The Inequalities* (2014–19)[1] addressed similar themes now implicating the

---

[1] *Beyond Caring* (2014), *Love* (2016), *Faith, Hope and Charity* (2019).

audience through direct address, making use of participatory techniques or strategies to produce proximity among audience members, and between the audience and the performance itself. Our view was that audience members were thus increasingly being called to imagine themselves in assembly to witness something together. The use of these devices and their echo with demonstrations beyond the theatre felt like a resurgence in contemporary theatre practice of an interest in collective politics very much less in evidence during neoliberalism's entrenchment in the 1990s and 2000s – a return triggered by the financial crisis and its lived ramifications.

Crisis, as Stuart Hall tells us, tends to ignite significant historical change. In a 2010 conversation with Doreen Massey, Hall reflects upon the concept of 'conjuncture' as a means of expressing its manifestation: 'a period in which the different social, political, economic and ideological contradictions that are at work in society come together to give it a specific and distinctive shape' (Hall and Massey 2010: 57). Where those contradictions become unmanageable, crisis occurs, and action is taken to 'resolve' them, thereby producing the conditions of a new conjuncture: his example is neoliberalism's supplanting of social democracy in the late 1970s. In the case of the financial crisis, as Massey notes, governmental narrativization of 'the public deficit' as the seat of the problem attempted to smooth neoliberalism's own contradictions by disaggregating 'the economic crisis from the philosophical one' (Hall and Massey 2010: 60) – an attempt that was not altogether successful, as protests and the increasing popularity of anti-austerity policies that arose throughout the 2010s show. Hall proposes crises as 'moments of potential change, but the nature of their resolution is not given' (Hall and Massey 2010: 57). As we write, we are living through another such embattled moment. In the context of Covid-19, governments have periodically and unevenly imposed stringent rules regarding public gatherings, but across the world the pandemic has witnessed an even greater 'profusion of protest movements' (Berger 2020). In Britain, demonstrations regarding racism, police brutality, violence against women, public services, economic support, LGBT+ rights, climate change and new legislation affecting civil liberties have taken place in contravention of government dictates. They have coincided with demonstrations by far-right groups, sometimes staged in reaction to protests with progressive aims, and actions in resistance to lockdown and vaccination measures (BBC News 2021). In this increasingly divisive political environment, the struggle over the content and contours of public discourse and its material consequences has been exacerbated by 'the social industry's culture wars and conspiracist panics' (Seymour 2019).

Made during the pandemic, the gentle qualities of the fifteen-minute-long digital piece that we discuss seem to be at some distance from this unresolved context of discord and uprising. But we argue here that in its content, form, and unfolding of histories of theatrical assembly, *In a Nutshell* carries implications for this wider public situation. In this respect, of particular interest to us is Hall's temporal conception of crisis as 'a break, a "ruptural fusion"' (Hall and Massey 2010: 60), in which past and present collide. We see theatrical pasts and presents at work in *In a Nutshell* via its recalling of bodies sharing space and time together. The performative power of co-presence is a concern likewise at the heart of Judith Butler's *Notes toward a Performative Theory of Assembly* (2015) – one of the primary theoretical touchpoints for the theme of public assembly of recent years. Butler argues that 'acting in concert can be an embodied form of calling into question inchoate and powerful dimensions of reigning notions of the political' (Butler 2015: 9). Though *Notes toward a Performative Theory of Assembly*'s focus is public demonstrations, protests and occupations, the actions and ambitions Butler discusses are shared by theatremakers. Across domains of theatrical and non-theatrical practice and experience, assembly carries a dramaturgical resonance: it implies spatial arrangement, narrative construction and modes of address. Within theatre buildings, assembly's 'acting in concert' entails, more often than not, a more formal and regimented organization of the audience than that experienced on the street (or even in immersive, site-responsive or site-specific modes of theatremaking). And challenging 'reigning notions of the political' is an aim that many theatremakers and theorists undoubtedly espouse. But as a commercial as well as state-regulated endeavour, the theatre is a more institutionally ambiguous scenario for the achievement of this aim. In its account of theatrical assembly, *In a Nutshell* speaks to that ambiguity.

In a Nutshell was originally slated to go offline after thirty days. We watched it first via The Place's website on what was ostensibly its last day of broadcast, in a situation that thereby approximated a live performance (or perhaps a show with an expiry date on Netflix or other streaming services, to which so many of us have had recourse during the pandemic). We furiously wrote notes and revisited it to take screengrabs, and each wrote a text immediately afterwards reflecting upon what we had seen, which we later spliced together in a makeshift dialogue. But then we discovered that the performance remained available on YouTube, so we could return to it and engage in a kind of detailed analysis that is not ordinarily possible for live theatre, and which also allowed us to look upon the performance, as well as our writing about it, with different eyes at different times. Despite its status as a digital work made for camera, we insist that *In a Nutshell* is a theatrical performance, which also functions as its own documentation. In our analysis and writing, we have pieced together our thoughts in the context of lockdown separation, utilizing 'assembly' as means of working things out. Here, we are inspired by the approach of feminist cultural critics including Sara Ahmed and Lauren Berlant, who invoke 'assembling' in relation to their own writing practices, methodologies and bringing together of archival materials. Our engagement with *In a Nutshell* reveals not only how long histories of assembly are implicated in contemporary performance, but also the dialectical and processual nature of theatre spectatorship: how changing circumstances cause our orientation to performance to shift. This text, written in phases, is very much a result of time passing, the gaps and twists in time of our experiences of lockdown, and the convoluted connection between our writing and our experience of modalities of time during the pandemic. We have learned something about how we make sense of, remember, what we see in the theatre, and how partial, selective and particular our experiences of theatre can be. We recall nights in the theatre via fragments of memory and incomplete associations; sometimes, these very particular experiences and ways of making sense of a piece of performance cannot be disentangled from the memory of the actual work. The next section of this essay, our dialogic account of the performance, speaks to that learning.

I: Assembling together

M: It is Thursday lunchtime. Both Lou and I have managed to make some (little but precious) time to 'go' to the theatre together. Like we've done so many times.

L: We have decided to attend Lost Dog's *In a Nutshell* – a fifteen-minute monologue performed by Ben Duke in which, 'sitting alone in an empty auditorium, a man explains to an unseen future generation, what live theatre was'. We've been to The Place together once before, but for the life of us we can't remember anything about the performance that we saw. We assemble in Zoom, muting ourselves and opening the performance in YouTube on an adjacent screen.

M: Theatre has been a constitutive element of our friendship over the past decade. Lou and I talk about the theatre; we gather and go to the theatre; we cry and laugh at the theatre. We have overpriced drinks and unhealthy snacks at the theatre. Sometimes, we are deeply sceptical of the theatre. And some other times, we believe in the theatre.

L: A man of about our age is sitting in the middle of a set of stalls seats. He talks to us about the theatre in what another friend of mine, like plenty of others, likes to call 'the before times', as if this experience of theatre is by now in the past, which at this moment it is. He says that seats are often red, because they disappear in the dark. Knowing that he is a performer, having introduced himself as such, at first I think he will go on to talk about the experience of being on stage, of not being distracted in performance by the sight of the red seats. Nicholas Ridout's discussion of Stanislavsky's Kostya's horror of the 'awful hole' (Ridout 2006: 35–9) of the darkened auditorium in his discussion of stage fright pops into my mind. But he doesn't talk about the experience of being on stage. He talks about the audience.

M: I am thinking of the energy of the theatre event; of what vibrates and affects oneself in any particular moment in the theatre. The performer Ben Duke, while sitting alone in the auditorium of an empty theatre, trying to explain what the theatre experience is like, reflects on that energy that travels through the auditorium and reaches one's body via the bodies of other audience members around you, strangers around you, 'very close' to you.

L: He talks about how, in the before times (or whatever), we would all come into the theatre and sit in these seats, lots of us, but that it wasn't 'a free-for-all', we would have tickets with numbers on. He is funny; his serious tone is funny. He says that we would sit in the seats and that we would keep ourselves to ourselves. Sometimes we would know people but everyone else was a stranger. Something like that. And that sometimes the person next to you, their leg would just fall against yours and they would leave it there. As he says this I laugh. At various moments in the performance I laugh.

M: I am looking at Lou laughing at the screen. A moment later I find myself laughing.

L: And I can see Marilena laughing too in the corner of my eye, but just slightly out of sync, maybe a couple of seconds behind.

M: I realize that despite our best attempts to start the streaming at exactly the same time, we have failed to press play at the very same moment. There is a lag – I am lagging behind by a second, or second and a half.

L: The time is slightly out of joint, as in *Hamlet*, one of the performances he says would happen a lot in the theatre. He suggests that we get a person and bring them near if they are around, or if we are alone we get a plant, an 'organism' to be near. Now I start to cry. He recalls performances, sketchily, in much the same way as I am attempting to recall his performance myself. The one with the Argentinians, the one with the woman with the 'terrible rage', the one with the woman in a red dress, the one with the horse, the one with a guy carrying a trident, like Aquaman, only not. He says that if he were to take off his shoe and throw it, it would hit the guy, because he's really there, not that he's ever seen that happen, but. So funny. Some of the performances he talks about I saw, others I did not, but I try to make educated guesses as to what they were.

M: He is remembering a moment from The Trojan Women - it doesn't matter when and where - but the memory of the moment when news of the loss of the child reaches the grandmother and former Queen who has now lost everything, that moment triggers a reflection on families, beyond the fictional framework... I am drifting off for a moment: I am thinking of the times that I missed theatre shows because my son, Nemo, was ill and the many times - since lockdown started - that I could not attend all these great shows or cool events online because they were happening at Nemo's bedtime and it is more complicated to attend events or theatre from home than work from home. I miss the theatre when I could actually go. It gave me a good reason to take a break even though yes, Duke is right in some other moments, theatregoing was a 'real hassle' as he says. 'I don't know why we were going', he says.

L: Now music plays – a melancholy air that I don't recognize as Henry Purcell's 'Dido's Lament', which a commenter on the YouTube video reveals it to be. He talks about coming on stage, as a performer, with a baby balanced on a shield that has been thrown from a wall, bringing the baby to the baby's grandmother, who in reality is not a grandmother herself but would like to be, her children are in their thirties and could do that, but her son is not ready, wants financial security. He talks about how she thinks about how her son could just be hit by a bus tomorrow, why wait. He talks about the relaxed feeling of a body in death. And he talks about how the baby balanced on the shield wobbles a bit, and so everyone, we, are alright.

M: Meanwhile Duke reminds us that after that moment when everything stands still, as we all connect individually and collectively, together and alone with the pain of the Trojan queen, after that moment where we both inhabit the actual here and now of our physical surroundings, in the theatre but also immerse ourselves in the then and there of the dramatic world, after that moment something happens – as the baby is lying on a shield, it wobbles (is that what he said?) and at that moment, the spell is broken: 'We know it's not a baby… we know, and we're okay now, we are all, we are all ok now.' We are back. We have landed.

L: He talks about how we sit there, in the theatre, to watch things, maybe only because we've paid fifty quid for them, even if they're a bit weird. He talks about how he's not sure if we, the audience, are there, that instead he's talking to an eye that's looking, a big eye, a camera lens, 'like a Cyclops'.

M: Back to the energy, travelling across bodies, transcending bodies. Contagious. I am thinking of Jill Dolan's *Utopia in Performance,* the moments in the theatre of intense intersubjectivity, those moments she describes as 'voluminous' (Dolan 2005: 5); these moments take up space, they leave a mark. These moments – rare and precious – are perhaps the reason why I kept on going back, returning to the theatre in the hope that something will happen. Waiting for something to happen. The possibility of something happening – that kept us going for years. And now that this possibility is not quite there, I don't quite know what I feel about the theatre.

L: We talk a bit about the performance. I've thought of 'things to say', and I say so: the performance as a discourse on theatricality, the production of empathy, the ground of empathy being the human body which itself is host to, in dialogue with, a mind that enables an understanding or apprehension of duality, that understands itself accordingly in relation to other human bodies. When he says 'offstage someone threw the baby from the top of the wall', and describes the women waiting, in my mind's eye I see him, a concrete wall, a gathering of women. In my mind's eye I'm looking at him, from the stage, at the women, from the stage, at the wall, from the stage, but also all of this from the auditorium – a bizarre concatenation of images which bears absolutely no relation to anything witnessed in reality. Maybe this is a piece of radio drama, really. Except it isn't. But all I want to do is cry, and I say that. I want to cry for my own experience of loss, about how perfectly this piece has captured something of the experience of loss. It is about infection – the infection of feeling in an auditorium, the organicity of our human bodies, like the plants he talks about, which means that for now it is not possible for us to assemble in auditoria.

M: And I am sitting on this empty carriage of the Jubilee line scribbling words in response to this show, while making my way to work. Today is one of the few times during this autumn term that I will actually get to see my students. Masked and 2m distance from each other but we will meet and share the same space. The first time I returned to my institution after almost seven months away and I stepped in the studio room for the first years' students' induction event, I was overwhelmed by this sensation of the familiar strange; the paradox of returning to what you have always known, which is not quite the same anymore. I was reminded of that sensation of being in a room with young people, so many times; in some ways, everything felt the same. But, like in a dream, everything felt like it was moving slower and was a bit out of place. The energy was a bit off and the effort to stay close while staying apart a bit harder. Time. Out of joint.

II: Assembling dramaturgies

So in what ways are histories of theatrical assembly relevant to this piece of work – a digital piece that features a man sitting alone, which we watch alone in our homes?

First, the dramaturgy of the piece: it is one of assembling elements, of piecing things together and making a virtue of gaps, interruptions and changes. The performer has been set the task of talking about the experience of the theatre to an audience that has no knowledge of the theatre. Throughout the first half of the performance, he seems to be 'trying out' different images for the audience, to construct a guidebook of sorts. He describes (the surroundings, the people, the characters who would appear onstage, the snacks, the drinks). He offers analogies (people as 'organisms'). He explains and offers detail ('they didn't know how long they were going to be inside for um so they might need they might need the snacks'). He even directs the audience into participating in an exercise in order to translate the experience in more tangible ways ('I want us to try something', he says, 'pause the video'). His address to camera, his way of looking at the invisible spectators zooming into him through the camera lens-eye of the Cyclops, his gestures (a hand choreography of sorts where he is reaching out to pull something in, to conjure something, to bring something to focus, to zoom in in his mind's eye and, in doing so, to evoke it in our imagination): all of those actions assemble, put together, ingredients of the theatre as it used to be.

These different means of making sense of the theatre through analogy render the performance a kind of haphazard teaching. Its haphazardness is essential to the sense of collectivity it is seeking to construct. His words are tentative, halting, difficult, hesitating, grasping at something that is challenging to describe, like trying to communicate what a colour is to someone who has no concept of that. The cultivated hesitancy is similar to the mode of delivery of stand-up comics who play with similar rhythms.[2] And at times it is really funny. The comedic quality of the piece both interrupts and amplifies a desire on our part as spectators to be with others, to laugh together. It also conjures a scene of togetherness: we are making sense of what the theatre was, together. A sidenote and a paradox: at an artist's talk in November 2020, Ben Duke revealed that while he had the support of filmmaker and editor Rachel Bunce in filming the work, he needed to feel alone to perform it. He asked her to hide. She lay down on the floor as he performed, squashed awkwardly among the seats (Ben Duke Q&A 2020). And although formally it is a short film, we must also see this work therefore as a theatrical performance whose dramaturgical techniques are very, very old, and which become reanimated in this digital form. Each segment of *In a Nutshell* is separated by a blackout, with an echo of the dramaturgical effect that choral songs performed in ancient tragedy. The piece's fragmented dramaturgy bespeaks Hans-Thies Lehmann's definition of tragedy as 'interrupted aesthetic experience' (Lehmann 2016: 168) that '*bring[s] the function of the spectator into play*' (Lehmann 2016: 154). There is insufficient space here to tease out in a more full way the many resonances between Lehmann's argument concerning tragedy and this piece, which invokes as an essential part of its functioning two key works in the Western tragic canon – Euripides's *The Trojan Women*

---

[2] See for example American comedian Nate Bargatze (Netflix is a Joke 2021).

and Shakespeare's *Hamlet*. Arguably *In a Nutshell* itself likewise constitutes an example of tragic drama, one which addresses itself to our collective plight under the conditions of the pandemic: our physical vulnerability, our losses, our isolation in lockdown, our confused sense of time. The blackouts, Ben Duke's faltering address to the spectator, render this a piece of theatre: one that seeks to remind us, to quote Lehmann again, that theatre means 'experiencing-together-with-others' (Lehmann 2016: 128).

The blackouts in the performance also open up space for different modalities of time to emerge. Each blackout lasts for a few seconds, yet can be imagined as stretching out to evoke months of life in the pandemic, months of closed theatres – or, as per the premise of this performance, a future where theatres never open again. These blackouts might also enable us as spectators to withdraw momentarily, to find a space of contemplation, in a process we might liken to day-dreaming. And while it stretches time out in these moments, plunging time into an imagined black hole, the performance also deeply condenses Western theatre history and myth. *In a Nutshell* is threaded through with classical and early modern allusions, one of which is its title, a phrase originating in the ancient world but for this purpose more likely drawn from *Hamlet*: 'O God, I could be bounded in a nut shell and count myself a king of infinite space, were it not that I have bad dreams' (II, ii). The psychic and material consequences of lockdown are writ large in this unspoken reference to Shakespeare's tragedy, and likewise the unspoken lyrics of Purcell's composition authored by Nahum Tate: 'When I am laid, am laid in earth/May my wrongs create/No trouble, no trouble in thy breast/Remember me, remember me, but ah! forget my fate.' The survival and grief invoked here are also tropes that figure in the mythical cycle of the Trojan war narrated in Homer's epics. Troy manifests in the background of *In a Nutshell*: in the image of Poseidon carrying the trident, in the story of Dido and Aeneas, which Purcell's opera tells, and in a figure that is never named, that of Odysseus, the man who tricked the Trojans and brought their downfall with a gift (the Trojan horse). On his way back home from Troy, the trickster-hero, the over-confident Odysseus meets Polyphemus, the Cyclops, son of Poseidon – and when he blinds the Cyclops to escape, he meets the god's wrath. Euripides's rendition of the myth in *The Trojan Women* opens with Poseidon's exchange with goddess Athena, protector of Odysseus – in an instance again where *In a Nutshell* draws threads together. Such processes speak of how narratives, fragmented and overlapping, are assembled and persist through repetition, echoing across the centuries, reproducing the Western dramatic canon. In a nod to its own title, the performance thus puts in a nutshell different references which may or may not thereby reverberate and multiply in the minds of the spectators, consciously or otherwise.

III: Assembling audiences

The performance also speaks to the theatre's role in the formation of the modern subject. In both content and form, it reflects on the place and function of theatre within industrialized capitalist societies and the role of the classical canon in class formation. In other words, *In a Nutshell* distils histories of gathering in the theatre, and their persistence and indeed active construction in our own theatrical present. The performance imagines audiences who sit facing forward, gazing upon a stage that is perhaps enclosed – protected, even – by a proscenium arch. This scene is 'the theatre' – despite the co-existence in contemporary British theatre culture of this kind of theatrical experience with other scenes of performance which do not take place in such spaces, and which have made it their business ostensibly to challenge or disrupt them. And furthermore we see Ben Duke sitting in a particular theatre – the Connaught Theatre, Worthing, converted in 1931 from a cinema building. We see the red velvet seats to which he refers with his words. Otherwise, it is words that construct 'the theatre' for us and remind us of its rituals: waiting in the foyer, purchasing snacks and alcohol, having bought a ticket in advance for the event, which is not a 'free-for-all'. Once in the auditorium, we are surrounded by 'strangers' who are 'eating snacks and coughing… sometimes a lot of coughing'. By contrast, in this digital situation, in which we watch alone in our homes, unseen by Duke, 'there's no… people to climb over, there's no embarrassment of leaving in the middle… no sense of value… you know… you're not there going "I spent 50 quid on this and I'm going to watch it no matter how weird and boring it is…" there's nothing holding you… you there.

The piece is therefore not talking about theatre 'as such' – there is no such thing – but a distinct historical formation of the theatre: the scene of the twentieth century, in which audiences came to be constructed increasingly as docile consumers of experience. In his discussion of early twentieth century theatre audiences, having surveyed other, more 'unruly' reactions to theatre, Baz Kershaw identifies 'popular' and 'genteel' as contrasting but dominant modes of audience patronage between the wars (Kershaw 2001: 141). These were specific to different class contexts of theatregoing, but as patronage, both positioned audiences as figures of authority in relation to what they saw onstage. In the post-war period, in response to moves on the part of theatre producers (or, in Kershaw's arch description, 'technicians of the cultural') who articulated their practices in terms of high standards, 'the authority of the patron was gradually hollowed out, and in its place was installed the subservience of the supplicant-client, and audiences became "better behaved"' (Kershaw 2001: 143). Kershaw argues that this 'better behaviour' runs hand-in-hand paradoxically with the reconfiguration of the audience member as choosing customer: this figure of sovereignty submits to the discipline of the theatre institution. Convenience and consumerism are writ large in Duke's words about interruption, embarrassment, value and enduring an experience that may or may not be 'weird and boring'. Ultimately, what emerges is an evocation of the theatre as a hallowed space in which other audience members are keeping you and your behaviour in check. The most disruptive behaviours referenced are coughing – formerly distracting, potentially lethal in the context of the pandemic – and a leg that falls against the leg of another. These are a far cry from the lively audience responses that Kershaw surveys in late-nineteenth-century and early-twentieth-century situations, much less the uninvited clapping, booing, fruit throwing, pissing, pickpocketing and prostitution which were common features of the early modern scene of theatre audiencing (Tichenor 2018). The audience member conjured by *In a Nutshell* is quiet, contained, deferent and now, in 2020, at home – although in our 'watch party' spectatorship of the piece (which may or may not have been adopted by others), we were able to see each other laugh, and laugh together.

Though we are nowhere near the theatre itself, the camera lens-eye of the Cyclops gives us a perspective as if from the stage. In a kind of reversal, we are gazing upon the performer sitting in the empty auditorium – a gesture of inversion similarly used by Australian company Back to Back Theatre in *Lady Eats Apple* (2016), which we attended together at the Barbican in June 2018, and in which we watched a love story play out in the theatre's circle from the vantage point of the stage. Duke is struggling to find words to capture what once unfolded onstage. Having described the audience settled in the auditorium, he attempts to conjure a sense of wonder: 'And we zoom into the stage and the stage is a magical place where all kinds of things can happen... for example....' But he cannot. It is futile. He stares confusedly into the middle distance for several seconds, eyes narrowed, grasping for a memory of a good moment: 'uh Hamlet, he was there a lot, he was on the stage a lot'. This funny introduction to the examples he talks through speaks to the persistence of 'bardolatry' – a phenomenon invented, Richard Schoch notes, by eighteenth-century actor-manager David Garrick, who proselytized Shakespeare as 'the great national poet': 'his country's triumphant answer to Homer and Virgil, the cultural expression of its growing worldwide economic and colonial power' (Schoch 2021: 25). The range of works that follows meanwhile speaks to the heterogeneity of contemporary British theatre presentation: new writing, experimental work from Europe, theatre for families, dance theatre. Duke's final example is his reference to *The Trojan Women*. The diverse aesthetics of these contemporary works are enclosed by the classics.

Meanwhile, a returning trope in the piece's choreography is Ben Duke turning his head to look around him – sometimes slowly, hesitantly, some other times faster. Duke is looking around for someone, perhaps an audience member, anyone to corroborate or endorse what he is thinking and saying. It is an act of comedic yet profound effect, reminiscent of the strategies of absurdist dramatists (Gardner 2020). He is alone, a survivor of whatever it was, in this version of events, that ended up closing the theatres for good. Often, the turn of his head cues in a blackout, suggesting that more time is passing. In this manner, Duke himself emerges as the figure of Odysseus which, as we have already noted, lingers in the background of the piece's web of references. He is a performer-castaway who longs for his companions (audiences, performers, technicians, stage hands) to return, a castaway who is stuck in this theatre for an unknown amount of time. The concertinaed temporality that the piece presents reduces him to someone who 'lacks depth', as he exclaims towards the end of the performance when reflecting on how he can possibly connect with a digital audience. The depthlessness he speaks of calls to mind performance in three dimensions, bodies in space. Reflecting on Pina Bausch's *Palermo Palermo* (1989) without naming it, he recalls a sensation: 'I could feel her going through something and that gave me a going through something feeling so we are going through something together... you know.' In this moment, Duke expresses uncertainty as to whether we, the digital audience, can feel the same, or if we feel anything – or, indeed, if we're still there at all.

Conclusion

Compare the sense of solitudinous uncertainty and absence that unsettles Ben Duke with the lively atmosphere conveyed in a recording of Judith Butler's visit to the Occupy Wall Street assembly at Liberty Square, New York in October 2011. Butler joined the assembly to extend solidarity and support to the movement. In the video, the 'human microphone' or 'people's mic' mediates Butler's speech to the assembly – a technique whereby a speaker's statement is repeated by those close by, and repeated again by others, and so on, to extend its reach across a crowd (Kahn 2011). The short phrases Butler reads aloud from their phone reverberate in the open air: the so-called 'impossible demands' of shelter, food, employment, as part of a larger insistence upon wealth redistribution, economic justice, social equality. These demands are reiterated by people around, who we cannot see on camera, but we can hear. This participatory address concludes with what is effectively a statement of Butler's argument in *Notes toward a Performative Theory of*

Assembly – that of the power and necessity of 'coming together as bodies in alliance, in the street and in the square' (Widyaratna 2011). Butler defines assembly in terms of action, 'an exercise – one might call it performative – of the right to appear, a bodily demand for a more liveable set of lives' (Butler 2015: 25). Though here they invoke performance in the 'everyday life' modality of performance studies, 'appearance' is also a highly theatrical metaphor. And acts of theatrical performance and spectatorship are writ large throughout Butler's text. At one moment Butler alludes to Brecht; at others, they invoke metaphors of acting, costume, gesture and chorus. And *Notes toward a Performative Theory of Assembly* correlates and extends the boundaries of what counts as 'public' with expansive understandings of the theatrical. Butler argues that the truth of the public sphere is its connection to state power; indeed, the state apparatus itself 'depends upon the regulation of the public space of appearance for its theatrical self-constitution' (Butler 2015: 85) by legislating for who or what may be seen there. The theatre's performative power in relation to assembled audiences has long been the prompt for state intervention and regulation – most notably, the official regime of censorship applied to British theatre between 1737 and 1968 (Priestman 1992: 123). As scholars in our own field such as Sophie Nield have previously argued (2012), there is substantial interplay, therefore, between gatherings in public space which make political claims, themselves underscored by a theatrical logic, and the space of the theatre, even though one may seem more 'free' than the other.

We understand *In a Nutshell* to capture many of these issues in its framing of theatrical assembly as an 'issue at once ancient and timely' (2015: 1), as Butler writes of assembly more broadly. While it describes itself in terms of the elegiac, the piece moves beyond a melancholic orientation towards theatres closed because of the pandemic, to evoke so much of what Western theatregoing is and has been. It describes practices which are modern and contemporary in nature. In conjuring them with words as opposed to images, it makes use of techniques of storytelling which predominated in ancient and early modern theatre practice, in which audiences are precisely that: people who listen. And as we have argued, Duke's words recall the specific customer protocols of the twentieth-century theatre industry and the success of artists' efforts to consolidate the gains of the theatre as an aesthetic domain for close, silent attention – part of an ongoing 'struggle for an autonomous stage' (Fisher 2017: 264), as Tony Fisher has framed it, waged by playwrights during the nineteenth and twentieth centuries to free it from censorship and other kinds of state intervention. In its complexity, *In a Nutshell* recalls the theatre as a crucial space of social gathering and empathetic connection with others. It offers moments for introspection, which themselves play a critical part in the intersubjective nature of the event. Conceived and performed in the midst of a hiatus of in-person theatre, *In a Nutshell* condenses the different facets of the theatre, its utopian potential and its social and economic limitations, all of them hinging on the practices and constitution of theatrical assembly – a manifestation of the 'interests of common life' (Fisher 2017: 265) and its governance.

In an observation about theatre under the conditions of the pandemic that echoes Fisher's argument, Rustom Bharucha proposes that 'we as theatre workers would like to imagine that theatre functions with its own autonomy' (Eastap 2021) within the wider context of society. Yet 'the sheer scale and synchronicity of the global closure of theatres worldwide' (Eastap 2021) in the service of public safety demonstrates the limits of that imagined autonomy. Bharucha's argument threads together theatre history, the earlier Spanish flu pandemic, and the persistence of assemblies in public space of the sort we referenced earlier. *In a Nutshell* does not seek explicitly to address the global closure of the theatres, instead offering a speculative fictional version of the future which speaks to that widespread closure. But in our analysis, the piece does offer a kind of diagnosis as to what Bharucha describes as the 'vexed relationship between theatre and the state and the integral role of theatre in civil society' (Eastap 2021) in the present time. It does so by sketching out the historical contours of British theatre, its pleasures and its status as a scene of transaction, attended by the discerning 'expert' theatregoer with access to disposable income, accruing knowledge and thus cultural capital with every visit. Even though *In a Nutshell*'s references to performances are framed in deliberately demystifying language ('one time it was just like a corridor of light and there was a horse', and so on), who are the audiences who would grasp them all? What were and are the economic and social conditions required to access this theatre that is now 'lost'? What might this suggest for the theatre of the future? What do we want and need to build anew? Bharucha's starting point is that, for him, the Covid-19 crisis did not reveal anything new with regard to the theatre; in fact, Covid-19 functioned as a 'catalyst' for his own thinking in relation to the theatre: 'coronavirus was merely activating what was already there' (Eastap 2021). Here, we might see Bharucha's thinking aligning with Hall's analysis of the relation between the conditions of a particular historical conjuncture, and the 'ruptural fusion' (Hall and Massey 2010: 60) represented by crisis, revealing and magnifying existing conditions. *In a Nutshell* subtly demonstrates the multi-layered and complex relation between theatre, the state and civil society before the crisis erupted, and in the pandemic present. It combines and juxtaposes many and varied references, which also correspond to 'out of joint', in-pandemic temporality. And as Ben Duke guides us to drift in and out, the performance captures something of what the experience of digital platforms feels like as a means of watching theatre, or interacting with people. Digitally mediated in this instance, the relation between theatre, the state and civil society is precisely a question of assembly: how and where we gather, under what conditions, and for what purpose. *In a Nutshell* – a summary, an enclosure, a condensation of so much into so little.

Acknowledgements

Many thanks to the organizers and attenders of *Dialogue, Performance and the Body Politic in the Twenty-First Century*, February 2021 (Charles University, Prague) and Warwick Theatre and Performance Studies Research Seminar, March 2021 for their insightful questions, and to Fintan Walsh for his helpful comments on a draft of this article.

References

BBC News (2021), 'Covid Vaccine: Speech Comparing NHS Medics to Nazis Condemned', *BBC*, 26 July. Available online: https://www.bbc.co.uk/news/uk-57962675 (accessed 27 July 2021).

'Ben Duke Q&A', Take Art Ltd Events, Thursday 26 November 2020, 4pm, online.

Berger, M. (2020), 'The Pandemic Is an Era of Protests – and Protest Restrictions', *Washington Post*, 3 October. Available online: https://www.washingtonpost.com/world/2020/10/02/coronavirus-pandemic-demonstrations-protest-restrictions/ (accessed 27 July 2021).

Butler, J. (2015), *Notes towards a Performative Theory of Assembly*, London and Massachusetts: Harvard University Press.

Dolan, J. (2005), *Utopia in Performance: Finding Hope at the Theater*, Ann Arbor: University of Michigan Press.

Eastap (2021), 'EASTAP Webinar Series: Rustom Bharucha', 3 March. Available online: https://eastap.com/2021/03/03/eastap-webinar-series-rustom-bharucha/ (accessed 27 July 2021).

Fisher, T. (2017), *Theatre and Governance in Britain, 1500–1900: Democracy, Disorder and the State*, Cambridge: Cambridge University Press.

Gardner, L. (2020), 'Review: Lost Dog, In a Nutshell', *Stagedoorapp.com*, 29 September. Available online: https://stagedoorapp.com/lyn-gardner/review-lost-dog-in-a-nutshel?ia=615 (accessed 27 July 2021).

Hall, S. and D. Massey (2010), 'Interpreting the Crisis', *Soundings*, 44: 57–71.

Kahn, C. (2011), 'Battle Cry: Occupy's Messaging Tactics Catch On', *npr*, 6 December. Available online: https://www.npr.org/2011/12/06/142999617/

battle-cry-occupys-messaging-tactics-catch-on?t=1627298619314 (accessed 27 July 2021).

Kershaw, B. (2001), 'Oh for Unruly Audiences! Or, Patterns of Participation in Twentieth-Century Theatre', *Modern Drama*, 44 (2): 133–54.

Lehmann, H.-T. (2016), *Tragedy and Dramatic Theatre*, trans. E. Butler, London: Routledge.

Lost Dog (2020), 'In a Nutshell by Lost Dog', 23 September. Available online: https://www.youtube.com/watch?v=CiMX1_bE7U8 (accessed 27 July 2021).

Netflix Is a Joke (2021),'Nate Bargatze: How to Tell Your Kid Their Dog Has Died', 31 January. Available online: https://www.youtube.com/watch?v=LWeaqISShHw (accessed 27 July 2021).

Nield, S. (2012), 'Siting the People: Power, Protest and Public Space', in A. Birch and J. Tompkins (eds), *Performing Site-Specific Theatre: Politics, Place, Practice*, 219–32, Basingstoke: Palgrave Macmillan.

Priestman, M. (1992), 'A Critical Stage: Drama in the 1960s', in B. Moore-Gilbert and J. Seed (eds), *Cultural Revolution? The Challenge of the Arts in the 1960s*, 118–38, London and New York: Routledge.

Ridout, N. (2006) *Stage Fright, Animals, and Other Theatrical Problems*, Cambridge: Cambridge University Press.

Schoch, R. (2021), *A Short History of Shakespeare in Performance: From the Restoration to the Twenty-First Century*, Cambridge: Cambridge University Press.

Seymour, R. (2019), 'Willing Servants', *New Humanist*, 14 October. Available online: https://newhumanist.org.uk/articles/5516/willing-servants (accessed 27 July 2021).

Tichenor, A. (2018), 'Elizabethan Theatre Etiquette and Audience Expectations Today', *Shakespeare and Beyond: Folger Shakespeare Library*, 25 September. Available online: https://shakespeareandbeyond.folger.edu/2018/09/25/elizabethan-theater-etiquette-audience-expectations/ (accessed 27 July 2021).

Widyaratna, K. (2011), '"If Hope Is an Impossible Demand, Then We Demand the Impossible." – Judith Butler at Occupy Wall Street Video', *Verso: Blog*. Available online: https://www.versobooks.com/blogs/765-if-hope-is-an-impossible-demand-then-we-demand-the-impossible-judith-butler-at-occupy-wall-street-video (accessed 27 July 2021).

14

Perspectives from the cascade

José Ramón Prado-Pérez, Clare Wallace,
Enric Monforte and Clara Escoda

'May you live in interesting times' is widely known in English as a Chinese curse. Like the oft-quoted remark by John F. Kennedy in 1959 claiming that 'in Chinese, the word "crisis" is composed of two characters – one represents danger and one represents opportunity' (Walsh 2019: 227), the attribution is erroneous, even while there is undoubtedly a certain aptness in the turn of phrase. Each of the chapters in this book has probed the relationship between theatre and crisis, artistic responses to risk and to opportunity that seek to illuminate something about the 'interesting times' we inhabit. As mentioned at the outset, work on this project was overtaken by the biggest public health crisis in a century and consequent radical alterations of shared collective and cultural spaces. While the first wave urgency of the situation has largely ebbed, what lies in store in the near future is uncertain, and the long-term consequences can only be guessed in the present moment. The global pandemic has by its very nature underscored the vulnerability of human existence in contrast with other crises that could perhaps be more easily blamed on human agency, such as the financial crisis of 2007/8, even though the Covid-19 pandemic equally exposes, among other things, the unsustainability of the way we live now. Even as this crisis becomes ordinary, as everyday life tentatively resumes, as mingling in public space is possible and theatres reopen, it is likely that the exploration of vulnerability and the precariousness of the extant model of social and political relations will continue to be the focus of new generations of playwrights, furthering a trend that arguably gathered momentum with the advent of the new millennium and the terrorist attacks of 9/11.

When confronting the current moment, it is tempting to look to the past to better understand the present. What legacies do the current generation of theatre-makers inherit and what distinguishes their responses to crisis in the twenty-first century from those of preceding periods of crisis? In various ways each of our contributors takes up this question. Through the widening fractures in the economic and sociocultural project of neoliberalism, hegemonic for the past forty years, we might glimpse another rupture at the end of the 1970s and the 1980s, which saw the dismantling of post-war consensus to be substituted by that same neoliberalism, then known in the UK as Thatcherism. Such a shift of economic paradigm with its social and cultural equivalent rooted in fierce individualism and greed, implied the reorganization of the theatrical landscape with the end of subsidy and the promotion of a thwarted culture of presumed excellence. The nascent Thatcherite period established a culture of crisis that became endemic, based on the theory of shock previously rehearsed in Augusto Pinochet's dictatorial regime in Chile. However, for the culture of crisis to crystalize and become naturalized among the population, it was necessary to accompany it with utopian narratives of infinite growth and economic myths of expansive austerity – also used later to make the case for Brexit – that would reverse the post-war consensus about the redistribution of wealth and the welfare state itself.

The British left, fractured by internal conflicts, was ill-prepared for the mesmerizing appeal of Thatcherite 'common sense' and dynamism that confronted the increasingly obvious signs of stagnation and exhaustion apparent in society by the late 1970s. Moreover, as theatre scholars like John Bull (1984, 1994) and D. Keith Peacock (1991, 1999) have amply documented, debates over and discontent with engaged theatre, be it agitprop, realist or epic in aesthetic, were rumbling throughout the 1970s in the work of Edward Bond, Howard Brenton, David Edgar, David Hare and John McGrath among others. Thatcher's governmental policies brought a seismic shift in this cultural discourse, overturning much of what was taken for granted about the value of artistic endeavour in British society, transforming the language of engagement and, as mentioned earlier, pressing forward with a severely contracted model of state funding for the arts. Looking back at this period from the vantage point of the twenty-first century and through the lenses provided by Bull and Peacock among others, we can recognize a period of 'ruptural fusion' (Hall and Massey 2010: 60) that prefigures the crises the contributors to this book explore in British theatre of the present and the continued, insidious impacts of commodification and exclusion.

Throughout the 1980s, British theatre underwent a period of initial disorientation and then readjustment when the aesthetic principles that had been upheld in ideological favourable times lost their validity, partly because they had been discredited by the ideological reconfiguration of the Eastern and Western blocks after the fall of the Berlin wall in 1989, partly because their artistic strategies and devices were appropriated by the new ideological turn or transformed into harmless, edgeless style, yet another consumer good to be culturally enjoyed. Among the early responses to the neoliberal impulse, it is significant that Caryl Churchill resorted to satire and parody in the form of Restoration comedy, in her formally experimental collaborative piece with Joint Stock, *Serious Money* (1987), where the financial world and the so-called Big Bang that ensued from the Thatcherite deregulation of the City in the late 1980s were portrayed. Both the Big Bang and *Serious Money* could be said to have inaugurated that culture of crisis, marking the systemic/structural reliance on destruction, and, on the artistic plane, issuing one of the first warnings about the social quantum leap that was in the making. The following 1990s decade, after neoliberal consolidation, produced an innovative generation of young playwrights that included the likes of Sarah Kane, Mark Ravenhill, Anthony Neilson or David Greig, all of whom had come of age in the 1980s. Though initially criticized as lacking a recognizable sense of political engagement, the new theatre of the 1990s vividly captured something of an end-of-century structure of feeling. Many, though certainly not all, of these new playwrights offered explicit images of sex or violence indicative of the dysphoric conditions offstage, and their dramatic provocations were strikingly synthesized by Aleks Sierz under the label In-Yer-Face theatre (Sierz 2000). This work reverberated with a youthful angst that can be traced to the existential environments of the post-Thatcher era, erupting in stage images of disorientating commodification, bodily harm and psychic alienation.

In 2016, Caryl Churchill again, concluded her ecological dystopian play *Escaped Alone*, with the words 'terrible rage', which captured the imagination of audiences and critics alike and seized the current zeitgeist ironically embodied by Mrs Jarrett, a character over the age of seventy. The playwright dramatized the double bind of facing global catastrophe while keeping on about our own business: rage that can and is destroying us, and rage that can propel us to act as well. Living in the midst of a conjuncture whose resolution is uncertain and whose prospects are negative judging from the external signals, the outcome seems to rest on the mobilization and channelling of affects such as rage. This is a conclusion that David Hare had suggested in 2003 in his verbatim play, *The Permanent Way*, about the Paddington railroad accident in London, built around his conversations with the victims of that crash. Anger is the emotion that the victims more readily articulate in their interviews, which Hare expands on by suggesting the possibility of being radicalized by grief and bereavement. Such stories of survival and the productive transformation of affective states into resistance or protest attest to the prominence of resilience, the stubbornness to persist and linger, from which we can set the foundations for what Hannah Arendt would call the 'power of promise', that is, 'the human capacity for action, for beginning new and spontaneous processes' (230–1).

British theatre in the twenty-first century, using a diverse array of aesthetic strategies, is strongly attuned to crises that are global, systemic and relational in ways necessarily distinct from the former century. It stands at the crossroads of a conjuncture where the previous state of the nation might be substituted by a more cosmopolitan state of the community approach that displaces the analysis of the big political questions in terms of well-defined and established ideological blocks, to embrace a regenerative approach focused on the restoration of the social fabric that has been systematically eroded during the hegemonic phase of neoliberalism. The success and consolidation of an alternative will depend, among other things, but most crucially, on the short duration of this coming interregnum; and the ability to forge alliances and affective networks that cut across the widest possible sections of society and the citizens. The performance and display of vulnerability on the stage brings to the fore the inequalities and injustice that have been obscured by neoliberal narratives of economic utopianism. It is not an exercise of self-deprecation but of visibility instead, reclaiming our extant humanity as a subversive, disruptive element of struggle. The restoration and celebration of human agency against the deterministic forces of the economy, be it by a redefinition of affective bonds or the restoration of the Arendtian notion of action, exposes the neoliberal construct and renders its contradictions open to scrutiny and ultimately substitution.

The theatrical and social communities that have emerged under globalization differ from those that established themselves in the 1970s and developed in the 1980s as a locus of resistance to Thatcherism, while still retaining a similar logic of resistance and celebration. Nowadays, projects such as those conceived by Welfare State, Ann Jellicoe or Ann Devlin and David Edgar in the 1980s have waned evolving towards the dramatization of vulnerability as strength that would apply, not only to the specific community where the artistic project originates, but to the wider community of citizens, in a process that aims at reverting the disaggregation of individuals back into a set of relations that constitute the essence of community. It is this extended relationality, not just amongst the members of a concrete group, but in myriad vectors that enriches the notion of community as a site of ongoing re-thinking and reshaping. It thus effects an appropriation of globalization with the performance of human agency and the critique of power structures.

In fact, the shape of the current crises, which are not novel but which have taken centre stage within the social and theatrical priorities, emphasizes that which makes us all equal in humanity: death would have been the answer in previous historical periods in order to underline the existential zeitgeist; however, now it is resilience and healing that stand out as our common ground of encounter, whether in non-epic narratives of migration, sexual abuse and women's liberation, institutional and ingrained racism, ecological activism or affective forms of politics and political engagement.

References

Arendt, H. (1998), *The Human Condition*, 2nd ed., intro. M. Canovan, Chicago: Chicago University Press.
Bull, J. (1984), *New British Political Dramatists*, Basingstoke: Macmillan.
Bull, J. (1994), *Stage Right: Crisis and Recovery in British Contemporary Mainstream Theatre*, Basingstoke: Macmillan.
Churchill, C. (1987), *Serious Money*, London: Methuen.
Churchill, C. (2016), *Escaped Alone*, London: Nick Hern.
Hall, S. and D. Massey (2010), 'Interpreting the Crisis', *Soundings*, 44: 57–71.
Hare, D. (2003), *The Permanent Way*, London: Faber and Faber.
Peacock, D. K. (1991), *Radical Stages: Alternative History in Modern British Drama*, Westport: Greenwood.
Peacock, D. K. (1999), *Thatcher's Theatre: British Theatre and Drama in the Eighties*, Westport: Greenwood.
Sierz, A. (2000), *In-Yer-Face Theatre: British Drama Today*, London: Faber and Faber.
Walsh, F. (2019), 'Editorial: Scenes of Crisis', *Theatre Research International*, 44 (3): 227–9.

Index

#MeToo 11, 40, 41, 45, 55, 56
#TimesUp 40

Abu Ghraib 178, 182
Adiseshiah, Siân 11, 77
Agamben, Georgio,
   contemporariness 189
ageing, adversarial ageism 11, 21–2,
   24–5, 27–9, 33–5
Ahmed, Sara 13, 33, 57, 150, 212
   happy/melancholic migrant 13,
     14, 162
   happy object 162
   promise of happiness 165
Alexander, Naomi 95–6, 101, 103
Almeida Theatre 39, 43, 50, 184, 209
Angelaki, Vicky 11, 23
   Social and Political Theatre in
     21st-Century Britain 9, 44,
     65–6, 82, 177–8, 189
   Theatre & Environment 47
Angel-Perez, Elisabeth 14
apocalypse, post-apocalyptic 11, 22,
   26, 29, 33–4, 113, 194, 196,
   198, 203
Appadurai, Arjun 6
Arendt, Hannah 183, 229–30
assembly 14–15, 209, 211–12, 216,
   219, 221–4
Aston, Elaine 10, 56
austerity, austerity policies 1, 4, 7, 12,
   56, 59, 74–5, 86, 90, 93–4, 97,
   101–5, 209–10, 228

Badiou, Alain 183
Bal, Mieke, migratory aesthetics 13,
   146–7, 150
Balestrini, Winnie 5
Barthes, Roland, *Camera Lucida* 178

Bartlett, Mike 12
   13 209
   Albion 12, 112, 118–19, 122–3
Bartley, Sarah 12
   'UK People's Theatres: Performing
     Civic Functions in a Time of
     Austerity' 91 n.2
Battersea Arts Centre 78, 82
Bauman, Zygmunt and Carlo
   Bordoni 5, 65
Bayley, Clare, *The Container* 13, 143,
   145, 147–51, 156
Beck, Ulrich 4
Becker, Howard, deviance 185
Benjamin, Walter 3
   catastrophe 23
   optical unconscious 181, 188
Berlant, Lauren 89, 212
   crisis ordinariness 5, 12, 23, 26, 90
   cruel optimism 15–16
Berlin wall 228
Bharucha, Rustom 14, 223
Big Bang, financial deregulation 73,
   90, 229
Billington, Michael 26, 41
Black British theatre 162, 163
Black Wednesday 90
Bloch, Ernst, nonsynchronism 30–1
Bourdieu, Pierre 4, 11, 73–4, 84
   habitus 181, 183, 187
Bradby, David and John McCormick
   96
Brecht, Bertolt 182, 222
   epic theatre 101
   estrangement 33
Breivik, Anders 186
Brexit 1, 7, 11, 12, 45, 86, 109–10,
   125, 128, 146, 178–9, 181,
   200–1, 228

Brighton Festival 95
Brighton People's Theatre (BPT) 12,
 89, 91, 93–6, 104
 'Come and Play' 103
 Tighten Our Belts 101, 103
Bull, John 228
Burstin, Haïm, protagonism 186
Butler, Judith 58, 167
 Frames of War 148, 182–3
 Notes Toward a Performative Theory of Assembly 14, 211, 221–2
Butterworth, Jez 12, 122–3
 Jerusalem 115–18
 The Night Heron 112–14
 The Winterling 114–15

Camden People's Theatre (CPT) 12,
 89, 91–5, 98
 Human Jam 99–101, 103
capitalism, capitalist system 3–4, 6–7,
 10–11, 23, 30, 47, 74, 85, 89,
 96, 134, 144, 146, 185, 219
 feminism 55–9, 61, 64–6
 patriarchy 40– 3
Cazdyn, Eric and Imre Szeman 6
Chamberlain, Prudence 56, 66
Charlie Hebdo 179
Christian, Jude 59–60
chrononormativity 30, 66
Churchill, Caryl 21 n.1
 Escaped Alone 11, 22, 29–31, 33,
  35, 41, 177, 181, 229
 Mad Forest 186
 Serious Money 229
Clegg, Nick 56 n.1, 128 n.1
climate crisis, climate change 2, 5, 14,
 195, 201, 206, 210
coalition government 56, 75, 127,
 128 n.1
community 2, 12, 14, 30, 61, 63, 74,
 103–4, 113, 136–7, 159, 180,
 183, 190, 230
 migrant minorities 155, 160, 163,
  165, 167, 169, 170–1, 173

 as resistance 79–85
 state-of-the-world global
  community 76–7
 temporality 99, 100–1
 theatrical practices 91–2, 94–5, 97
conjuncture 7, 13, 65, 73, 127–8, 133,
 139, 210, 223, 229–30
Connaught Theatre 219
Conservative government,
 Conservative Party 7, 29, 56,
 73, 75, 86, 89, 93, 97, 102,
 127–9, 131, 138
 Boris Johnson 80, 130 n.3
 David Cameron 56 n.1, 75
 John Major 73
 Theresa May 155 n.2
containment, uncontaining,
 container play 13, 143–56
Cook, Peter 126
Cottesloe Theatre 127
Covid-19 pandemic 2, 10, 14–15,
 21, 45, 81, 104, 151, 177, 193,
 209–12, 218, 220, 222–3, 227
Cox, Emma, theatre of migration
 143, 144, 145, 146, 155, 156
Crimp, Martin 51, 177
 Attempts on Her Life 51
 The Treatment 50, 51
crisis of care, care crisis 11, 25, 33,
 39–40, 41, 42, 43, 45–6, 49–52,
 57, 60, 62–3, 75
crisis chronology 65, 67
Crouch, Colin 126
Crouch, Tim 10, 193
 An Oak Tree 197
 Beginners 195
 *Total Immediate Collective
  Imminent Terrestrial Salvation*
  14, 193, 195–207
Curtis, Neal 6

Daddario, Will and Theron Schmidt 2
Delanty, Gerard 6, 74
Delgado, Maria and Caridad Svich 8

Diamond, Elin 9
Dinshaw, Caroline 68
Dobry, Michel 183
Dolan, Jill, utopian performatives 12, 77, 83, 85, 215
Duffy-Syedi, Kate, Rosanna Jahangard 152, 153, 154
Dufourmantelle, Anne 178
Duggan, Patrick and Lisa Peschel 9
Duke, Ben 212, 213, 214, 215, 217–19, 220, 221, 223–4

écriture féminine 48
Edgerton, David 110
Edinburgh Fringe Festival, Edinburgh International Festival 78, 147, 151, 185, 193
Edwards, Gemma 110
eerie 12, 112, 114, 118–20, 122–3
Englishness, Deep England 12, 109–18, 120, 122–3
equality, inequality 5, 11, 39–40, 44, 46, 67, 90, 96, 110, 126, 136, 161, 209, 221

Fabian, Johannes, denial of coevalness 30
Featherstone, Vicky 11, 56
Federici, Silvia 11, 55–8, 61, 64–5
female genital mutilation, FGM 13–14, 159, 160, 162–73
  The Cruel Cut Channel 4 documentary 159
feminism 9, 13, 42, 44, 47, 49, 55–9, 61, 66–8, 160–3, 168, 172–3
Festinger, Leon, Henry Riecken, Stanley Schlachter 194–5, 203
financial crisis 2007/8 4, 7, 12, 45, 56 n.1, 74, 77, 102, 125, 209, 210, 227
Fisher, Mark 6, 12, 112, 114, 118, 120, 123
Fisher, Tony 9, 222–3

Fragkou, Marissia 9, 82, 155, 182
Franzmann, Vivienne, *Bodies* 11, 56, 60–3

gestus 182
Gilleard, Chris and Paul Higgs, third age 21, 25
Gilpin, William 111–12, 118
Goddard, Lynette 163
Goodman, Joel, 'New Years Night Revellers' 178–81
Graham, James 10, 13, 126
  Labour of Love 13, 125, 127, 133–8
  This House 13, 127–33
Gullette, Margaret 24

Hager, Philip 9, 85
Haiven, Max 6
Hall, Stuart 23
  with Doreen Massey 6, 7, 11, 65, 73–5, 127, 210–11, 223, 228
Hamidi Kim, Bérénice, people's theatre 92, 101
Hare, David 126, 228
  The Permanent Way 229
Harrison, Dawn 152–4
Harvey, David 4
Harvie, Jen 8, 22, 29, 56
Haydon, Andrew 8
Headlong theatre company 133
Herrin, Jeremy 128, 133
Hickson, Ella, *The Writer* 11, 39–52
homelessness, housing crisis 79–81, 83, 90, 98–100
HS2 project 99–100

Jadhav, Rachana 197, 200, 202, 204–6
James, Charlene, *Cuttin'it* 13, 159–60, 163–7, 172–3
James, Karl and Andy Smith 199
Jeffers, Alison 146, 153–5
Jelinek, Elfriede, *Wut (Rage)* 179, 180
Johnson, Boris 80, 130

Katsouraki, Eve 9, 15
Kent, Nicolas 147
Kershaw, Baz 219–20
Kirkwood, Lucy 11
  The Children 11, 22, 26–9, 31, 34–5
  Chimerica 14, 178, 184–5
  NSFW 209
Klaić, Dragan 1
Klein, Naomi 2, 4–5

Labour Party/government 73–5, 79, 80 n.1, 82, 93, 98–9, 110, 125, 127–9, 131–8
  Tony Blair 7, 75, 98, 134
Latour, Bruno 14, 196, 201, 203–4, 206
Lehmann, Hans-Thies 217–18
Lewis, Sophie 61–3
Logan, Brian 93–4, 99–100
Longman, Simon, *Gundog* 12, 112, 120–3
Lorey, Isabell 5
Lost Dog, *In a Nutshell* 14, 209, 211–24
Lung theatre company *E15* 12, 73–4, 78–86
  Helen Monks and Matt Woodhead 78–9
Lustgarten, Anders, radical optimism 77
Lynn, Cordelia, *Lela & Co.* 11, 56, 59–62, 64–8

MacDonald, James and Miriam Buether 22
male monoculture 11, 44, 46
Massana, Elisabeth 11, 14
Matless, David 109
McGuigan, Jim 6
Megson, Chris 77
migrant/refugee/asylum seeker 13, 62, 97, 143–56, 165
  immigrant, immigrant community 13–14, 143–4, 155, 159, 161–5, 167, 172–3

Mishra, Pankaj 74
Monforte, Enric 12
Mouffe, Chantal, agonism 13, 126–7, 129, 132
multiculturalism 13, 159–66, 172
Musca, Szabolcs and Graça P. Corrêa 143, 146, 151–2

Nail, Thomas 147
Nield, Sophie 222
neoliberal, neoliberalism 2–13, 25, 27, 30, 58, 61, 64, 73–5, 77–9, 81, 83–6, 125–7, 132–4, 136, 138–9, 189, 210, 227–30
NHS 159, 171
Nöel Coward Theatre 133
non-text-based performance, community chorus 99–100
Nübling Sebastian 179–80

Occupy Wall Street 221
O'Hanlon, Dom 10
Okin, Susan Möller 13, 161–2, 165
optimism, hope, hopefulness 77, 82–3, 86, 129, 207
Owen, Louise 14

Parekh, Bhikhu 161
Park Theatre 160, 170
Pattie, David 12
Peacock, D. Keith 228
Pedwell, Carolyn 162–3, 170, 172
Phipps, Alison 91
Phosphoros Theatre *Dear Home Office* 13, 143–4, 151
photodramas, photography 14, 177–89
Pirandello, Luigi, Pirandellian 198, 203
political cynicism 130
political theatre, political performance 9, 66, 92, 137, 138, 177
Prado-Pérez, José Ramón 13
Priestley, J.B. 11–12

Rancière, Jacques, postdemocracy, postdemocratic 13, 58, 125–7, 129, 132, 134–5, 138
Readman, Paul 110, 112
Rebellato, Dan 9, 77
reproductive work 11, 55, 57, 62, 68
resilience 2, 15, 45, 136, 178, 229–30
Ridout, Nicholas 213
Rodríguez, Verónica 13–14
Royal Court Theatre 8, 10–11, 22, 26–7, 29, 31, 55–6, 59, 66, 74, 78, 84, 160, 163, 182, 193, 209
ruptural fusion 7, 74, 211, 223, 228

satire 126, 129–30, 229
Schinkel, Willem 24
Scott-Bottoms, Stephen 14
Seguro, María Isabel 13–14
Sierz, Aleks 137, 229
social realism 66, 168
Sontag, Susan 24–5, 27, 34, 182
Stephens, Simon 10, 21, 189
   Motortown 182–3
   Rage 14, 178–81

Tank Man, the Unknown Protester 178, 184–7
temporality, *kairos*, crisis 7, 30–1, 65, 178, 184, 187, 221, 223
Thatcher, Margaret, Thatcherism 7, 73, 133, 135, 228
Thorne, Jack, *Hope* 12, 73–5, 78
Thorpe, Chris 14
   I Wish I Was Alone with Hannah Jane Walker 185
   Mysteries 185
   There Has Possibly Been an Incident 14, 178, 184, 185–9

Tiananmen Square 184, 187
Tiffany, John 74, 77–8
Tirado, Marta 13–14
Tomlin, Liz 9
Turner, Lindsey 184
Turner, Victor, *communitas* 83

Underbelly Med Squad 151
Unity Theatre 92, 97–8

van Erven, Eugène, radical popular plays 101
verbatim theatre 8, 73, 78, 152, 177, 229
volkstheater 91

Walby, Sylvia, crisis, cascade 2–5, 11–12, 15, 23, 26, 42, 44–7, 49–50, 52, 57, 64–5, 74–5, 79
Watts, Rupert 97
Weinstein, Harvey 41, 56
Welfare Reform Act 80, 103
Wheatley, Ben *A Field in England* 109, 112, 122
Williams, Gloria, *Bullet Hole* 13, 159–60, 163, 167–8, 170, 172
Williams, Raymond 3, 110
Wilmer, Steve 152, 155
women's labour, work 58
Wright, Patrick 109, 111
Wright, Tom 147

Young Vic Theatre 147, 148, 160
YouTube 209, 211–12, 214

Zaroulia, Marilena 9, 14, 58, 78, 85, 146
Zoom plays 10, 212

www.ingramcontent.com/pod-product-compliance
Lightning Source LLC
Chambersburg PA
CBHW062137300426
44115CB00012BA/1964